Science for Sale in the Autism Wars

Medically necessary autism treatment, the court battle for health insurance and why health technology academics are enemy number one

Sabrina Freeman, Ph.D.
Foreword by: Gary S. Mayerson, J.D.

Any errors and omissions are the responsibility of the author.

Library of Congress Control Number: 2003092216

National Library of Canada Cataloguing in Publication Data

Freeman, Sabrina Karen, 1958-
Science for sale in the autism wars : medically necessary autism treatment, the court battle for health insurance and why health technology academics are enemy number one / Sabrina K. Freeman.

Includes bibliographical references and index.
ISBN 0-9657565-3-X

1. Autism in children--Treatment--British Columbia. 2. Medical care--British Columbia--Needs assessment. 3. Medical technology--British Columbia--Evaluation. I. Title.
RJ506.A9F73 2003 362.1'98928982'009711 C2003-910550-4

Co-published by:

SKF Books, Inc.,
20641 46th Ave.,
Langley, B.C. V3A 3H8

SKF Books USA, Inc.,
413B 19th St. #322,
Lynden, WA 98264

Printed in the United States of America
First Edition

Contents

Foreword

By Gary S. Mayerson,* J.D.

Science for Sale in the Autism Wars is a story crying out to be told. Dr. Sabrina Freeman, author of the popular "Teach Me Language" series, expertly describes in her direct, no-holds-barred fashion precisely how health technology science was hijacked and distorted by British Columbia government ministries and their supporters, all in an effort to deprive children with autism of a "medically necessary" autism intervention that would appear to be *the* intervention. Dr. Freeman pulls no punches in naming names. She exposes how and why government functionaries placed in charge of ***protecting*** children with autism have breached the public trust and why they continue to do so, despite multiple adverse court rulings.

The autism intervention in question—intensive one-to-one Applied Behavior Analysis ("ABA")— is not some experimental or unproven fad treatment. To the contrary, as Dr. Freeman explains, decades of research published in respected, peer-review journals have supported intensive, one-to-one ABA as the singular autism intervention that has the capacity to significantly remediate autism's devastating impact.

---

*Gary Mayerson is the founder of Mayerson & Associates, a law practice in Manhattan dedicated almost exclusively to the representation of children and adolescents diagnosed with autism spectrum disorders. Mr. Mayerson has testified before the United States House of Representatives on the subject of autism-related litigation brought under federal law. His chapter, "Notes From the Front, The Current Wave in ABA Litigation" appears in Dr. Lovaas' most recent book, *Teaching Children With Developmental Delays* (Pro-Ed 2003).

In the most well known of the published studies, first published in 1987, Dr. Ivar Lovaas and his colleagues at UCLA reported that approximately 47% of young children in an experimental group receiving 40 hours per week of 1:1 ABA interventions for 2-3 years were succeeding in *mainstream* educational settings and passing as "indistinguishable." While the remaining 53% of the children in the experimental group did not become "indistinguishable," they still improved markedly. Even today, there is no outcome data that rivals the outcomes reported in Dr. Lovaas' 1987 study—a study that the Surgeon General of the United States has blessed as a "well designed study." No longer does the diagnosis of autism necessarily have to be the equivalent of a death sentence.

The story behind the now famous *Auton* court case—a case that the government lost at the Supreme Court level as well as on appeal to the British Columbia Court of Appeal, presents a pitched battle that has been waged for centuries. Ever since Galileo was hauled before the Inquisition, fact-based science has been forced to fight orthodoxy and the institutional *status quo.* As Robert Ingersoll wrote in 1877, "every science has been an outcast." Intensive ABA has been no exception, ostensibly because of its initial financial cost.

What makes the *Auton* case different from the prior confrontations, however, is that the ***government*** spent a tidy fortune hiring a phalanx of so-called "experts." These experts, holding themselves out as scientists, were compensated handsomely by the government to offer the opinion that the ABA intervention is not "medically necessary." The government's experts offered excuse after excuse and pretext after pretext as to why the published research supporting the efficacy of ABA is imperfect, and not to be relied upon.

Stephen Jay Gould, the late evolutionary biologist and paleontologist, wrote "The essence of science is intelligent sampling, not sitting in a single place and trying to get every last one."* The "intelligent sampling" approach, however, was lost on the government's witnesses. The government's experts demanded a level of "sampling" perfection that has, to date, still not been achieved by any scientist in the world studying the efficacy of intensive ABA interventions. Since every child with an autism spectrum disorder will present *differently*, it would be difficult, if not impossible, to conduct subject selection

*Gould, S. J. *Dinosaur In A Haystack.* New York: Harmony Books, 1995, p. 153.

sampling any better than Dr. Lovaas and his colleagues did. Significantly, none of the government's witnesses ever conducted subject selection sampling (for autism) at the level they insist Dr. Lovaas should have adhered to. Hence, the origin of Dr. Freeman's chapter, "When Academics Go Bad."

As Dr. Freeman explains, the *Auton* case turned into a case essentially pitting science against pseudoscience or non-science. Everyone may be entitled to their own beliefs, but certainly no one is entitled to their own "facts." Fortunately, the British Columbia Supreme Court and a unanimous British Columbia Court of Appeal saw through the government's hollow evidentiary presentation. Both courts held that intensive ABA *is* "medically necessary." Undaunted, the Government of British Columbia is continuing to press an appeal to the Supreme Court of Canada. Undoubtedly, one day, someone will quantify the extent of the fortune the government continues to spend trying to prove that intensive ABA is not "medically necessary." It goes without saying that these public funds could be put to a more noble use.

Dr. Freeman, a skilled and articulate advocate, performs the investigatory equivalent of an autopsy, wielding a razor-sharp scalpel. With the reported incidence of autism clearly on the rise, Dr. Freeman's analysis of the *Auton* case has profound implications for a whole generation of young children (and their families) very much at risk. Dr. Freeman sends a powerful message about the search for truth, and how that search is being distorted and corrupted by handsomely compensated health technology scientists who are allowing their integrity to be compromised. These academics and scientists would be well served to adhere to the first commandment in the Hippocratic Oath: "First, do no harm."

Gary S. Mayerson, J.D.
New York, New York

Introduction

Science for Sale in the Autism Wars is a book about a very important part of the Autism Wars in Canada — the role played by government funded academics against parents, in the difficult struggle to provide children with publicly funded health care insurance for medically necessary autism treatment that is their constitutional right. *Science for Sale in the Autism Wars* takes a close, hard look at the Health Technology Assessment movement through the lens of what amounts to a rare case study opportunity — the Auton et al. v. British Columbia court case, which attempted to gain publicly funded autism treatment for children. The case study shows that health technology has become a biased enterprise conducted by academics who seem to view themselves as the guardians of Medicare, the publicly funded health care system in Canada. This book exposes advocacy research from an academic group that is not accustomed to the limelight of scrutiny. One usually does not hear much about them, but they have the close ear of government and have tremendous influence regarding what gets into — and is kept out of — the health care system. In that sense, exposing the government's autism wars agenda exposes the health technology movement as a whole and acts as an inoculation kit against biased, anti-autism treatment advocacy research of the Health Technology movement. *Science for Sale in the Autism Wars* is also dedicated to helping those in need of expensive autism health-care who are fighting to have that treatment covered, whether by government or private health insurance. Although the group of academics discussed here are situated in Canada, there are health technologists everywhere. So work done in Canada has grave implications for parents of children in the United States and the rest of the world. American insurance companies and physician journals have already incorporated the autism report written by health technologists in Canada into their web-sites as justification for not funding or supporting intensive behavioral treatment for children with autism. Damage the health technology movement has done in the aftermath of their far-reaching report is discussed in some detail in the book.

Parents of children with autism fighting for their children's rights to medically necessary health care for autistic disorder have been at the sharp end of the Health Technology Assessment stick for only one reason: Health Technology tried to convince the courts, at the behest of government, that the science-based standard for autism treatments, Dr. I.O. Lovaas' "Intensive Behavioral Treatment" (autism treatment), is a purportedly experimental, unsubstantiated therapy, unworthy of health insurance coverage. This health technology argument, rejected by superior courts of British Columbia, is still being made by this group of health policy academics.

Part I of *Science for Sale in the Autism Wars* provides an in-depth analysis of the British Columbia Office of Health Technology Assessment (BCOHTA) report on Intensive Behavioural Treatment, also referred to as Lovaas Autism Treatment. The BCOHTA report, entitled *Autism and Lovaas Treatment: a systematic review of effectiveness evidence,* was produced at the request of the B.C. Ministry of Health for specific use by government lawyers in legal defense of the government in British Columbia Supreme Court. This case pitted children with autism against the government of the third largest province in Canada, and one of the most affluent G-8 nations in the world. The BCOHTA was brought in by government essentially as academic mercenaries to convince the court that government does not have a legal obligation to fund science-based treatment for autism because according to government's beholden health technology academics, there *is* no proven autism treatment at this time. As academics affiliated with the University of British Columbia, BCOHTA researchers were expected to use science to discredit the Lovaas Autism Treatment Protocol and the favourable economic consultant's cost-benefit analysis presented by families in court. Part I details the techniques used by the BCOHTA to distort and misrepresent the state of the science in autism treatment to discredit legitimate research underlying Intensive Behavioral Treatment pioneered by Lovaas and colleagues; as of this publication, the Lovaas protocol is the only proven treatment for the intractable disorder of autism.

Part II of *Science for Sale in the Autism Wars* describes the outcome of the B.C. Supreme Court case and the scathing rejection by the court of the BCOHTA report. In addition, the book documents the rejectionist and arrogant conduct of the BCOHTA subsequent to the court ruling on Lovaas treatment and the biased health technology research paper.

Throughout *Science for Sale in the Autism Wars*, we use the term Lovaas Autism Treatment as a convenient shorthand for the ground breaking behavioral treatment method pioneered by Dr. Lovaas and colleagues in the late 1960s and refined during 30 years of research to become widely known as Early Intensive Behavioural Intervention (EIBI). Aside from reducing a long name to a more conventional short one, is the need to differentiate the treatment protocol developed by Dr. Lovaas and colleagues from generic Applied Behavior Analysis or ABA, which is a very large field with only a small fraction of the research applied to autism and pervasive developmental disorders. More recently, this type of autism treatment has been referred to as science-based Intensive Behavioral Intervention (IBI). It is considered to be science-based insofar as it is based on decades of sound, generally accepted research, the foundations of which were originally formed by Dr. Lovaas and carried forward for decades by academics who followed. Lovaas' treatment protocol is often referred to as Early Intensive Behavioral Intervention because it is ideally a treatment that should begin from the moment of diagnosis, preferably as early as age two and is delivered "intensively," meaning approaching or exceeding 40 hours per week of treatment. Research has shown that although children of any age benefit from intensive behavioural intervention, the youngest children make the most remarkable gains. Although some academics may be mildly troubled by the term "Lovaas Autism Treatment," for a parent, this is the most direct way, specifically, to refer to what parents of children with autism are in fact demanding for their children and what the community of professionals recommend as medically necessary, best practice treatment for autism spectrum disorders. Therefore, for clarity and to help differentiate the "genuine article" from terms often deliberately used to obfuscate and generate confusion, the term Lovaas Autism Treatment is used throughout *Science for Sale in the Autism Wars*, as it was used in the B.C. Supreme Court case against the government of British Columbia and is still used in health technology literature today.

There is an afterword that documents findings of the B.C. Court of Appeal which heard the Government of British Columbia's appeal of the Auton case. After a second legal defeat and continued refusal to fund medically necessary autism treatment, the Government of British Columbia applied to the Supreme Court of Canada for a final opportunity to appeal the landmark Auton decision on medically necessary autism treatment. Now that the Supreme Court of Canada has chosen to hear this case, it is possible children with autism across Canada will finally be welcomed into the national medicare system on equal terms with those who suffer from physical ailments. The ultimate effectiveness of science sold in the cause of government's legal battle against children with autism remains to be seen.

Part I

BCOHTA's Attempt To Discredit Lovaas Autism Treatment

Chapters in Part I

Part I presents an analysis of the Lovaas Treatment report the British Columbia Office of Health Technology Assessment (BCOHTA) introduced into B.C. Supreme Court in the Auton case. The report has been dissected, point by point, because it is primarily in the details where the BCOHTA agenda is laid bare. Due to the complexity of the analysis, summaries of each section are provided in the margins of each page. In this way, the highlights of the analysis can be read quickly, but the entire analysis is also provided for readers interested in the details.

The highlights of this analysis have been summarized using a thematic approach to expose the variety of techniques the BCOHTA uses to discredit Lovaas. Although their report was written to discredit the work of Dr. Lovaas and colleagues in a court case, the same techniques can be used by unscrupulous academics to produce advocacy research on other topics. The tool box is generic.

The analysis is divided into seven sections that present information on who the BCOHTA is and how it attempted to discredit the entire field of Early Intensive Behavioral Intervention.

Chapter 1

What is the B.C. Office of Health Technology Assessment

In This Chapter

- B.C. Office of Health Technolgy Assessment: Independent or agent of government?
- What's the True Mission?
- BCOHTA is Dependent on Government Funding
- Health Technolgy in Over Their Heads with Autism

A thorough analysis of the British Columbia Office of Technology Assessment (BCOHTA) report on Lovaas Treatment must include a discussion about the nature of the BCOHTA as an organization. An examination of the BCOHTA is necessary because this government funded "research" organization is cloaked in academic legitimacy and claims to be unbiased, yet its works has been found by the Supreme Court of British Columbia to be, "obviously biased."

B.C. Office of Health Technology Assessment: Independent or agents of government?

The BCOHTA's desire to study Lovaas was a *direct* result of a court case against the government that is *the* source of the BCOHTA's funding.

Although physically located at the University of British Columbia, from a financial and functional standpoint, the Centre for Health Services and Policy Research (CHSPR) appears more closely tied to provincial government than to the University. The Centre was officially opened by the Minister of Health in 1991. Funding supporting the research work at the Centre comes from the province, through a, "*Sustaining grant to the center from the B.C. Ministry of Health and Ministry Responsible for Seniors.*"[1] According to the B.C. Comptroller General, the Ministry of Health grant to the University in 1998-1999 was nearly 8 million dollars.[2] The BCOHTA is part of the CHSPR and receives funding from the Ministry of Health through the Centre.

Since the BCOHTA relies upon Ministry of Health funding, the Office cannot be looked upon as a center of independent, disinterested scholars. *There is a very real possibility that the money received by the Office from the Ministry of Health serves to bias the research agenda as well as the outcome of research conducted by the Office analysts.* The BCOHTA research on Lovaas Treatment is a case in point. The research agenda was set by government Ministries in late 1999 when the government called upon the Office to help defend them in court to discredit the autism treatment developed by Lovaas and colleagues. The Report states that:

> *Three BC government Ministries... jointly requested the BC Office of Health Technology Assessment (BCOHTA) to assess the effectiveness evidence regarding a program of intensive behavioural therapy known as "Lovaas treatment."*[3]

The Report also states that:

> ***"The assessment request reflects particular issues raised in legal proceeding filed against the Government of BC"*** (emphasis added).[4]

Office analysts admit that the government's request for research is based on the issues that flow from the lawsuit that parents launched against the government. In other words, the BCOHTA's desire to study Lovaas was a *direct* result of a court case against the government that is *the* sole source of the BCOHTA's funding.

The BCOHTA gives government the "academic" legitimacy to support what can amount to a restrictive policy on developing health technologies.

The BCOHTA sees its role as promoting:

> *...the use of health technology assessment research* ***appropriate to issues of policy planning,*** *and* ***utilization at governmental*** *operational, and clinical* ***levels***[5] (emphasis added).

The Report goes on to state that its

> *"primary purpose" is "to examine scientific evidence on the effectiveness of current and developing health technologies [so BCOHTA can] identify* ***the best use of limited resources..."***[6] (emphasis added).

Put simply, the BCOHTA receives Ministry of Health money to advise government on how best to make health care resource allocation decisions. The BCOHTA gives government the "academic" legitimacy to support what can amount to a restrictive policy on the *developing health technologies* deemed to be expensive and ineffective, and therefore, a threat to the sustainability of the health care system.

The BCOHTA researchers also see themselves as close advisors to the Ministry of Health. Their web site states that the Office's ability to identify "the *best use of limited resources...*" provides *"valuable assistance to both public and private sectors in their policy and development planning"*[7] (emphasis added). In other words, they understand their role as the "gate keepers" to Canada's Medicare system as well as to U.S. health insurance companies.

B.C. Government dependence upon the Centre (CHSPR) and the Office (BCOHTA) is in some ways similar to the relationship deputy ministers and senior bureaucrats enjoy. Meetings between the government and senior Centre employees happen on a regular basis to give policy advice and support. This relationship was described in some detail on the Centre's web site in 1999.

According to the Centre, CHSPR analysts, *"regularly present relevant research findings to [health] ministry staff."*[8] They also show that the Center *"is a **source of advice and assistance** to external agencies, both **governmental** and non-governmental organizations in B.C., Canada and abroad"*[9] (emphasis added). In addition, the Center is *"engaged in a number of endeavors designed to disseminate research results [including] **participation in health policy-related committees**"*[10] (emphasis added). Their research agenda is clearly influenced by the B.C. Government, based on the fact that *"continuous communication with provincial and federal governmental bodies assures that the **research agenda** is both **relevant and timely**"*[11] (emphasis added). The Centre's web site in 1999 included the following description of its Director:

> *[The Director] of the Centre for Health Services and Policy Research at UBC... and was in 1998 **one of five external (non-government) members of the Advisory Committee on Health Services**, which reports to the Federal/Provincial/Territorial Conference of Deputy Ministers of Health*[12] (emphasis added).

In short, a claim of unbiased, objective scientific enquiry in which these purportedly disinterested academics work to add to the body of knowledge is *deceptive*.

The Centre's financial dependency on government money and their close relationship with the B.C. Government shows that the research agenda of the BCOHTA is largely set by the agenda of government, rather than the interests of science and academe. Consequently, at the outset, the agenda of the Office regarding research of Lovaas Treatment is the agenda of government facing a lawsuit by parents seeking publicly funded autism treatment. In short, a claim of unbiased, objective scientific enquiry in which these purportedly disinterested academics work to add to the body of knowledge is *deceptive* in the extreme.

What's The True Mission?

Who is the BCOHTA and what does it do? As previously mentioned, the BCOHTA is an organization funded by the B.C. Government to help them evaluate new health technologies and treatments, including a cost-benefit perspective, so as to save limited public health care dollars which support Medicare.

Consistent with its mission, the BCOHTA was enlisted to fight the Autism War for government and used every weapon at its disposal to undermine the credibility of the research done by Dr. Lovaas and colleagues in the area of intensive behavioural treatment for children with autism. Based on the BCOHTA report, the B.C. Government argued in court that the treatment was experimental and therefore undeserving of public health care funding.

The Centre for Health Sciences Policy Research (CHSPR) and the B.C. Office of Health Technology Assessment (BCOHTA) are breaking University ethical guidelines and policies.

BCOHTA is Dependent on Government Funding

All accredited universities have ethical rules or guidelines which researchers at the institution must follow. The University of British Columbia (UBC) is no exception. In fact, the University has very clear conflict of interest guidelines which all affiliated researchers must honor. UBC's Policy Number 97, entitled *Conflict of Interest*, states that:

> *The University is a forum for critical discussion and debate and a locus of **unbiased enquiry**." It is responsible for advancing and disseminating knowledge. **It is important to retain the public's trust and confidence** in order to play such a role"*[13] (emphasis added).

The UBC policy also states:

> *The university expects each of its members - faculty and staff - to act ethically and with integrity. Among these obligations, **members acting on the University's behalf, must avoid** ethical, legal, **financial** or other **conflicts of interest.**"*[14] (emphasis added).

The U.B.C. policy defines conflict of interest as:

> ***a breach of an obligation to the University that has the effect*** *or intention of advancing one's own interest or the interests of*

> *others in a way **detrimental to the interests or potentially harmful to the integrity or fundamental mission of the University**"*[15] (emphasis added).

The UBC policy regarding conflict of interest goes on to state that:

> *Conflict of interest in the conduct and reporting of research/creative/professional work can take many forms. In addition, the University's commitment to liaise with industry and transfer technology will often result in arrangements which are potential conflicts of interest."*[16]

The Office had at the very least an apparent financial conflict of interest when it undertook to do the Lovaas report for the court case.

In the same way that outside funding from industry can result in potential conflicts of interest, it is also true that funding from government can result in potential conflicts of interests. The BCOHTA is particularly susceptible to a conflict of interest when the Ministry of Health's research agenda is determined by its *legal defense needs* before the Supreme Court of British Columbia. UBC's participation in the Auton case is a pure example of conflict of interest.

As previously mentioned, the Centre, which funds the BCOHTA, regularly receives millions of dollars from the B.C. Government through a sustaining grant from the B.C. Ministry of Health. The existence of the Centre that operates the Office is dependent upon funding from the government. At the time the Report on Lovaas was written, this same government was being sued in the Supreme Court of British Columbia by parents of children with autism seeking Lovaas Autism Treatment. *The Office had at the very least an apparent financial conflict of interest when it undertook to do the Lovaas report for the court case.* As a result, it is suggested that the BCOHTA Report does not meet the test of disinterested, impartial scientific enquiry. It's for the University of British Columbia to determine what penalties should apply for violation of its conflict of interests rules.

Health Technology in Over Their Heads With Autism

The authors of the BCOHTA report on Lovaas Treatment lack expertise in disciplines related to autism. Specifically, expertise in psychology, neurology, psychiatry, neuropsychology, pediatrics, or applied behavioral analysis is strikingly absent amongst BCOHTA faculty and staff. The first author of the BCOHTA report on Lovaas Treatment is Dr. Ken Bassett, an Assistant Professor in the Department of Family Practice. His current research interests are in technology assessment theory and health policy related to genetic testing of diverse cultural groups. The senior author is also the chair of the Drug Assessment Work Group of the Therapeutics Initiative, in the Department of Pharmacology and Therapeutics. His department conducts systematic reviews for government of all drugs licensed for sale in British Columbia.

None of the three analysts who wrote the *Report on Lovaas Effectiveness* have any expertise, training or experience in autism diagnosis, research or treatment.

The Associate Director of the Center for Health Services and Policy Research, and the third author of the report is Dr. Arminee Kazanjian, the founding chair of the B.C. Office of Health Technology Assessment. Dr. Kazanjian holds a Masters of Arts Degree in Sociology from the University of Toronto and a Doctor of Philosophy in Sociology from the Sorbonne.

The second author of the BCOHTA report on Lovaas Treatment, Ms. Carolyn Green, is a research coordinator at the BCOHTA. She has been project leader on "technology assessment" projects including pharmaceutical, diagnostic and screening technology, and complementary therapy. Ms. Green's research interests also include research update in health policy and planning and the dissemination of technology assessment findings. She has a Masters of Science degree in Health Care and Epidemiology and a Bachelor of Health Science in Physiotherapy.

In short, none of the three analysts who wrote the *Report on Lovaas Effectiveness* have any expertise, training or experience in autism diagnosis, research or treatment. The authors of the BCOHTA report admit they do not have the necessary expertise in autism research, when they state that:

> *While it is* ***outside the expertise of BCOHTA*** *researchers to interpret the validity of this critique or the responses by Lovaas et al. these comments are included because they raise important issues regarding the base line characteristics of the study population*[17] (emphasis added).

The BCOHTA authors further expose their lack of knowledge and autism expertise when they state that:

> *Several authors discussed the relative merits of various tests of psychosocial development. Again, these issues are* ***beyond the expertise of BCOHTA*** *researchers...*[18] (emphasis added).

Most scholars and outside observers would agree that an in-depth understanding of psychosocial intervention is *crucial* for researchers who publish a report analyzing effectiveness of behavioural autism treatment. The BCOHTA report on Lovaas Treatment fails *terribly* in this regard.

Based on the qualifications of analysts at the BCOHTA and the content of their reports, it is apparent that there is a bias, albeit perhaps unintended, away from the analysis of technologies relating to neurological disorders, such as autism.

Based on the qualifications of analysts at the BCOHTA and the content of their reports, it is apparent that there is a bias, albeit perhaps unintended, away from the analysis of technologies relating to neurological disorders, such as autism. Below is the complete list of BCOHTA Projects appearing on the Office web site at the time of the Lovaas Report's publication:

- Acupuncture in the Treatment of Drug and Alcohol Dependency
- British Columbia Prostate Cancer Trends and Service Utilization in the Post PSA Era
- Effectiveness of Coronary Stents: Update
- Cholesterol Testing and Treatment in Women
- Does Famciclovir Cause Post-Herpetic Neuralgia?
- Effectiveness of Lipid Lowering Drugs in Women and the Elderly
- Endovascular Graft Treatment of Infrarenal Aortic Aneurysms
- Health Policy and the New Genetics
- Hearing Screening
- Hereditary Cancer Screening
- Hip Replacement Surgery: A Briefing Paper
- Lipid Lowering Therapy
- 'Normal' Bone Mass, Aging Bodies, Marketing of Fear
- The Predictive Value of Methods for Assessing Fracture Risk
- Relative Efficacy and Safety of Low Molecular Weight Heparin Preparations for Non-Hospital Prophylaxis and Treatment of Venous Thrombo-Embolic Disease
- Review of Triple Marker Screening in British Columbia
- The Role of Clinical Practice Guidelines in Health Policy
- Rules of Scientific Inquiry and Clinical Trials: Improvement is Needed
- Strategic Framework for Public Health Nursing
- A Systematic Review and Critical Appraisal of the Scientific Evidence on Craniosacral Therapy

- Tibet: The Final Frontier
- Utilization of Lipid Lowering Drugs in B.C.

See the BCOHTA web-site (www.chspr.ubc.ca/bcohta) for the complete articles.

Highlighting the lack of autism expertise is the striking absence of BCOHTA research in the fields of mental health, child development, neurology or psychiatry. Although there is no expectation that Health Technologists be experts in the field of autism, they should have enough knowledge to understand the debates from the literature before they present report conclusions harmful to children with autism. Autism research and treatment has simply never been an area of focus or health research priority for the B.C. Office of Health Technology Assessment. Such a restricted view of human health and a lack of BCOHTA autism expertise are important issues when considering the Office's analysis of Lovaas Autism Treatment. These issues suggest that Office analysts may have, in effect, "bitten off more than they could chew" when attempting to evaluate psychosocial autism treatment. Apparent expertise in pharmaceutical interventions does not qualify an organization to evaluate autism treatment.

The physical versus neurological research bias that characterizes health technology assessment in the U.S. is a component of health insurance practices that often discriminate against mental disabilities in terms of funding policies for treatments.

The lack of expertise in neurological disorders on the part of the BCOHTA is not surprising and certainly not uncommon. In the United States, where health insurance is largely detached from government, the health technology assessment industry primarily works for the private health insurance industry. The physical versus neurological research bias that characterizes health technology assessment in the U.S. is a component of health insurance practices that often discriminate against mental disabilities in terms of funding policies for treatments. The American Federal Government and several state governments have responded to this widespread discrimination by enacting Mental Health Parity legislation. In several U.S. States, it is now required that health insurance fund mental health treatments on the same basis as physical treatments.

The American Psychological Association states that:

> *Discrimination in insurance for mental health services must end if all Americans are to receive truly fair and equitable health care. Indeed, public outcry for fairness in mental health insurance coverage has led to laws requiring fairer coverage*

> *for these services. Maryland, Minnesota, Maine, New Hampshire, and Rhode Island, among other states, have enacted laws to require that coverage for mental illness services be on a par with services for physical health. Several other states are considering similar legislation.*[19]

The U.S. Congress has also acted. In 1996, Congress passed the Mental Health Parity Act. This landmark legislation prohibits insurers from imposing lifetime and annual benefit limits on mental health services that insurers do not impose on services for physical health.[20] In other words, under U.S. law, health insurance companies are not allowed to discriminate against children with autism when it comes to coverage for autism treatment.

The B.C. Government finds itself in an awkward position as it functions in both the role of the *only* health insurance "company" as well as the sole regulator of that B.C. health insurance company; clearly a conflict of interest.

The U.S. National Institute of Mental Health also recognizes that this discriminatory practice is widespread. It states that:

> *In general, Americans find that the level of services for their mental illnesses is less than that for other illnesses such as cancer, diabetes, or heart disease. An American with Parkinson's disease, one kind of brain disease affecting the neurotransmitter dopamine, might have full coverage, while another with schizophrenia, a brain disease that also affects dopamine, might have none. The bottom line of this reality is that many Americans with mental disorders do not receive treatment. Even those who do have access to treatment might not have appropriate or high quality care.*[21]

In addition to U.S. Federal legislation, Mental Health Parity Act of 1996, the following U.S. States have enacted mental health parity legislation:

> *...Arkansas, California, Colorado, Connecticut, Delaware, Florida, Georgia, Hawaii, Indiana, Louisiana, Maine, Maryland, Minnesota, Missouri, Montana, Nebraska, New Hampshire, New Jersey, North Carolina, Oklahoma, Rhode Island, South Dakota, Tennessee, Texas, Vermont and Virginia.*[22]

The California bill is a good example of legislation enacted to contend with bias of health care insurance plans against mental disabilities. California Law (Assembly Bill no. 88) states that:

> *...this bill would require a health care service plan contract or disability insurance policy issues, amended, or renewed on or after July 1, 2000, to provide coverage for the diagnosis and* ***medically necessary treatment*** *of severe mental illnesses, as defined, of a person of any age, and of serious emotional disturbances of a child, under the same terms and conditions applied to other medical conditions*[23] (emphasis added).

The BCOHTA and the Ministry of Health typically concern themselves with saving money rather than protecting the individual's right to treatment.

The California mental health parity legislation defines "severe mental illnesses" to include:
(1) Schizophrenia
(2) Schizo-affective disorder
(3) Bipolar disorder (manic-depressive illness)
(4) Major depressive disorders
(5) Panic disorder
(6) Obsessive-compulsive disorder
(7) Pervasive developmental disorder or autism
(8) Anorexia nervosa
(9) Bulimia nervosa[24] (emphasis added).

In contrast to the United States, in British Columbia (as in the rest of Canada), health insurance is owned and operated by provincial governments. *There is, in practice, only one insurance "company" per province.* The need for mental health parity protection in British Columbia is comparable to the need in the U.S. However, the B.C. Government finds itself in an awkward position as it functions in both the role of the *only* health insurance "company" as well as the sole regulator of that B.C. health insurance company; clearly a conflict of interest. In B.C., the need for government regulation to protect the health insurance rights of the neurologically disabled, competes with the needs of running a health insurance agency that is cost effective. The BCOHTA and the Ministry of Health typically concern themselves with saving money rather than protecting the individual's right to treatment.

This is a structural problem that will likely persist, in large measure due to a profound lack of transparency and accountability in B.C.'s government-run health care system. The public has no means (and regrettably no sanctioned right) to peer into government's health policy committee process along the model of public affairs windows such as C-SPAN (U.S.) or CPAC (Canada).

Vitally important decisions on health insurance policy in B.C. are routinely made without public knowledge or input. Those who wield the disproportionate influence are an elite club of university health policy technocrats who are unaccountable to the public yet routinely advise and guide government health ministries and departments of health to an extent few comprehend.

Chapter 2

When Academics Go Bad: Bias in Health Technology Research

In This Chapter

- University of British Columbia Does Government Advocacy Research for Court
- Strawman of Autism Cure vs. Loss of Autism Diagnosis
- Spotlight on Lovaas Only: BCOHTA ignores all other treatments
- The Double Standard: ABA is okay but Lovaas is experimental
- Exclude What Hurts: BCOHTA falls far short of exhaustive research

It is useful for this discussion to broadly categorize research into three types:

(1) clinical/scientific,
(2) academic, or
(3) research intended for advocacy — "advocacy research."

According to this typology (Hanson, 1998), a person using a clinical approach gathers and reviews comprehensive data, and then makes a decision regarding the content of the data. The person using the academic approach gathers data and makes a statement based on its synthesis, often times disregarding the political/socioeconomic consequences of a given issue. The person using the advocacy approach pushes for the model solution; the research contains all the information necessary to sway policy in their direction only.

BCOHTA researchers use "selective analysis" in the conduct of their advocacy research.

University of British Columbia Does Government Advocacy Research for Court

Based on the evidence presented throughout this chapter, research conducted by the BCOHTA falls into the third category — a research orientation that advocates, in this case, for current B.C. Government policy regarding children with autism. In keeping with the research orientation of advocacy, Office researchers elected to conduct an analysis of Lovaas Treatment using only the information necessary to sway the court opinion in favour of their funding source and the same organization that requested and paid for the autism study — the B.C. Government.

Broadly speaking, BCOHTA researchers use "selective analysis" in the conduct of their advocacy research. Their report appears to use four "selective analysis" techniques which are summarized here, and analyzed in more detail later in this chapter:

- **Building the straw-man of a "cure":** The Office sets out to determine whether or not the UCLA protocol (Lovaas Treatment) "cures" children with autism. This selective and overly restrictive research purpose excludes a thorough examination of overall autism treatment "effectiveness" or "best practices." If they can provide evidence that shows Lovaas did not "cure" autism, then this finding can be used to justify denial of treatment funds.

• **Exclusive Spotlight on Lovaas:** Office analysts frame their question narrowly and examine only Lovaas Treatment. A BCOHTA analysis of the scientific validity of alternate so-called "treatment" options, including those currently funded by the BC government, is conspicuously absent. This selective and restricted purpose also serves to avoid a thorough examination of autism treatment "best practices." If they do not compare all other autism interventions, they will not leave themselves open to arrive at the uncomfortable conclusion that Lovaas and colleagues may present the most compelling data regarding bona fide, effective autism treatment.

Office analysts incorrectly present Lovaas Treatment as a purported "cure" for autism, and inaccurately define legal claims in B.C. as based upon the supposed "curative claim."

• **The double standard:** BCOHTA researchers accept, without question, the science behind Applied Behavioral Analysis, which is very closely linked to the work of Lovaas and colleagues. In addition, they do not perform a rigorous analysis of the Treatment and Education of Autistic and related Communication-handicapped Children protocol (TEACCH) (a competitor) which they introduce in a perfunctory way only. Further, they accept the research conducted by Jocelyn et al. (another Canadian competitor) as "ground breaking," despite a lack of significant successful treatment outcome. Only with the Lovaas landmark study do they perform a detailed and highly critical analysis that ultimately rejects the science behind the treatment protocol developed by Lovaas. The research agenda of the BCOHTA authored Lovaas report is clearly determined by the legal imperative of the government to defend itself in court, and not to add to the body of knowledge.

• **Exclude what hurts:** Despite a supposedly exhaustive literature search, the BCOHTA study *did not include articles that hurt the advocacy objective of the research.* The failings of the BCOHTA report in this regard does not appear to result from research incompetence; the research bias may instead be explained by the advocacy nature of the report and the litigation context.

Strawman of Autism Cure Versus Loss of Diagnosis

Setting up the Straw Man

From the first page of their report, Office analysts incorrectly ascribe an "autism-cure" claim to Dr. Lovaas, and inaccurately define legal claims in B.C. as based upon the supposed "curative claim."

BCOHTA researchers state:

> *This systematic review examined whether early, intensive behavioural therapy for children with autism results in normal functioning, or* ***essentially a cure.*** *The scientific validity of this* ***curative claim is central****, both to legal proceedings brought on behalf of several children in British Columbia against the Province seeking an intensive behavioural program; and to cost-benefit analyses and clinical guidelines used for planning autism treatment programs* [1] (emphasis added).

Defining successful Lovaas research outcomes as "essentially a cure" amounts to the construction of an easy target to discredit with advocacy research.

They further state:

> *At issue in this report, however, is the stronger assertion, conceivably also to be inferred from the Autism Action statement, that scientific evidence supports behavioral therapy as a means to alter beneficially the natural course of the condition, or all the symptoms of the conditions, and as a result a substantial number of children will achieve 'recovery' or* ***'cure'*** [2] (emphasis added).

Dr. Lovaas has never referred to Intensive Behavioral Treatment as a "cure;" nor has this claim ever been made by bona fide researchers in the field or by families seeking legal redress in British Columbia. It can be argued that framing the BCOHTA Lovaas Autism Treatment analysis as a search for "*scientific validity of this curative claim,*" is in fact, *a purposefully selective research goal with a predetermined outcome*. In other words, it is generally accepted that at this time there is no known cause or cure for autism. No scholar, researcher or clinician has made that claim in the autism case that was before the B.C. Supreme Court. Therefore, defining successful Lovaas research outcomes as "essentially a cure" amounts to the construction of an easy target to discredit with advocacy research. Such a narrow, inaccurate definition of the Lovaas Treatment protocol also serves a second, important advocacy purpose — to divert attention from the principle of "best practice" and the growing consensus that intensive behavioural treatment currently constitutes "best practice" in autism intervention.

BCOHTA researchers misrepresent Lovaas when they state, as a given, that Lovaas and colleagues claim to have cured autism:

> *The published literature on autism contains only one report, from a controlled clinical trial, in which the authors claim that their treatment normalized or* ***cured*** *children with autism (Lovaas 1987, with McEachin 1993)*[3] (emphasis added).

Dr. Gresham has been an ardent critic and academic rival of Dr. Lovaas, and he is known to have attributed the "cure claim" to Dr. Lovaas.

Again, there is nothing in the Lovaas Treatment literature to support the Office's view that Lovaas researchers have claimed to "cure" autism. Their report has no evidence from Lovaas' articles to support this view. As has been argued above, the BCOHTA researchers are not experts in autism treatment. However, it appears they did accept and adopt the arguments of another expert retained by the B.C. government in the litigation: Dr. Frank Gresham. Dr. Gresham has been an ardent critic and academic rival of Dr. Lovaas, and he is known to have attributed the "cure claim" to Dr. Lovaas. The following passage from Dr. Lovaas illustrates this point:

> *An issue which surfaces periodically is the assertion that the UCLA project claimed to "cure" autism. Gresham and MacMillan (1997) report: "We argue in this article that the (UCLA project) is far from providing a cure for autism. With the exception of (studies from UCLA) <u>none</u> claim to have a cure (of) autism." They go on to cite Rutter (1996) to back up their accusation that the UCLA project has claimed a "cure." Referring to the Lovaas (1987) and McEachin, Smith, & Lovaas (1993) studies, Rutter (1996) argues that one of the reasons for being cautious about the acceptance of the "strong claims" of these articles are based on " the claims of cure." Rutter argues that the claims of cure run "counter to both clinical experience and what might be expected on the basis of prevailing theories."*[4]

> *The UCLA project has never claimed to cure autism. The term "cure" implies removal of the original cause of the problem. Because this cause of autism is unknown, claiming a cure would certainly be unjustified and unethical. In contrast, it is possible to enable a child with autism to achieve normal functioning without finding a cure for autism, just as it is possible for a physician to recover patients to normal functioning without having found a cure for their illness. Hodgkin's disease is a case in point. It can only undermine parent's and professional's confidence in the UCLA project to imply that we have made unethical claims.*[5]

The "all-or-nothing" position taken by Office analysts in adopting the "curative claim" premise is a severe flaw in their analysis.

In other words, Lovaas' research has shown that it is possible to treat a child with autism to the point where the child is *functionally* normal, despite not having been *cured* of the underlying cause of the condition. There are parallels in physical medicine other than Hodgkin's disease, where physicians treat patients to the point where they are functionally normal without having been "cured." Other examples include publicly funded treatments for Parkinson's, diabetes and AIDS, where significant health care dollars are expended by physicians, and the Medicare system as a whole, to improve the quality of life of patients, even though there is no known "cure" for the underlying disorder.

The BCOHTA cites another critic of Lovaas, Gary Mesibov, to support their view that Lovaas makes a curative claim. BCOHTA researchers state:

> *Mesibov raises the principal concern with this approach: "..readers might jump to the conclusion that the children have been* ***cured****. This has been an unfortunate consequence of other presentations and studies published by these authors."*[6] (emphasis added).

Ironically, it is not casual "readers" who have jumped to the conclusion of cure, but rather, it is sophisticated Office researchers themselves who have jumped to conclusions that Lovaas Treatment protocol makes curative claims. A thorough review of the original Lovaas literature confirms that no curative claim has ever been made. Again, this may reveal the advocacy nature of the BCOHTA study.

It is only possible to ignore a large range of significant treatment-based improvements in autism if one frames the debate as cure versus no cure. The "all-or-nothing" position taken by Office analysts in adopting the "curative claim" premise is a severe flaw in their analysis. The flaw is as simple as it is obvious: BCOHTA researchers have excluded a significant proportion of children from the analysis — those children who achieved *significantly* improved outcomes along a continuum, which spanned a range up to the most successful outcome of normal functioning.

It is obvious that an unbiased analysis of Lovaas Treatment should also have discussed the considerable degree to which another 43% improved — but this was ignored.

Instead of exclusively focusing on the 47% of children whose outcome rendered them indistinguishable from their peers in the landmark 1987 Lovaas study, it is obvious that an unbiased analysis of Lovaas Treatment should also have discussed the considerable degree to which another 43% improved — but this was ignored by health technology academics at UBC. Even children who were classified as retarded and autistic made significant gains with Lovaas Treatment in Smith et al., 1997. As discussed above, the Ministry of Health and British Columbia's medicare system both widely fund treatments that improve the condition of several disorders so as to improve quality of life, without "curing" the disorder. Treatments are not accepted or rejected by B.C. physicians based on this "all-or-nothing" criterion. In fact, patients often receive drug or surgical interventions that may not always achieve the optimal outcomes seen in research. Often there may be a full expectation of near-term death, yet significant publicly funded treatments are administered nonetheless. Simply because some patients may not respond to treatment does not mean that all patients should be denied treatment. Chemotherapy, surgery and radiation treatment are regularly delivered to cancer patients, at considerable public expense, yet some of these patients do not recover, or even improve.

The BCOHTA placed strong emphasis on the "curative claim" argument against public funding for Lovaas Treatment. It is true there is no proven cure for autism, yet there are many costly health care programs for conditions that cannot be cured, even terminal illness. For example, there is public funding for palliative care and the Ministry of Health has a generous program of individualized funding where no expectation exists that the patient will be "cured." The Choices in Independent Community Living (CICL) program provides individualized funding for in-home palliative or longer term nursing care so that patients are able to stay in their homes for the rest of their lives. The spouse is entrusted with management of a $36,000 annual budget to hire

nursing and other support staff. *Of note is that the CICL program* ***is not means tested*** *as applied to palliative care, and is not "cure" dependent."*
In the case of childhood autism, the Office apparently sees no contradiction or moral issue with withholding public funding — in the absence of a cure — for best practice autism treatment that has been shown to significantly improve the quality of life for children with autism.

Competent delivery of Lovaas Autism Treatment can make children indistinguishable from their peers in the best case scenario. However, those who may still have symptoms of autism after treatment have been shown to achieve a substantially higher quality of life. Whether they make large or modest gains, the treatment is nonetheless beneficial.

In addition, it is noteworthy that the BCOHTA is so dismissive of the "published literature" despite the fact that this literature is peer-reviewed.

Autism is a behavioural diagnosis. As result, when a child no longer demonstrates the symptoms associated with the condition, the condition is no longer apparent. Where all the symptoms are controlled or extinguished, the child becomes "functionally normal." Yet the BCOHTA researchers appear to misunderstand or misinterpret the nature of autism diagnosis when they state:

> *However, Lovaas and his research colleagues have not limited their effectiveness claims to achieving developmental gains. Instead, they have permitted and even fostered the premise that appears throughout the published literature, associating their therapy with a notion of achieving 'normal functioning' for as many as half a given population of children with autism.*[7]

In addition, it is noteworthy that the BCOHTA is so dismissive of the "published literature" despite the fact that this literature is peer-reviewed.

When Office Analysts Wish to Appear Balanced, They Exclude the "Curative Claim" and Refer to "Functioning."

There is notable inconsistency in the BCOHTA report. The research question the BCOHTA report posits is not the research question they answer in their Lovaas treatment report. They seek evidence for *"improved overall outcome versus alternative management strategies,"*[8] whereas they conclude that there is not enough evidence to support children achieving *"normal functioning."*[9]

This undisciplined "wiffle waffle" illustrates that the Office's report on Lovaas does not meet the most basic test of well conducted research: it does not contain clear and consistent research questions and answers.

The Office sets out two different research questions: (1) improved overall outcome, and (2) normal functioning. These cannot be used interchangeably since they are very different questions. It is notable that, conspicuously, neither research question mentions "cure."

BCOHTA researchers *ask*:

> *What is the effectiveness evidence that early, intensive behavioural treatment programs for preschool children with autism results in* ***improved overall outcome*** *versus alternative management strategies?*[10] (emphasis added).

Their conclusion *answers* a different research question:

> *The Lovaas et al (1987) and McEachin (1993) study, while methodologically stronger than published reports of alternate comprehensive therapies, is inadequate to establish the degree to which this form of therapy results in children achieving* ***'normal' functioning,*** *however defined*[11] (emphasis added).

The Report toggles between "cure" and "improved outcome" on a regular basis. At the outset, the BCOHTA analysis appears to have a different and contradictory focus — that of "cure" rather than "improved overall outcome" or "normal functioning."

> ***At issue in this report****, however, is the stronger assertion... that scientific evidence supports behavioural therapy as a means to [improve autism or its symptoms] and as a result a substantial number of children will achieve "recovery" or "****cure****"*[12] (emphasis added).

Then, the BCOHTA further contradicts the curative "issue" above with the improvement in overall function "issue" below:

> ***At issue in this review*** *are comprehensive behavioural treatment programs designed to alter the outcome in autism, and* ***improve the overall function*** *of affected individuals*[13] (emphasis added).

This undisciplined "wiffle waffle" illustrates that the Office's report on Lovaas does not meet the most basic test of well conducted research: it does not contain clear and consistent research questions and answers. This could be due to the conflicting practices and goals of advocacy versus academic research. This inconsistency is likely agenda-based rather than an issue of research competence.

Spotlight on Lovaas Only: BCOHTA ignores all other treatments

This bias in how the research is framed completely undermines the Office's ability to scientifically evaluate health technologies from a comparative, relative effectiveness standpoint for various autism treatments.

At the outset of the BCOHTA report, Office researchers acknowledge the BC Government approached BCOHTA to request an efficacy study on Lovaas Treatment. These researchers further acknowledge that the research request was in the context of legal action against several B.C. Government Ministries. According to the B.C. Office of Health Technology Assessment, *the research question has been narrowly defined by government, and consequently by the BCOHTA, to spotlight only the Lovaas Treatment protocol for evidence as to its effectiveness. They completely neglected to conduct a review — even a rudimentary one — of research evidence for the large number of alternate autism interventions, management strategies and "support" options.*

In short, all the scientific evidence supporting or refuting major so-called treatment options is excluded from the BCOHTA analysis. *This bias in how the research is framed completely undermines the Office's ability to scientifically evaluate health technologies from a comparative, relative effectiveness standpoint for various autism treatments.* This is particularly important in a field where dozens of competing, scientifically unsubstantiated, treatments are offered. Of particular note is that the Office did not evaluate any of the government-funded autism services for their real-world effectiveness.

The government sponsored BCOHTA report attempts to dilute the exclusive attention paid to Lovaas Treatment by conducting an arbitrarily narrow comparison between a method referred to as TEACCH (popular with many school districts due to perceived economy) and Lovaas. However, the discussion of TEACCH falls far short of "exhaustive" because BCOHTA researchers fail to conduct even a basic literature search on TEACCH, as well as the many alternative autism treatment and management options. The Office may be aware they are "exposed" in this area, *i.e.* conducting a purposefully narrow, government-petitioned review of Lovaas only. Possibly to rectify this academic vacuum, the Office (at the time of this publication) collaborated with The Canadian Coordinating Council Office of Health Technology Assessment (CCOHTA) to produce a more comprehensive report on autism treatment. The CCOHTA web site cited the following autism study with BCOHTA collaboration at the time of the court hearing (April 2000):

> ***Treatment and Support for Children with Autism***
> ***In collaboration with researchers at BCOHTA.***
>
> *Project Team: Lynda McGahan (CCOHTA);*
> ***Ken Bassett (BCOHTA);***
> ***Carolyn Green (BCOHTA)***
> *Status:* ***Ongoing*** [14] (emphasis added).

In other words, the Office had no intention of looking for any evidence to support the autism intervention and management practices government contractees used on B.C.'s children at the time of the legal action against the government.

The obvious question raised by the autism collaboration between the BCOHTA and the CCOHTA is, "why were *all* major "*Treatment and Support*" options purposely excluded by BCOHTA researchers in the case before the Supreme Court in July 2000?" After all, the issue of effectiveness in terms of autism treatments is at the heart of the action: parents and a significant number of mental health care professionals did *not* view the existing government autism services as adequate or effective. It must be stressed that *all* government service providers and contractees were conveniently excluded from the BCOHTA analysis. In other words, the Office had no intention of looking for any evidence to support the autism intervention and management practices government contractors used on B.C.'s children at the time of the legal action against the government. Not surprisingly, ineffective B.C. Government funded and approved special needs services, proportedly intended for children with autism, were spared the critical eye of Office researchers in the context of the court case on autism treatment.

If the BCOHTA were truly an independent body of impartial university researchers, it would have conducted a broader review at the outset. Perhaps it would have done so approaching the comprehensive nature of the review published by the New York State Department of Health. Instead, the Office only shines the spotlight on the work of Lovaas. If BCOHTA researchers were pressed to share the spotlight and *impartially* analyze all that currently constitutes B.C. Government intervention services for children with autism, they may have had to agree with the New York Department of Health in concluding that:

1) intensive behavioural treatment is the intervention of choice, and

2) Lovaas' research on intensive behavioural treatment is the most methodologically sound and has the most compelling outcome data of any other autism research conducted to date.[15]

BCOHTA researchers have not adequately contended with the autism treatment "best practices" issue. They cannot ignore the fact that work by Lovaas and colleagues has influenced the entire field. Undaunted, for its advocacy research in the B.C. Government's court battle, the BCOHTA exploits the systematic review conducted by Gina Green, which is supportive of Lovaas' work. They quote Gina Green, Ph.D.:

Office analysts cannot ignore the fact that work by Lovaas and colleagues has influenced the entire field.

> *Green, in the systematic review that conducted the least critical appraisal, draws the strongest conclusions in favour of Lovaas treatment. She states that "applied behavioural analysis is the treatment of choice..."*[16]

BCOHTA researchers cite Green as a scholar who considers Lovaas Treatment as the "treatment of choice" (the Best Practices argument). In apparent agreement, BCOHTA states:

> *The absence of corroborative evidence of 'recovery from autism' does not devalue the* ***effectiveness of early, intensive and comprehensive treatment programs in achieving significant developmental gains*** (emphasis added).[17]

The above BCOHTA opinion is contradicted by BCOHTA discussion below:

> *The Lovaas et al (1987) and McEachin (1993) study, while methodologically stronger than published reports of alternate comprehensive therapies, is inadequate to establish the degree to which this form of therapy results in children achieving* ***"normal" functioning,*** *however defined* (emphasis added).[18]
>
> ***At issue in this review*** *are comprehensive behavioural treatment programs designed to alter the outcome in autism, and* ***improve the overall function*** *of affected individuals* (emphasis added).[19]

If, as BCOHTA researchers state, Lovaas Treatment has value as an effective early, intensive and comprehensive treatment program *"in achieving significant developmental gains,"* then one is left to wonder why the treatment is not recommended by the Office.

The Double Standard: ABA's okay but Lovaas is experimental

While critical of Lovaas' research, BCOHTA analysts had to tread lightly on Applied Behavioural Analysis because of the vast literature on the subject.

Lovaas Treatment is partially based upon, and is an outgrowth of, the discipline of Applied Behaviour Analysis (commonly known as ABA). While critical of Lovaas' research, BCOHTA analysts had to tread lightly on Applied Behavioural Analysis because of the vast literature on the subject. The Office presents the following disclaimer at the outset of the report:

> *This systematic review does not consider the literature on focal treatments directed either at reducing specific behavioural problems associated with autism, such as sleep disturbances and escape behaviours; or at increasing behavioural successes such as social interaction with peers and symbolic play.*[20]

They also state:

> *Matson et al. draw similar limited conclusions in favour of behavioural therapy for children with autism. The authors describe 271 published studies evaluating behavioral techniques directed at target behaviors, which are divided into categories of aberrant behaviour, social skills, language, daily living skills, and academic skills.*[21]

Unfortunately, BCOHTA researchers fail to state that the 271 published studies on ABA use primarily single-subject case designs which would fail the BCOHTA efficacy criteria because they did not "involve random assignment to different treatment conditions." Simply stated, the majority of ABA studies do not employ a control group, yet are apparently accepted at face value by BCOHTA analysts. Designs without a control group (also referred to as "within subject" designs) do have their place in science; however, the BCOHTA uncritically accepts the ABA studies where typically no control group exists, yet has serious "research" concerns with Lovaas studies that *do* use control groups. Again, this serves to illustrate the advocacy-focus of their report.

Another possible explanation for this inconsistency is a simple lack of knowledge and expertise regarding research in the field of autism. Either possibility should give rise to concern if this is how decisions about health care resources are to be made.

The academic reality, perhaps unintentionally overlooked by the Office, is that Lovaas is, in fact, part of the ABA "universe." The Lovaas protocol is built upon the past successes of hundreds of ABA studies. Lovaas employed many of the Applied Behaviour Analytic techniques methodically developed in the ABA literature and unconditionally accepted by the Office analysts. Lovaas combined established ABA techniques into a comprehensive prototype of autism intervention. Following decades of follow-up success in studies and in the real world, the protocol is now widely known as *intensive behavioural treatment* or the *Lovaas Autism Treatment* protocol. What sets Dr. Lovaas apart from other ABA researchers is his compelling protocol and research design. Lovaas employed an experimental and control group — a research design commonly accepted as comparatively more robust or stronger when studying many different elements.

The Office must either reject ABA research methodology as it does not meet standards BCOHTA has put forth for Lovaas Treatment, or BCOHTA must *accept* Lovaas research, since it builds upon the same ABA research Office analysts accept indiscriminately at the outset of their report.

It is difficult for BCOHTA researchers to have it both ways. On the one hand, they cannot accept the vast body of ABA research that does not meet the criteria they have laid out for Lovaas' research and, on the other hand, apply stringent standards to the singular researcher in autism treatment research — Lovaas — who has tested ABA principles (accepted at face value by BCOHTA) in a comprehensive and controlled manner.

Put simply, the Office must either reject ABA research methodology as it does not meet standards BCOHTA has put forth for Lovaas Treatment, or BCOHTA must *accept* Lovaas research, since it builds upon the same ABA research Office analysts accept indiscriminately at the outset of their report.

Moreover, when BCOHTA researchers conducted a literature review, they reported the following, "*... Approximately 150 articles met the minimum [BCOHTA] inclusion criteria and were retrieved... However, only four controlled studies of treatment programs were identified* ***that reported overall outcome for children...***"[22] (emphasis added).

It is telling that in the "exhaustive" BCOHTA literature search, only 150 autism articles were worth retrieving. Of the 150 articles retrieved, a mere 4 articles met the Office criteria for controlled treatment studies with overall outcome for children. From this select group of autism treatment studies — 4 of 150 — chosen by the BCOHTA as acceptable research, it is highly relevant that three were either Lovaas or attempted Lovaas replication studies. It is important to note that *no studies encompassing the autism treatment, management or support practices of the BC government, or its special needs contractors, have been cited by the B.C. Office of Health Technology Assessment as meeting its 'minimum' selection criteria for research articles.* In other words, BCOHTA found no research evidence that meets its scientific criteria to support the BC government's claim that "things are working well," and that public dollars currently spent on autism services produce successful outcomes in autism intervention. Aside from the three Lovaas Treatment studies or replications that met the Office criteria for good research, the fourth is a study of the TEACCH philosophy of autism intervention which is irrelevant since there were no government funded TEACCH classrooms in B.C. at the time of the legal proceedings.

From a select group of autism treatment studies — 4 of 150 — chosen by the BCOHTA as acceptable research, it is highly relevant that three were either Lovaas or attempted Lovaas replication studies.

In short, the BCOHTA find themselves in a bit of a quandary. They have adopted very stringent criteria which Lovaas' study does meet on the whole. Yet they have uncritically accepted the vast literature of applied behavioural analysis which, strictly speaking, does not meet the NIH criteria which BCOHTA is using to evaluate Lovaas' research. Specifically, ABA research which the Office uncritically accepts, wholesale, does not meet BCOHTA criteria in the following areas:

1) They do not compare various approaches to treatment; these studies generally are designed to treat, then withdraw and treat again.

2) They do not involve random assignment to different treatment conditions; these are within-subject designs which compare the child to himself at several different intervals.

3) They do not represent a cross section of children with autism as the BCOHTA researchers require.[23]

Exclude What Hurts: BCOHTA falls far short of exhaustive research

It is, therefore, more than a little surprising to find highly relevant autism articles, reports and books missing from the BCOHTA "exhaustive" search.

The BCOHTA researchers pride themselves on the ability to conduct "exhaustive research" and in their ability to find not only published literature, but also "fugitive" literature.

The BCOHTA states:

> *Health Technology Assessment projects are conducted by faculty and staff (including medical consultants) who are expert in systematic review methodology. Electronic bibliographic databases and fugitive literature (that is, literature not indexed or distributed publicly) are searched using predefined inclusion and exclusion criteria based on a specific search strategy.*[24]

The Office devotes five pages in their report to provide readers with meticulous detail regarding their exhaustive search vis-à-vis autism treatment. It is, therefore, more than a little surprising to find highly relevant autism articles, reports and books missing from the BCOHTA "exhaustive" search.

Most notable of the reports the BCOHTA omitted from its analysis of Lovaas Treatment, is a seminal report entitled *Mental Health: A Report of the [U.S.] Surgeon General.* In this report, Dr. David Satcher, M.D., Ph.D., U.S. Surgeon General, discusses Lovaas' work. Dr. Satcher states:

> *Thirty years of research demonstrated the efficacy of applied behavioral methods in reducing inappropriate behavior and in increasing communication, learning and appropriate social behavior.* ***A well-designed study of a psychosocial intervention was carried out by Lovaas and colleagues (Lovaas, 1987; McEachin et al., 1993).*** *Nineteen children with autism were treated intensively with behavior therapy for 2 years and compared with two control groups.* ***Follow-up of the experimental group in first grade, in late childhood, and in adolescence found that nearly half the experimental group but almost none of the children in the matched control group were able to participate in regular schooling.*** *Up to this point,*

> *a number of other research groups have provided at least a partial replication of the Lovaas model (see Rogers, 1998)*[25] (emphasis added).

Another notable omission from the BCOHTA report is a book which details the "mechanics" of the Lovaas home-based early, intensive intervention programs. Based on the Lovaas Treatment protocol, Drs. Leaf and McEachin have authored a significant autism treatment publication entitled *A Work In Progress*. The book is a detailed blueprint of the Lovaas Treatment protocol and additionally illustrates how much Lovaas Treatment has advanced from the original *The ME Book* written by Lovaas in 1981. Although Leaf and McEachin (1999) is not an outcome study, it should most certainly have been included by the Office since both *The ME book* by Lovaas and *Behavioural Intervention for Young Children with Autism* by Maurice, were included in the "exhaustive" BCOHTA literature search.

Eaves and Ho find that no children with autism in B.C. improve with available government services. Exclusion of this study from the so-called exhaustive research of the BCOHTA further points to the advocacy nature of the report.

Under the category of "Exclude what hurts," it is highly significant to note that Office researchers omitted a very relevant article by Eaves and Ho (1996). This BC-based study conducted by Sunnyhill Hospital researchers, looks at outcomes of children with autism who have "gone through the system" in B.C. *Eaves and Ho find that no children with autism in B.C. improve with available government services.* Exclusion of this study from the so-called exhaustive research of the BCOHTA further points to the advocacy nature of the report.

Chapter 3

How Health Technology's Attack on Lovaas Autism Treatment Fails

In This Chapter

- The Charge Lovaas Didn't Compare Different Approaches to Treatment
- How Children Were Grouped in Lovaas' Autism Research
- Is It Ethical to Deny Treatment to Children?
- The Claim That Lovaas Does Not Measure 'real life' Data
- Psychological Assessment of Children in Lovaas' Research
- Did Lovaas Provide Enough Details On How the Treatment is Implemented?
- Is the Treatment Still Effective Over Time?
- Have Others Replicated the Success of Lovaas Treatment?
- The Classic Aversives Ruse

The BC Office of Health Technology Assessment accepts, without question, various criticisms made by academic rivals of Dr. Ivar Lovaas. Essentially, the most vicious critics view the favourable research results achieved by Lovaas as "too good to be true." Rival autism intervention researchers have not been able to achieve anything approaching outcomes of the Lovaas autism intervention protocol. A few have become outspoken critics of Lovaas, in essence claiming, "it's just not possible... autism is a lifelong, intractable condition." Therefore, the assumption is that Lovaas' outcomes must be exaggerated, likely based on poor research design, or simply fraudulent.

The most vicious critics view the favourable research results achieved by Lovaas as "too good to be true."

Lovaas et al. (1989) address the question of "believability" regarding reported outcomes of their behavioural treatment research. Lovaas states:

> *Three aspects of our intervention may account for the favorable outcome we reported: First, our intervention was* ***very intensive****; children were in a one-to-one teaching situation for most of their waking hours for several years. Second, it contained many empirically derived teaching techniques, including some that other investigators have not made full use of such as discrimination training and contingent aversives. And third, it improved on previous treatment programs (e.g., Lovaas, Koegel, Simmons, & Long, 1973) by* ***emphasizing early intervention****, by involving parents more extensively, by being* ***conducted in children's homes*** *instead of clinical settings, and* ***by explicitly teaching children to learn from and interact with "normal" peers in normal settings, such as school.****"*[1] (emphasis added).

Despite sound rationale for Lovaas' autism treatment success, there remain ardent critics of his work. This chapter will discuss these critiques in greater detail. Of note is that Office researchers have accepted, seemingly on a wholesale basis, these critiques without applying the rigorous, exhaustive analysis to these papers that supposedly is a hallmark of the BCOHTA. Following is a discussion of BCOHTA's critique of Lovaas autism treatment research, organized along the same research guidelines used in its report submitted to the B.C. Supreme Court in the defence of government against families of children with autism.

The Charge Lovaas Didn't Compare Different Approaches to Treatment

The BCOHTA criticizes Lovaas' experiment because they claim that:

> *Lovaas did not compare two different therapies, but only compares two levels of intensity in a single form of behavioral intervention. There were insufficient details provided from the second control group to determine what therapies were applied.*[2]

When Lovaas began his groundbreaking research in autism treatment, there were no competing therapies that could lay claim to any academic legitimacy.

This criticism is problematic for historical reasons. When Lovaas began his groundbreaking research in autism treatment, there *were* no competing therapies that could lay claim to any academic legitimacy. In the era when Dr. Lovaas began his research (the mid sixties and early seventies), institutionalization was the typical "medical model" for children suffering with autism. Those children less afflicted by Autistic Disorder and fortunate enough to avoid institutionalization, were offered what are generically known as "support services" and special education classes. For a severe, lifelong condition with no known cause and no effective treatment, a system of social services supports evolved. Even when the Auton court case was heard (April 2000), the support (versus treatment) model for autism was the prime intervention strategy used by the B.C. Government.

For his time, Dr. Lovaas did something that was genuinely groundbreaking: he introduced scientific rigor into the field of autism research. Much to his credit, he did not merely establish one control group for his study, but rather, *he created two control groups so that he could test intensity of treatment received, as well as the alternatives received by children in the community*. It is generally recognized that the "alternatives" in the community were simply traditional special education rather than specifically defined treatment interventions. Lovaas states:

> *Lovaas (1987) compared intensive behavioral treatment to minimal behavioral treatment and placement in special education. These interventions were provided to the experimental group, Control Group 1, and Control Group 2, respectively.*[3]

BCOHTA criticism regarding Lovaas' groundbreaking autism research, for example *"Lovaas did not compare two different therapies,"* suggests the BCOHTA's complete ignorance with respect to the field of autism and the vacuum that constituted autism "intervention" for children at the time of Lovaas' research. Indeed, at that time, the notion that uncaring, "refrigerator" mothers cause autism (a theory proposed by Bettelheim) had only recently been challenged and discredited.

How Children Were Grouped in Lovaas' Autism Research

Lovaas utilized an assortment of recognized psychometric measures to evaluate prospective study subjects, and thereby ensured that all children accepted into the study were closely matched.

Following is a discussion surrounding the spurious "random assignment" critique raised by Office analysts against Lovaas autism treatment research. Fundamentally, at question regarding group assignment, is whether groups in the Lovaas (1987) study were the same or different at the outset of the study. When researchers use the true random method of assigning subjects to conditions in an experiment, researchers and readers have a high degree of confidence that the groups are identical. When true, or pure, random assignment is not possible for various reasons — such as ethical considerations documented by Lovaas — other valid, recognized measures must be used to ensure that groups have essentially the same characteristics at study intake. In the landmark Lovaas study, pure "random" assignment was not used due to an outcry from parent groups against its use. In place of true random assignment, and with the approval of the U.S. National Institute of Mental Health (the granting agency supporting the Lovaas study), an alternate assignment method was decided upon. This method is known as quasi or "functional" random assignment. Lovaas utilized an assortment of recognized psychometric measures to evaluate prospective study subjects, and thereby ensured that all children accepted into the study were closely matched.

Quasi-random or Functional Random Assignment

Professor Donald Baer (1993), a highly regarded academic and considered by many to be the father of Applied Behaviour Analysis, is given only passing reference in the BCOHTA report regarding his opinion on the report's main criticism — lack of true random assignment. However, the remarks of Dr. Baer (1993) are highly relevant to sorting out the important issue of whether groups in the Lovaas study were identical at intake. Baer's analysis is quoted correctly, albeit narrowly, by the Office.

Baer states:

> *Besides, it is typical of many of us in the science community to suspend the rules and impose our judgment in their place when we do not like the outcome of following the rules of competent design. Perhaps some of the audience who will dismiss these [Lovaas] results because subject assignment was not pristinely random are actually dismissing the procedures that produced these results and the theory that produced these procedures...*[4]

Moreover, the rigour of Lovaas' study design is rooted in the use of no less than eight different psychological measures to ensure close matching of groups.

Dr. Baer has a profound understanding of the political nature characterizing the autism treatment field. He gives us valuable insight into the motivation driving critics of Lovaas' Treatment. With respect to matching of subjects in the landmark Lovaas study, *Baer is satisfied that the groups are the same at intake because most subjects were simply assigned on the basis of therapist availability.* Moreover, the rigor of Lovaas' study design is rooted in the use of no less than eight different psychological measures to ensure close matching of groups. Collectively, due to the result of subject matching based on such a large number of well regarded measures, Dr. Baer regards the groups in the Lovaas study as "functionally random" and therefore valid from a research standpoint.[5]

The heavy emphasis on pure random assignment by BCOHTA may be explained by the researchers' bias towards physical sciences research assessment (e.g., drugs, medical devices) as opposed to psychological research involving children in particular. Pure random assignment in that context cannot be supported on ethical grounds. The lack of appreciation of this context is a flaw in the BCOHTA report and serves as a major stumbling block to accurate assessment of the Lovaas study.

Baer also indicates that on possible predictors of "best" outcome children, the psychometric measures are very similar amongst *all* children in the landmark Lovaas study. Baer states:

> *The experimental and control subjects [in the Lovaas study] had* ***strikingly similar averages*** *on most of those, and those*

> *on which they differed somewhat do not strike me as predictors of treatment success...*[6] (emphasis added).

In other words, all children in the Lovaas study were functionally the same according to generally accepted psychometric measures, particularly those measures relevant to autism.

By contrast, the Office states:

> *However, support for unbiased group assignment is negated by Lovaas and his colleagues who admit that group assignment was also based on family factors, geographic location and stage of research.*[7]

All children in the Lovaas study were functionally the same according to generally accepted psychometric measures, particularly those measures relevant to autism.

This criticism further confuses the issue of random assignment. Family factors and geographic location are random by their very nature. They clearly have no bearing on how well children with autism will respond to treatment. Although children who lived far away were not randomly assigned, from a functional standpoint, their place of residence is a random issue unrelated to severity of autism.

Two children in the Lovaas study lived over an hour from the clinic which made it unfeasible for the child to receive intensive intervention. Therefore, the child was excluded from the experimental group receiving intensive treatment (forty hours per week). We would expect BCOHTA researchers to agree that an hour's drive from UCLA does not make an autistic child higher or lower functioning. Consequently, assignment of that child to the Lovaas study control group, although not truly random, is nonetheless a *functionally random assignment*, because place of residence is not a psychometric variable and cannot be manipulated by the researchers. Assertion to the contrary is indeed a spurious allegation.

Another mistaken BCOHTA criticism is that the Lovaas study did not control the variable of "stage of research." In other words, all the children in the study did not start treatment at the same time. The Lovaas study accepted children into the study as they contacted the UCLA clinic. Although this was not *true random assignment*, it meets the test of functional random assignment because researchers did not have any control over who contacted the clinic, or when they contacted the clinic. This random event is clearly unrelated to severity of autism, which again casts doubt on the BCOHTA critique that lack of control for stage of research is relevant to the issue of group similarity.

Regarding the BCOHTA's critique that "family factors" could possibly degrade the study design, McEachin suggests that this argument is unfounded. McEachin describes the families:

> *Subjects' families ranged from high to low socioeconomic status, and, on average, they did not differ from the general population (Lovaas, 1987). Thus, although our treatment required extensive family participation, a diverse group of families was apparently able to meet this requirement.*[8]

Office analysts argue that there was selection bias in the Lovaas study, implying that Lovaas deliberately selected higher functioning children with possibly better prospects for treatment success for the intensive treatment group.

Subject Selection Bias

Office analysts argue that there was selection bias in the Lovaas study, implying that Lovaas deliberately selected higher functioning children with possibly better prospects for treatment success for the intensive treatment group. However, there is no support for this allegation.

The BCOHTA researchers state:

> *Lovaas only included children between 40-46 months if they had echolalia, "a symptom widely recognized (also by Lovaas, 1981) as a characteristic of autistic children with a better prognosis."*[9]

They appear not to have taken Lovaas' explanation into account. Lovaas states:

> *Schopler et al. (1989) claim that our selection criteria were intended to produce a biased sample. In fact, the purpose of these criteria was twofold: First, to ensure that our subjects were reliably diagnosed, we excluded children with low PMA scores (equivalent to a deviation IQ below 30) because it is difficult to differentiate autistic children with such low IQs from other profoundly retarded children (Wing, 1981). Second, we extended the age limit from 40 to 46 months for echolalic children. Eight of our 38 subjects (4 in the experimental group*

> *and 4 in the control group) were included by this criterion. We thought that, because we would not need to establish speech in these children, we might still have enough time to prepare them for regular preschool (a central goal in our program). We found that we did not bias the outcome by doing this because only 1 of the 4 experimental group subjects included by the echolalia criterion attained normal functioning.*[10]

With respect to prorated mental age and the exclusion of profoundly retarded children from the study, it is correct that Lovaas excluded children whom he suspected of suffering not only from autism but also severe mental retardation. However, such exclusion was not an attempt to "cream" high functioning autistic children. As part of competent study design, Lovaas acted to ensure the subject pool was comprised of children who suffer *only* from autism. In all, only 15% of the children were excluded from Lovaas' landmark study.[11]

Office analysts make another argument which suggests that Lovaas "creamed" subjects for the experimental group but not for the control group.

Office analysts make another argument which suggests that Lovaas "creamed" subjects for the experimental group but not for the control group. In a discussion of scientific validity, the BCOHTA states:

> *Any treatment will appear effective or perhaps curative if it is applied to the (relatively small) subset of children who will do well regardless of specific treatment. The appearance of treatment effect will be further enhanced if, at the same time as children likely to benefit are assigned to receive treatment, children with poorer prognosis are assigned to a "matched" control group.*[12]

BCOHTA also states:

> *... (b) the control group had fewer higher functioning clients than one would expect in groups of this size: typically, 20% to 30% of people with autism are higher functioning, irrespective of the services that they receive...*[13]

There is no support for this contention. The variables used to match groups in the Lovaas study are widely considered in psychology as the most likely predictors of prognosis in children with autism. It is simply not possible for competent researchers to successfully argue that *"the control group had fewer*

No statistically significant differences occurred in the key psychometric measures used to match the groups.

higher functioning clients" than the experimental group insofar as no statistically significant differences occurred in the key psychometric measures used to match the groups. Such measures include: prorated mental age; sum pathology; abnormal speech; self-stimulatory behavior; appropriate toy play; any recognizable words. Measures such as these would have differed significantly had the groups not been matched correctly. In short, Lovaas utilized a variety of measures generally recognized as part of highly competent research design, even by present day standards.

In addition, the BCOHTA selectively state that, *"In the case of 5 children, assessment was conducted in conjunction with the children's parents."*[14] Lovaas describes exactly what happened as *"Five subjects were judged to be untestable (3 in the experimental group and 2 in Control Group 1)."*[15] Those children with autism deemed "untestable," typically might be behaviorally out-of-control to the extent that they are unable to sit in one spot and comply with testing. Other children with autism may be so withdrawn into their own world that they are functionally oblivious to what goes on around them. By having three "untestable" children in the experimental group and two in Control Group 1, if there were any advantage given — which is debatable in itself — Lovaas may have given a slight advantage to the control group.

In this context it is useful to highlight an important study[16] that only included children with *severe autism and mental retardation.* Smith et al. 1997 found that even for this most severely affected group of autistic children, the experimental group achieved positive outcome, *i.e.*, severely retarded, autistic children who received Lovaas Treatment made significant gains.

Smith et al. state:

> *At follow-up, children in the experimental group obtained a higher mean IQ and evinced more expressive speech than did those in the comparison group. Behavior problems diminished in both groups. Results indicate that intensively treated children achieved clinically meaningful gains relative to the comparison group but remained quite delayed.*[17]

The I.Q. scores of the children changed significantly:

> *The mean IQ of the experimental group increased from 28 at intake to 36 (SD = 13.14) at follow-up. By contrast, the mean IQ of the comparison group decreased from 27 to 24 (SD = 8.23).*[18]

These results are statistically significant ($p < .05$). In short, even the most challenging group of children, children with both autism and mental retardation, significantly improved using Lovaas' treatment protocol. Although this study was included in the BCOHTA references, it is not analyzed or discussed in the body of the report despite (or perhaps because of) its importance in addressing the subject selection bias issue.

The most challenging group of children, children with both autism and mental retardation, significantly improved using Lovaas' treatment protocol.

Sex Differences Between Experimental and Control Group

The B.C. Office of Health Technology Assessment researchers cite Boyd (1987) in its report to argue that the sex inequivalencies between the experimental group and the control group account for most of the difference between the two groups (rather than the treatment). Yet in a perplexing omission, Office analysts then omitted Boyd's key opinion regarding the Lovaas study. Dr. Boyd states, "*in Control group 2, the sex ratios were well within the accepted range.*"[19]

It is an interesting hypothesis that sex differences partially account for the differences between groups. However, Lovaas' original study matched for I.Q. and there were no *statistically* significant differences in I.Q. between groups.[20] In addition, if two of the three girls in the treatment group of Lovaas' study achieved best outcome, and they were "functionally" randomly assigned, as Baer confirms, then perhaps the original studies which made the claim that autistic girls have lower I.Q. than autistic boys need further replication. It is important to keep in mind that Lovaas did attempt to exclude all girls and boys with severe mental retardation from his study so he could keep children with non-autism issues from clouding conclusions about treatment efficacy. One variable that may account for apparently lower I.Q. for autistic girls is the following: some girls with a lower I.Q. relative to boys may suffer from Rett's Syndrome which is characterized by very low I.Q. and only occurs in girls. This may not have been adequately screened out in the various studies cited by Boyd since Rett's Syndrome can look very much like autism at a young age.

Lovaas, by excluding severely retarded children, may have also eliminated the relationship between the variable of sex and I.Q.

Boyd also states:

> *Certainly the fact that significant improvement occurred for a group of autistic children is noteworthy, potentially significant, and deserving of further study. Moreover, this research group [Lovaas researchers] should be commended for engaging in a long-term follow-up treatment study that employed a control group, a rare occurrence in autism research.*[21]

The outcome of the study suggests that it would be unjustified to give this treatment to boys and not girls, because the girls in the experimental group benefitted significantly.

Boyd further discusses the relevance of the sex difference in particular. He states:

> *While seeming group inequivalence along sex may not negate the power of the treatment, it might temper our judgment of which autistic children would benefit from its use.*[22]

Boyd can certainly be challenged on this point since *two of the three girls in the experimental group achieved best outcome.* In other words, since two thirds of the girls achieved the most favourable outcome from Lovaas Treatment, it is clear the treatment works extremely well for girls. If it can be confirmed that girls, in the aggregate, are more severely impacted cognitively than boys — still a contentious issue — then clearly the girls in this study did not follow that model. The outcome of the study suggests that it would be unjustified to give this treatment to boys and not girls, because the girls in the experimental group benefitted significantly.

Is Random Assignment of Children to Treatment and Control Groups "Feasible and Ethical"

The BCOHTA has indicated that it sees no ethical problems with random assignment of autistic children to experimental and control groups for the purpose of replicating and reaffirming the effectiveness of Intensive Behavioural Treatment. BCOHTA researchers state:

> *Random assignment of children to treatment and control groups has been recently shown by Jocelyn et al. to be both*

> *feasible and ethical in Canada, the most relevant context for this review.*[23]

Pure random assignment of children for study of a treatment protocol regarded as best practice is most certainly not ethical. Presumably if we know an autism treatment works in the United States, then, in Canada, it would be morally repugnant to assign children to a control group (the group that does not get the treatment).

The British Columbia Government's Office of Health Technology Assessment has indicated they it sees no ethical problems with random assignment of autistic children to experimental and control groups for the purpose of replicating and reaffirming the effectiveness of Intensive Behavioural Treatment.

The second ethical problem with random assignment in any future autism treatment research concerns the ground-breaking report from the New York Department of Health (conveniently side stepped by the BCOHTA). According to the New York Report on clinical best practices in autism treatment, the entire Jocelyn et al. study, highly touted by the BCOHTA, can be deemed as unethical since it did not include twenty hours of behavioral treatment. The New York Report makes this quite clear in three of its recommendations:

> 1) It is recommended that principles of applied behavior analysis (ABA) and behavior intervention strategies be included as an important element of any intervention program for your children with autism.[24]
>
> 2) It is recommended that intensive behavioral programs include as a minimum, approximately 20 hours per week of individualized behavioral intervention using applied behavioral analysis techniques (not including time spent by parents).[25]
>
> 3) While not explicitly stated in these sections, the panel considered use of an ineffective assessment or intervention method as a type of indirect harm if its use supplants an effective assessment or intervention method that the child might have otherwise received.[26]

In other words, by not informing and educating parents regarding early, intensive behavioral intervention (EIBI), Jocelyn et al. (1998) actually kept the possibility of EIBI treatment from autistic children in her study because many of the parents might have opted for EIBI if they knew about it (and could afford it). According to the New York State Department of Health Report, withholding EIBI is actually *harmful* to the child (New York Report, pages 1-10). Therefore, pure random assignment is in fact *unethical,* unless researchers are prepared to provide all children the EIBI and then randomly assign them to experimental and control groups to test some other type of therapy.

It is also highly noteworthy that the study highlighted by BCOHTA, Jocelyn et al. (1998), actually did not produce any meaningful success in outcomes. In order to get around this inconvenient conclusion, BCOHTA states:

> *While their study is ground-breaking in this area of research, it was, as the authors note, too short to determine ultimate treatment effect.*[27]

Those familiar with the field of autism, such as psychiatrists and psychologists, are fully aware of the efficacy of intensive behavioural treatment and would likely not consider pure random assignment as ethical research practice.

In view of the fact that intensive behavioural treatment is currently considered "best practice" for autism by the New York State Department of Health, and the U.S. Surgeon General recommends it as the treatment of choice for children with autism, BCOHTA support for random assignment would appear to be a breach *UBC ethics* in human subject research. University of British Columbia Policy states:

> *It is the purpose of the University to ensure that where a human subject is involved in a research or other study: the safety, welfare, and rights of the subject are adequately protected;*[28] ...

The parents of disabled children are entitled to give *informed* consent when volunteering their children for human subject research. It is the solemn responsibility of university researchers to fully inform those parents as to best practices, so that parents can protect their children's best interests. Based on our current knowledge about intensive behavioural treatment, any proposal for autism research incorporating pure random assignment would clearly be unethical.

Is It Ethical to Deny Treatment to Children?

As seen above, the BCOHTA report supports pure random assignment despite the ethical problems with this approach. In fact, BCOHTA goes as far as saying that pure random assignment is necessary:

> ***Randomized trials*** *of alternative early intensive treatment programs* ***are ethical*** *and feasible to advance research knowledge, and absolutely necessary if* ***resource utilization*** *is to be justified in this area*[29] (emphasis added).

In short, Office analysts use the lack of "pure random assignment," as an apparent justification to deny publicly funded intensive behavioural treatment for children with autism. Following through to the logical conclusion of this circular argument is that children with autism can never receive publicly funded behavioural treatment until we get more purely randomized studies. However, that kind of research can never happen because it is no longer ethical. So, according to this health technology argument, in the meantime no public spending on autism can be justified.

Based on our current knowledge about intensive behavioural treatment, any proposal for autism research incorporating pure random assignment, would be "unethical."

The Claim That Lovaas Does Not Measure 'Real Life' Data

By their own admission, the Office recognizes that the Lovaas landmark study has done much to use standard intervention protocols which capture a wide range of skills and symptoms, under both laboratory and "real life" situations.

The BCOHTA indicates that the Lovaas treatment protocol can be credited with "moving *therapy beyond the clinic and laboratory into real life settings such as home and community.*"[30] Indeed, the Lovaas treatment protocol sets an autism research "gold standard" in this regard.

No other autism interventions or therapies have a similar commitment to *"moving therapy beyond the clinic and laboratory into real life* ."[31] Lovaas' research can be greatly credited for removing children with autism from the clinics and institutions and delivering intensive treatment in their own homes, under their parents' watchful eyes.

Once BCOHTA offers Lovaas perfunctory credit, it then goes about qualifying the praise. Office analysts state:

> *It should be noted, however, that while criterion 3 is clearly met [the study should use standard intervention protocols that*

> *capture a wide range of skills and symptoms, under both laboratory and 'real life' situations*], *criterion 6 (**details of the application of that method**) is not*"[32] (emphasis added).

This is a misleading statement. Details of the Lovaas treatment protocol are very clearly set out, particularly in his publication, *Teaching Developmentally Disabled Children: The Me Book* (Lovaas, 1981). In addition, *A Work in Progress* (Leaf and McEachin, 1999), further sets out details of the intensive behavioural treatment protocol. Although the BCOHTA perceives itself as a group of researchers who conduct so-called "exhaustive" research, it is indeed unfortunate that they did not review the work of Leaf and McEachin, cited above. This would have given the Office greater insight into what constitutes bona fide intensive behavioural treatment based on the Lovaas protocol.

Lovaas' research can be greatly credited for removing children with autism from the clinics and institutions and delivering intensive treatment in their own homes, under their parents watchful eyes.

Moreover, the BCOHTA failed to acknowledge, perhaps deliberately, that Lovaas researchers were scrupulous in taking detailed data on the program of *each child* in the study. This surely satisfies their requirement for *"details of the application of that method."*[33] which BCOHTA researchers misleadingly claim Lovaas' landmark study lacks. The voluminous data taken for each individual child's program has not been published by Lovaas, because this is not customary and would serve no purpose. It should be noted that treatment staff in every well-run Lovaas Treatment program today continue to follow the protocol established by Lovaas — they take detailed data on each child they treat. A minimal knowledge of Lovaas' autism treatment work and the numerous replication sites around the world would have avoided the BCOHTA's embarrassing error in asserting that Lovaas did not provide details of the application of his treatment method.

In short, the BCOHTA criticism regarding criterion 6 [details of the application of the method] is unfounded. It shows either a profound lack of understanding on the part of Office analysts regarding what constitutes the Lovaas Treatment protocol, or an attempt to confuse the judge about generally recognized and well defined parameters of Lovaas' treatment protocol.

Psychological Assessment of Children in Lovaas' Research

The BCOHTA regard Lovaas' use of outside evaluators at intake and at school entry as flawed. It is significant to note that Office researchers may not have analyzed the evaluation procedure in the Lovaas study because they do not describe the evaluation at intake. *What Office analysts have done, however, is describe the intake procedure through a secondary source* — Gresham and McMillan — rather than conducting what is customary in academe, a review of the primary source. BCOHTA quotes from this secondary source, "*5 children were not evaluated by , but by the parents.*"[34]

Academic honesty dictates researchers from the BCOHTA should have gone to the source material to investigate what actually happened.

Academic honesty dictates researchers from the BCOHTA should have gone to the source material to investigate what actually happened. It is not apparent from the report that such primary research was done.

In reference to the use of at intake, Lovaas states:

> *Testing was carried out by graduate students in psychology who worked under the supervision of clinical psychologists at UCLA or licensed Ph.D. psychologists at other agencies. The examiner chose the test that would best accommodate each subject's developmental level, and this decision was reached independently of the project staff. Five subjects were judged to be untestable (3 in the experimental group and 2 in the Control Group 1). Instead, the Vineland Social Maturity Scale (Doll, 1953) was used to estimate the MAs (with the mother as informant). To adjust for variations in MA scores as a function of the subject's CA at the time of test administration, PMA scores were calculated for a CA at 30 months (MA/CA x 30).*[35]

The central point here is that were used for *all* but five children. As discussed previously in this section, those five children were deemed untestable. A subset of autistic children are untestable. This is a concept familiar to anyone with even a limited background in autism. In reference to the five children, Lovaas states, "*these interviews were given for children who were too noncompliant to complete tests of intellectual functioning.*"[36]

Lovaas did the next best thing — he used a Vineland Social Maturity Scale with a parent. Other scholars are also of the opinion that Lovaas did an outstanding job in the use of at intake. Rogers (1998), whom BCOHTA researchers rely upon extensively in their critique of Lovaas, describes Lovaas' procedure at intake as follows:

> *Children in all three groups were diagnosed by independent clinicians, and virtually all the children came from the same large diagnostic clinic in the Psychiatry Department at the University of California, Los Angeles from faculty members recognized* ***internationally*** *for their expertise in autism*[37] (emphasis added).

Five children were deemed untestable. A subset of autistic children are untestable. This is a concept familiar to anyone with even a limited background in autism.

In terms of outcome measures at the beginning of school entry, BCOHTA researchers acknowledge that independent evaluators were used for testing, but emphasize the point of Gresham and McMillan's that, *"school performance and behavior was reported by parents and teachers, not by ."* It is an obvious contradiction on the part of Office to state that teachers are *not* , *i.e.*, not outside the study. Moreover, teachers most certainly are expert evaluators of children in terms of what constitutes typical, acceptable in-class behaviour and classroom performance.

Here it is valuable to reference the description that Lovaas gives regarding school placement. Lovaas states:

> *All children who successfully completed normal kindergarten successfully completed first grade and subsequent normal grades. Children who were observed to be experiencing educational and psychological problems received their school placement through Individualized Educational Plan (IEP) staffings (attended by educators and psychologists) in accordance with the Education For All Handicapped Children Act of 1975.*[38]

Lovaas goes on to explain why the educational system is a good outcome measure:

> *These children then entered normal first grade classes on their own merits. They remained there without any special*

> *intervention and were passed from grade to grade using the same criteria applied to all other children in such classes.* ***This is significant because schools in Los Angeles conduct extensive, independent assessments on all exceptional children, and they virtually always place children whom they identify as autistic in special education classes***[39] (emphasis added).

Those familiar with autism would agree that untreated children with autism who are a) assigned to a regular classroom and b) have no front line support, are highly unlikely to progress and advance through the regular educational system. *When such progress occurs in regular classrooms, it indeed functions as a true indicator of success in overcoming autism.* In the realm of regular education, successful, unsupported progress of an autistic child is a salient measure from highly relevant "" — regular education teachers in the real world.

In the realm of regular education, successful, unsupported progress of an autistic child is a salient measure from highly relevant "outside evaluators" — regular education teachers in the real world.

BCOHTA misrepresentation of the outcome evaluation of Lovaas' study further suggests a profound lack of knowledge on the part of Office researchers regarding autism. It also reflects the Office's bias to uncritically accept opinions put forth by Lovaas' academic rivals. This further supports the claim that the BCOHTA review of Lovaas Treatment is little more than advocacy research clearly influenced by the litigation context in which it was created.

Did Lovaas Provide Enough Details On How the Treatment is Implemented?

It is clear, even to the uninitiated reader, that the BCOHTA unfairly favours any argument that supports its position without critically evaluating the argument itself. A case in point: the Report uncritically presented the internal validity argument that Gresham and McMillan provide, by stating:

> *BCOHTA researchers concur with Gresham and MacMillan. In neither the Lovaas 1987 study report, nor in the subsequent discussions do Lovaas et al. provide details of which elements and how much of the therapeutic intervention individual children received.*[40]

The BCOHTA further states:

> *Clearly -defined treatment activities are essential if treatment effect is to be distinguished from extraneous variables influencing the outcome of children with autism.*[41]

The study did have high compliance with the defined treatment protocol, based on the operations manual that Lovaas published, as well as the tight supervision of the therapists by the research team. Rogers (1998), upon whom BCOHTA relies heavily, states:

The study did have high compliance with the defined treatment protocol, based on the operations manual that Lovaas published, as well as the tight supervision of the therapists by the research team.

> *There was tight control of the treatment delivery by those who had developed the treatment program.*[42]

The BCOHTA critique further points to a *profound* lack of knowledge regarding the intractable nature of autism and how extraneous variables do not have enough power to influence the outcome of children with autism to substantively change manifestations of the condition. It is significant to note that Office analysts have adopted this critique from Gresham and MacMillan as their own.

Gresham and MacMillan state:

> *Some treatments, particularly those delivered by different therapists, may be effective not because of the efficacy of the treatment per se, but rather because of therapist's characteristics (e.g., rapport, warmth, encouragement).*[43]

The Gresham and MacMillan critique appears to be a cousin of Bettelheim's discredited theory that autism is caused by cold "refrigerator" mothers. Most competent autism professionals have moved away from the "rapport and warmth" school of autism etiology. It is most unfortunate, therefore, that Gresham and MacMillan, as well as BCOHTA researchers, perpetuate the "refrigerator mother" myth and unwittingly lend credence to the academic descendants of Bettelheim's lineage.

Lovaas speaks to Gresham and MacMillan's contention that *"rapport, warmth, encouragement"* are effective in autism treatment. Lovaas states:

> *The idea [e.g., rapport, warmth, encouragement] is the basis for many treatment programs for children with autism, including psychoanalysis, Gentle Teaching, Holding Therapy, Options, Theraplay, and other "relationship therapies." Nevertheless,* ***it has fared extremely poorly in research, as much evidence indicates that children with autism derive no particular benefit from attention*** *and may be harmed by it under many circumstances (Lovaas et al., 1989; Smith, 1993). To put this another way, attention, warmth, and so on are probably necessary components of treatment, but they are not sufficient to help children with autism."*[44] (emphasis added).

The Gresham and MacMillan critique appears to be a cousin of Bettelheim's discredited theory that autism is caused by cold "refrigerator" mothers.

BCOHTA researchers make an additional criticism regarding the possible use of prescription drugs in the Lovaas landmark study as a possible reason for improvement amongst the children. The report states:

> *Also omitted are details of the type and amount of alternative (perhaps pharmaceutical) therapies received by the experimental group.*[45]

The criticism exposes a "drug and physical-medicine bias" of the Office towards the treatment of illness, in this case applied to autism. This BCOHTA bias once again constitutes an expertise blind spot that blocks necessary understanding of psychosocial treatments for autism.

Speaking directly to the BCOHTA pharmaceutical criticism, it can be said there is no reason that the experimental group in the Lovaas study would have received more or less pharmaceuticals than the control group. Because Lovaas did not study pharmaceuticals, if any drugs were unknowingly in use, most impartial observers would agree that such pharmaceutical use would be evenly distributed amongst children in all groups. To suggest that *"alternative (perhaps pharmaceutical) therapies [were] received by the experimental group,"* [46] *and selectively not administered to the control group,* is a most serious allegation that should not be made lightly by BCOHTA researchers. This is an implicit accusation that Lovaas has not been honest and forthcoming in reporting his study methodology — the Office suggestion is that Lovaas may have withheld methodology information.

The autism expertise vacuum within the Office comes into sharp focus when discussing drug interventions to treat autistic disorder. Pharmaceutical options for children with autism, at the time of Lovaas' study (1970's - 1980's) were crude and ineffective. Even today, most B.C. children in Lovaas Treatment programs are not given drugs for the simple reason that there are no drugs that *effectively* treat autism on a global level; some drugs administered to autistic children also have unwelcome side-effects. Dr. E.J. Garland, M.D., F.R.C.P.(C) a British Columbia psychiatrist well aware of the pharmaceutical options for children with autism, states:

> *it is my opinion that it is unacceptable to withhold funding for intensive early intervention with a program which clearly works when we do not have any other effective treatment for Autistic Disorder.*[47]

The autism expertise vacuum within the Office comes into sharp focus when discussing drug interventions to treat autistic disorder. Pharmaceutical options for children with autism, at the time of Lovaas' study (1970's - 1980's) were crude and ineffective.

The BCOHTA report also puts forth its contention regarding the purported difficulty of administering Lovaas Treatment. Office researchers argue that Lovaas treatment is a complex autism treatment protocol.

> *Replication of the Lovaas (1987) treatment benefit requires replication of the comprehensive treatment model including parents, therapists and pre-school institutions. This could be extremely problematic.*[48]

Indeed, the Lovaas Treatment protocol *is* complex. It is not an easy treatment to design or administer. However, to say that delivery of a complex treatment model is "*extremely problematic*"[49] is simply not the case. Today, the treatment protocol is being replicated throughout British Columbia, with many children and with tremendous success. However, a complex, comprehensive treatment protocol cannot be designed and implemented by unqualified professionals. To be effective, an intensive behavioural treatment program must be designed and implemented by competent, experienced Lovaas Treatment consultants.

Perhaps due to an ignorance about autism and the privately funded autism treatment reality in British Columbia, BCOHTA researchers hold the incorrect view that it is simply parents, therapists and preschool institutions that must attempt to "replicate" Lovaas Treatment success. In fact, parents who desire bona fide Lovaas Treatment, currently import — of necessity and at private

Indeed, the Lovaas Treatment protocol *is* complex. It is not an easy treatment to design or administer. However, to say that delivery of a complex treatment model is *"extremely problematic"*[55] is simply not the case.

expense — highly qualified U.S. Lovaas Treatment consultants to set up and customize autism treatment programs for their children. The process of replicating the treatment protocol utilized in Lovaas' 1987 article is costly for British Columbia families, but can hardly be viewed as *"extremely problematic"* by any knowledgeable, disinterested observer.

The BCOHTA concludes by stating:

> *In summary, despite the detailed material regarding the Lovaas method, the research reports provide virtually no details regarding the actual application of that material. In fact, the absence of description of the amount, quality, and consistency of the applied behavioral analysis techniques is one of the most striking aspects of Lovaas and McEachin's work.*[50]

Gresham and MacMillan had already made this point in their critiques of Lovaas. Lovaas replies, in terms of amount of treatment:

> *On the contrary, we specified that all children received an average of 40 hours per week (Lovaas, 1987), and we provided data on the time between the end of treatment and follow-up (McEachin et al., 1993). We might add that, because of holidays, illnesses, and so forth, the number of treatment hours fell below 40 in some weeks, but we made up missed sessions to maintain the average of 40 hours.*[51]

In terms of treatment quality, Lovaas describes:

> *Each subject in the experimental group was assigned several well trained student therapists who worked (part-time) with the subject in the subject's home, school and community for an average of 40 hr per week for 2 or more years. The parents worked as part of the treatment team throughout the intervention; they were extensively trained in the treatment procedures so that treatment could take place for almost all of the subject's waking hours 365 days a year. A detailed presentation of the treatment procedure has been presented in a teaching manual.*[52]

Regarding the treatment integrity, Lovaas states:

> *We documented treatment integrity in the manner recommended by the investigators cited by Gresham and MacMillan (Johnston & Pennypacker, 1980). These investigators have contended that the best way to know what aspects of a treatment make it work is to study individual components of the treatment separately before performing an outcome study (see also Johnston, 1988). This is what we did (see Newsom & Rincover, 1989, for one review).*[53]

It is disturbingly apparent that Office researchers have once again elected to adopt, as their own, the critique of Lovaas' most scathing academic rivals — Gresham and MacMillan.

In short, it is disturbingly apparent that Office researchers have once again elected to adopt, as their own, the critique of Lovaas' most scathing academic rivals — Gresham and MacMillan. Unfortunately, BCOHTA researchers elected to exclude from their purportedly "exhaustive" review, Lovaas' significant reply to the critique of Gresham and MacMillan (1997), as well as Schopler et al. (1989). Such is the nature of advocacy research.

Is the Treatment Still Effective Over Time?

The BCOHTA admits that the Lovaas 1987 study uses longitudinal designs that evaluate treatment effects, both during the treatment itself, and at set points after the intervention. However, they fault the study based on the criticism of Schopler et al., 1989, in stating that classroom placement and IQ measures are used excessively by Lovaas (this criticism has already been addressed). In terms of IQ measures, Office analysts present the points of several critics regarding I.Q., *i.e.*, Schopler, et al., 1989; Mesibov, 1997; Mundy, 1997, and Gresham and MacMillan, 1997. In typical advocacy research fashion, BCOHTA researchers elected to exclude from their report Lovaas' responses to I.Q. as an outcome measure. This shortcoming in the Office report is addressed below:

BCOHTA states:

> *Schopler et al. also note that "Improvement on IQ measures may reflect improvement in compliance rather than in cognitive function. Higher scores on follow up IQ tests will then reflect improved test-taking skill rather than improved intellectual functioning.*[54]

In typical advocacy research fashion, BCOHTA researchers elected to exclude from their report Lovaas' responses to I.Q. as an outcome measure.

Lovaas neutralizes the BCOHTA critique via his response to Schopler:

> *Schopler et al. (1989) question our IQ data. Yet, we reported a very conservative estimate of IQ increase (using a ratio pretreatment IQ rather than a deviation IQ because ratio scores tend to be higher). We also optimized the children's performance on pretreatment IQ tests by reinforcing compliant behavior, a deviation from standard test administration procedures that is commonly used with autistic children (Freeman, 1976). Nevertheless, we found a 20-point gain in posttreatment IQ in our experimental group as a whole and a 37-point gain (to the normal range) in the 9 children we classified as normal functioning. The improved functioning occurred with strict adherence to standardized test administration procedures at follow-up. Schopler et al., however, suggest that the normal IQs obtained at follow-up were indicative of the children's true intelligence and that the retarded IQs obtained at intake were underestimates resulting from the children' uncooperativeness. The notion that autistic children actually have a normal intelligence and that their disturbances present them from showing it was widely held in the 1940s and 1950s. It was abandoned when numerous studies showed that autistic children have severe intellectual deficits no matter how cooperative they are (Rutter, 1983). For example, mute children (like half of our subjects at intake) or children who repeat others but have little or no communicative speech (like the remainder of our subjects at intake) score low on IQ tests mainly because they lack language, not because they refuse to do tasks.*[55]

The BCOHTA's further reliance on Mesibov's critique of Lovaas states:

> *Mesibov similarly notes that "Many skills required for normal functioning have not been measured by McEachin et al (1993). They did not report on the student's social interactions, friendships, conceptual abilities, and social communication skills, skills likely to differentiate children with autism from their peers without handicaps.*[56]

The BCOHTA report also presents Mundy's critique, which is similar to Mesibov's. Smith and Lovaas (1997) respond to this as well. They state:

> *...while two measures were used at the age 7 follow-up (i.e. IQ and school placement), 33 were used at the age 12 follow-up. Gresham and MacMillan discuss only 1 of these 33 measures (full scale IQ) in their critique. Plainly, this is a severe shortcoming in their analysis.*[57]

In addition, McEachin et al. (1993) state:

Lovaas found a 20-point gain in posttreatment IQ in his experimental group as a whole and a 37-point gain (to the normal range) in the 9 children he classified as normal functioning.

> *A wide range of measures was administered, avoiding over reliance on intelligence tests, which have limitations if used in isolation (e.g., bias resulting from teaching to the test, selecting a test that would yield especially favorable results, failing to assess other aspects of functioning such as social competence or school performance) (Spitz, 1986: Zigler & Trickett, 1978).*[58]

As discussed previously, the following points must be raised:

> 1) When Lovaas-treated children are deemed "indistinguishable from their peers," based on evaluation by psychologists trained to diagnose autism,
> 2) They are functioning independently at school, and
> 3) They cannot be identified at school as autistic, then we most certainly have a valid measure of successful autism treatment outcome. Moreover, this outcome is a valid indicator that these children no longer meet the criteria for autism. It is understandable that rival autism academics, who have yet to achieve similar outcomes, may find such "school success" outcomes troubling. However, academic rivalry, no matter how heated, does not degrade the significance of a valid outcome measure.

The BCOHTA mentions Gresham and MacMillan's critique regarding measurement instruments used by Lovaas 1987 at baseline. *To their credit, Office analysts acknowledge they do not understand the criticism, presumably owing to their lack of expertise in psychology and autism.* However, in the

BCOHTA report, Office staff still choose to include an analysis they openly admit they do not understand. Typical to advocacy research, the BCOHTA excludes Lovaas' defense, which again supports the contention that the review was primarily motivated by the desire to defeat the parents' claims in the B.C. litigation.

Instead of simply viewing Gresham and MacMillan's critique through the advocacy filter of the BCOHTA, it is most telling and impartial to review the *entire* discussion between Smith and Lovaas, 1997 and Gresham and MacMillan, 1997. Based on the exchange between these academics, it is apparent that Lovaas is a competent researcher. Below is the complete dialog between these academics. The statements are made by Gresham and MacMillan and the answers are made by Lovaas and Smith.[59]

Office staff still choose to include an analysis they openly admit they do not understand.

> ***Statement:*** *The EIP made use of a psychometrically questionable scaling procedure Lovaas (1987) called the prorated mental age (PMA) (p. 189).*
>
> ***Answer:*** *If Gresham and MacMillan do not like this statistic, they are free to use the ratio or deviation IQ, each of which we also reported (Lovaas et al., 1989) and which could, in any case, have been readily calculated from the prorated mental age.*
>
> ***Statement:*** *How Lovaas (1987) was able to derive deviation IQ scores from the PMA formula is unknown, since the formula is based on the ratio IQ formula (p. 189).*
>
> ***Answer:*** *Basically, what the PMA score did was translate children's performance into a score that could either be converted to a ratio IQ or looked up in the norms tables for deviation IQs in Bayley (1969) or the supplemental tables by Naglieri (1981). These tables contain deviation IQs for children with chronological ages up to 30 months. Because most of our children were a few months older than this, we used PMA to estimate what they would have scored at 30 months so that we could obtain a deviation IQ for them.*

Rather than viewing Gresham and MacMillan's critique through the BCOHTA advocacy filter, the *entire* discussion between Smith and Lovaas, 1997 and Gresham and MacMillan, 1997 makes it apparent that Lovaas is a competent researcher.

Statement: *Lovaas (1987) presented no data concerning the CA (means or) ranges (at intake) in any of the three groups. (p. 189).*

Answer: *Means appear in the second and third column of Table 1 (Lovaas, 1987) and the range is presented in Table 2 of this article.*

Statement: *We simply do not know how to interpret the posttest IQ results given that posttest measures primarily were scaled as deviation IQs . . . and pretest scores were based on PMA (p. 189).*

Answer: *This issue is discussed at length by Lovaas and Smith (1988) and somewhat more briefly by Lovaas and colleagues (1989). To summarize, we presented deviation IQ at intake in addition to PMA (Lovaas et al., 1989). If we had used deviation IQs throughout (as Gresham and MacMillan apparently advocate), our estimates of IQ gains would have been much larger than what we presented (29 points rather than 20 at the age 7 follow-up). We chose to be more conservative.*

Statement: *Lovaas and his colleagues (1989) reported that experimental group and Control Group 1 children's IQ scores at pretest were optimized by reinforcing compliant behavior ... [but] do not describe how this compliant behavior was reinforced (p. 190).*

Answer: *On the contrary, we cited a journal article that detailed the procedure we used (Freeman, 1976). This procedure is standard in the testing of children with autism (e.g., Marcus, Lansing, & Schopler, 1993), many of whom would be untestable if standard administration procedures were employed.*

Statement: *Lovaas and his colleagues reported that strict adherence to standardized test administration procedures was* *achieved at follow-up (p. 190). Hence, pre- and post-treatment evaluations were conducted "under completely different experimental conditions" (p. 190). As a result, the results are "uninterpretable" but "might be expected to have a conservative bias" (p. 190).*

Answer: *Obviously, results cannot be both "uninterpretable" and "conservatively biased." Which is right? As noted by Lovaas and colleagues (1989), optimizing scores at intake but not follow-up yields a conservative estimate of improvement. Gresham and MacMillan (1997) contradict their own assertion that the results are uninterpretable, as they offer many interpretations in subsequent sections of their article.*

"Gresham and MacMillan (1997) contradict their own assertion that the results are uninterpretable, as they offer many interpretations in subsequent sections of their article."

Statement: *Schopler, Short, and Mesibov (1989) suggested that improved test scores could reflect increased "compliance" and "test-taking skills" (p. 190) rather than enhanced intellectual functioning.*

Answer: *This effect occurs in children from impoverished families (as noted by Gresham and MacMillan), but not in children with autism (Freeman, Ritvo, Needleman, & Yokota, 1985; Lord & Schopler, 1988; Rutter & Bartak, 1973; see Rutter, 1983), as we pointed out already in answer to Schopler and colleagues (1989: Lovaas et al., 1989). Moreover, the effect is much smaller than the gain we obtained (typically about 10 points for a maximum of 4 years, not 20 points over a 10 year period, including many years without treatment, as we reported).*

Statement: *As Schopler and colleagues (1989) pointed out, "Improvement on IQ measures may reflect improvement in compliance rather than in cognitive functions" (p. 190).*

Answer: *As we have previously noted, this old psychoanalytic notion has been overwhelmingly refuted by research (Rutter, 1983), including studies by Schopler and colleagues, that have failed to obtain IQ increases with treatment (Lord & Schopler, 1988).*

> ***Statement:*** *IQ test results were "influenced to an unknown degree by the so-called Flynn effect," (p. 190) which refers to the gradual improvement that has occurred in the performance of children on intelligence tests over time in the United States and elsewhere.*
>
> ***Answer:*** *On the contrary, the influence of the is known with some precision from the manuals for the tests used for the large majority of the children in our study at intake (Bayley, 1993, Table 6.10) and the age 7 and age 12 follow-ups (Wechsler, 1993, Table 6.9). Table 1 in this article presents intake and follow-up scores with and without Flynn corrections. Flynn-corrected scores are presented as ranges rather than precise numbers, in keeping with the format used by Bayley (1993) and Wechsler (1993). They are extrapolated from the tables because Flynn corrections were presented not for each possible score, but for each 5-point (Bayley, 1993) or 15-point (Wechsler, 1993) increment in IQ. Plainly, Flynn corrections have only a trivial influence on the interpretation of the results. For example, without Flynn corrections, we reported that the mean deviation IQ of the experimental group rose from 54 at intake to 83 at age 7 and 85 at age 12. As shown in the first row of Table 1, with Flynn corrections the ranges at each assessment are 46-55, 76-80, and 78-82, respectively.*[60]

"As we have previously noted, this old psychoanalytic notion [Improvement on IQ measures may reflect improvement in compliance rather than in cognitive functions]has been overwhelmingly refuted by research."

When one carefully examines the above discourse between Gresham and MacMillan, and Smith and Lovaas published in the Journal of Behavioral Disorders (1997), it is evident that Smith and Lovaas have a credible defense to every allegation. *It is clearly unjustified on the part of BCOHTA researchers to arrive at the conclusion that "the studies by Lovaas (1987) and McEachin (1993) suffer from several major methodological limitations."*[61] In every study there is likely room for improvement, but many practitioners, reviews, and organizations, such as the U.S. Surgeon General and the New York State Department of Health, do not hold the view espoused by BCOHTA researchers. The opposite is true. Any organization or academic that is disinterested and thinking purely about the role of science in developing effective treatments for autism, considers the work of Lovaas and colleagues as groundbreaking, of high quality and a landmark achievement in the field of autism treatment.

Have Others Replicated the Success of Lovaas Treatment?

The BCOHTA report tends to discount or omit relevant information flowing from research designed to replicate Lovaas' original research. Office analysts evaluate the work of Birnbauer and Leach (1993) and Sheinkopf and Siegal (1998) and conclude that due to the poor quality of these studies, "*it is impossible to determine any causal inference relating to the limited gains reported for these children.*"[62]

Many practitioners, reviews, and organizations, such as the U.S. Surgeon General and the New York State Department of Health, do not hold the view espoused by BCOHTA researchers.

In fact, *there are two other studies that BCOHTA researchers omitted from their report,* despite the fact that their "exhaustive" literature search did uncover those studies (Smith et al., 1997; Anderson et al., 1987). These two studies are discussed here because they offer additional evidence as to the efficacy of the Lovaas autism treatment protocol.

In their report on Lovaas Autism Treatment, Office analysts have tightly framed the debate such that if evidence cannot be found that a given percentage of children are "cured," then the treatment protocol has failed. The "straw man of cure" (versus loss of diagnosis) has been discussed previously; in this section, the highly relevant yet neglected issue is that in every Lovaas Treatment study done, autistic children significantly improved. This remains true whether the study was well done and strictly controlled, such as Lovaas, 1987, McEachin et al, 1993, or Smith et al, 1997, or loosely or completely unaffiliated with U.C.L.A., such as Birnbauer and Leach (1993), and Sheinkopf and Siegel (1998). The fact remains that autistic children improved significantly with behavioural treatment based on the Lovaas model.

BCOHTA does state that:

> *They report that, after 24 months, 4 of the 9 treated children had non-verbal IQs of 89 or higher; the language levels of the treated group doubled that of controls.*[63]

The BCOHTA also reports that in Sheinkopf and Siegal (1998):

> *The treatment group had a mean IQ 25 points higher than the control group (mean of 90 versus mean of 64; p = .01). All 10*

> *children in the treatment group with outcome data improved on IQ measures, usually by 20 or more points.*[64]

In Smith et al., 1997, a study done with *severely autistic, mentally retarded subjects,* the children made substantial gains subsequent to Lovaas treatment. Smith et al. state:

> *At the follow-up evaluation, the intensively treated children achieved a higher mean IQ (36 vs. 24) and demonstrated more expressive speech than did the minimally treated children. Ten of the 11 intensively treated children spoke in words and used them to label objects and express needs at follow-up, whereas only 2 of 10 minimally treated children did so.*[65]

The BCOHTA report tends to discount or omit relevant information flowing from research designed to replicate Lovaas' original research.

In the Anderson et al, 1987 study, outcome was as follows:

> *Most of the 14 children who participated in the study demonstrated significant gains in their language, self-care, social, and academic development, as evidence by the results of standardized assessments and individual treatment data." (Anderson et al., 1987: 352). Of note, is that these children received only 20 hours of treatment a week over a two year period. At the end of the study, most children remained in special education. They describe the school placement as follows: "The results of school placement ratings indicate that only one child (n=11) participated in socially integrated school placement at the time of her admission into the program. At the end of one year of participation in the program, 23% of the children (n=13) were integrated at least two hours a week. This percentage had increased to 31% (n=13) by the time the study had been completed. Nevertheless, all children continued to require specialized services and none were mainstreamed full-time in a regular kindergarten or first grade classroom.*[66]

What is apparent from these various studies is that the Lovaas treatment protocol is robust to the extent that even when insufficient training or oversight of research staff (therapists) occurs, the children still make *very* significant gains. Given that autism is a severe and historically intractable condition, such favourable results are very encouraging and clearly support the efficacy of the treatment protocol. *The various studies cited above can be viewed as instantiations of the original Lovaas study insofar as children made significant gains.* They also teach us another very important lesson. These studies, which were run without sufficient oversight and training of staff, strongly show that the Lovaas protocol, although robust, must be delivered in a disciplined and competent manner if outcomes approaching the U.C.L.A. young autism project are to be equalled. This strongly supports the view that "good enough" is not good enough to overcome or adequately ameliorate the condition of autism. Effective behavioural autism treatment programs require close supervision by highly qualified, trained professionals.

The fact remains that autistic children improved significantly with behavioural treatment based on the Lovaas model.

The Classic Aversives Ruse

A favorite tool in the anti-Lovaas "kit-bag" is to exploit the spurious issue of aversives. Office analysts do not hesitate to exploit this easy, push-button topic to manipulate with fear. Below is a discussion surrounding the topic of aversives the BCOHTA raises.

The BCOHTA suggests that without the use of physical aversives, the Lovaas treatment protocol may not be effective. In the original study, four of the children were subjected to one aversive procedure, which was a slap on the thigh. The BCOHTA states:

> *On the other hand, they recommend excluding certain aspects of the initial Lovaas treatment program that have become socially unacceptable. For example, the authors recommend against use of physical aversives as part of the applied behavioural analysis program, but without noting that this may have been an essential component of the initial Lovaas (1987) treatment success.*[67]

Smith and Lovaas (1997) dispense with this BCOHTA critique through a reply to Gresham and MacMillan. Smith and Lovaas state:

> *This was true in Lovaas (1987) [the use of physical punishment to decrease inappropriate behaviors], but it is not true of the*

> *current UCLA project because we believe research advances since the time the study began (the 1970s) have rendered such procedures unnecessary. Hence, it is incorrect to say that "physical punishment is used" in the UCLA project. Such a statement needlessly deters other sites from adopting the UCLA treatment model, and it gives the erroneous impression that the treatment has not evolved over time as research has progressed.*[68]

Moreover, in none of the replication studies, such as Birnbauer and Leach, 1993; Scheinkopf and Siegal, 1998; and Anderson, et al., 1987, were physical aversives used; yet the results for the treatment groups were still significant and impressive.

A favorite tool in the anti-Lovaas "kit-bag" is to exploit the spurious issue of aversives. Office analysts do not hesitate to exploit this easy, push-button topic to manipulate with fear.

Office analysts present the elimination of physical aversives as a consequence of the lack of social acceptance of this procedure. There are methodological reasons Lovaas abandoned physical aversives. In an interview with the Canadian Broadcast Corporation's *Nature of Things* program, Lovaas describes the problem of "satiation" with physical aversives. The basic concept of satiation is this: if a small physical aversive is given to a child with autism, the first time, it may be effective. With subsequent use of the aversive, the child may not respond because it is no longer aversive. The child has satiated on a low level. As one increases the level incrementally, the child satiates on the aversive incrementally. Clearly one cannot continually increase the level of the aversive. Therefore, if only from a research standpoint, it is preferable not to use physical aversives at all.

A child that is continually positively reinforced in treatment is being rewarded for success. Success then begets success, and the vast majority of behavioral issues can be extinguished by withholding positive reinforcement rather than through the use of aversives. To provoke and incite general resistance to Lovaas treatment, rival academics regularly exploit society's compassion towards special needs children by distorting the issue of contingent aversives in Lovaas treatment, both past and present. The exaggerated critique regarding contingent aversives is an artifact of academic politics and rivalry amongst scholars, rather than a relevant academic topic in intensive behavioural treatment of autism.

Chapter 4

BCOHTA's Deceptive Use of Research

In This Chapter

- State of the Science in Autism
- Do Children with Autism Do Well Without Treatment?
- Is Daycare Good Enough to Treat Autism?
- A Strategy to Ration Autism Diagnoses?
- Questionable Use of Other Scholars' Research
- BCOHTA and the American Psychological Association

The BCOHTA study is replete with references and scholarly citations, giving the appearance of a sophisticated and well researched report. However, it is important to note that BCOHTA was highly selective in its use of citations. Specifically, the authors identify quotations from the literature which support their argument, and present the quotations out of context. In this manner, they avoid presentation of a balanced view regarding what the cited researchers have actually written about the Lovaas protocol. In addition, BCOHTA researchers choose to highlight topics with little relevance to the issues, such as discussion on the tiny percentage of children who do well without treatment, or highlighting a study with very poor outcome data. On the flip side, they devote a very small amount of "analysis" and discussion for significant evidence that supports a "best practices" argument for Lovaas Treatment — their superficial evaluation of the New York Report being a prime example.

The BCOHTA devote a very small amount of "analysis" and discussion for significant evidence that supports a "best practices" argument for Lovaas Treatment.

State of the Science in Autism

The first major example concerns the article written by Bristol, et al., 1996. In this work, the entire state of the science in autism is reviewed and organized into working groups for diagnosis, epidemiology, pathophysiology, brain mechanisms, communication/social/emotional development, medical intervention, and social and behavioral intervention. Office analysts utilize the misleading citation below to make the following claim:

> *The weaknesses of current knowledge are documented in the report "The state of the Science in Autism" by the US National Institutes of Health, which notes that "Only a few longitudinal studies of children with autism have been conducted."*[1]

However, the BCOHTA study fails to note that the same organization, the NIH, also concluded:

> *Although there is no cure,* ***autism is treatable*** *through educational interventions of various types. Early intervention may be particularly effective, presumably because of the plasticity of the neural systems at that time*[2] (emphasis added).

In addition, the NIH researchers state:

> *It is also clear that* ***persons of all ages and levels of ability can benefit from access to consistently available, proven treatment.*** *It is also known, however, that treatment response is not uniform within the population. Although* ***many children may be brought to the point of near-normal functioning,*** *others are much less responsive to social/behavioral intervention programs*[3] (emphasis added).

The BCOHTA omission of key NIH citations can only be interpreted as further evidence that BCOHTA functions for, and is devoted to, advocacy research on behalf of the provincial government.

The position of the U.S. NIH is strikingly different from that which BCOHTA researchers portray. The BCOHTA citation is, therefore, highly misleading. The BCOHTA omission of key NIH citations may therefore be interpreted as further evidence that BCOHTA functions for, and is devoted to, advocacy research on behalf of the B.C. Government.

Do Children With Autism Do Well Without Treatment?

The next area BCOHTA researchers address concerns the notion of spontaneous "recovery" from autism. Office analysts present a research citation to suggest there are a significant number of children with autism that do well on their own, without *any* autism treatment. This builds a foundation for a later BCOHTA argument that Lovaas may have "creamed" from such a pool of children, and hence, achieved remarkable outcomes. Remarkable outcomes can be called into question if an argument can be made that those subjects came from a subset of children who would have "recovered" or done very well anyway.

Again, BCOHTA relies upon the strategic, selective use of research citations such as Howlin, 1997, and Nordin and Gilberg, 1998, to support the claim of supposedly spontaneous "recovery" from autism. BCOHTA researchers state:

> *Howlin concludes that: "over the years, there has been improvement in the levels of functioning attained by people with autism." While the majority of individuals are ranked as "fair" or "poor," 10%-20% of people in the latter years are*

> *in their own homes and in work. Howlin qualifies the conclusions by noting the "direct comparisons between studies are complicated, because of differences in methodology, in the subjects involved, and in data analysis."*[4]

What is excluded, however, by BCOHTA's selective citation is Howlin's reasoning for the improvements in the levels of functioning attained by people with autism. *Howlin suggests that some of the change may be due to better treatment and education,* although she admits the statistics are misleadingly strong, due to the deinstitutionalization movement. Howlin states:

The BCOHTA report claim that suggests 10%-20% of autistic adults spontaneously fall into the "paid employment" category.

> *Obviously, these changes cannot be* ***directly*** *attributed to better treatment and education - the decrease in hospital care, for example, is mostly due to the widespread closure of large institutions - but they are encouraging."*[5] (emphasis added).

An additional statistic BCOHTA researchers elect to highlight is Kanner's findings regarding purportedly positive outcomes for people with autism. Kanner claims that 11% to 12% of adult autistics are "doing well." This finding is problematic because, according to Howlin, early reports — of which Kanner was the earliest — are not representative of autistic persons followed into adulthood. Significantly, we do not know what "doing well" is because the term is not defined by any explicit, recognized measures. Presumably BCOHTA researchers do not know what constitutes "doing well" either. There are two reasons for this:

1) Office analysts acknowledge they are unfamiliar with psychology and do not possess expertise in psychosocial treatment and
2) the BCOHTA appears to have relied exclusively on secondary source material. The bibliography does not even include the Kanner article they rely upon in their analysis. Instead, they have quoted Kanner through a secondary source (Howlin); Kanner's findings were reported and interpreted by Howlin.

Howlin offers the following conclusion regarding the issue of spontaneous recovery from autism:

> *Early reports of adults with autism were largely anecdotal (33,39) but towards the end of the 1960's Michael Rutter and*

> *his colleagues conducted a detailed follow-up of 63 autistic individuals initially diagnosed during the 1950's and 1960's. Amongst those who had reached adulthood, over half were in long stay hospitals, eleven were still living with their parents and three were placed in special autistic communities;* ***only three were in paid employment*** *(87, 137, 138)*[6] (emphasis added).

The position of Howlin regarding "spontaneous recovery" is strikingly different from that which Office analysts portray. The BCOHTA citation is, therefore, misleading. Howlin's findings are more in line with the generally held view amongst psychologists and psychiatrists, that autism is an intractable disorder that, if left untreated, severely compromises the independence and quality of life of autistic adults.

Office analysts appear to have misrepresented the arguments and findings of Howlin to support the BCOHTA advocacy position.

Howlin's work shows that a mere 4.8% of the autistic people researchers followed into adult life were sufficiently independent and teachable so as to be gainfully employed. This sharply contradicts the BCOHTA report claim that suggests 10%-20% of autistic adults spontaneously fall into the *paid employment* category.

Regarding behavioral treatment, Howlin's view is *strategically* excluded from the BCOHTA analysis. Howlin states:

> *There is little doubt that the* ***use of behavioural procedures has resulted in major improvements*** *in the education, management and treatment of children with autism over the last three decades*[7] (emphasis added).

Office analysts therefore appear to have misrepresented the arguments and findings of Howlin to support the BCOHTA advocacy position.

Is Day-Care Good Enough to Treat Autism?

In order to inject Canadian content into the discussion, and come up with a Canadian solution, the researchers at the BCOHTA present the Jocelyn et al. 1998 study as a supposedly "groundbreaking" study. They claim the study is groundbreaking due to the use of random assignment of subjects to experimental and control groups. They describe the study as follows:

> *This study, although only 12 weeks in duration, is particularly relevant because it shows randomization is suitable for empirical validation of an early (24-72), intensive community-based integrated treatment program. While their study is ground-breaking in this area of research, it was, as the authors note, too short to determine ultimate treatment effect.*[8]

Such misleading and inappropriate use of the term "intensive" can only be attributed either to a profound lack of knowledge regarding psychosocial treatment, or a deliberate attempt to mislead the reader.

BCOHTA researchers attempt to mislead the reader regarding Jocelyn et al. in terms of the study's *intensity* and *treatment outcomes.* At this point, it is important to briefly describe the Jocelyn et al. study.

First, the children in both the experimental and control group attended *preschool* for an average of 21.4 hours a week (4.28 hours a day). Each child was given a *child-care worker* who attended the preschool with the child. The program upon which the Jocelyn et al. study is based is not intensive and does not constitute treatment delivered by competent, qualified autism treatment personnel. Jocelyn et al. describe the supposed "intervention:"

> ***Intervention was directed primarily at the parents and day-care staff rather than the child.*** *In this model, caregivers were helped to develop understanding and empathy for the child's view of the world, as a means of predicting behavior, understanding its communicative aspects, and enhancing mutual enjoyment of interactions. They were taught how to perform a functional analysis of behavior and to plan and evaluate strategies for changing behavior. Facilitating language and social development as a proactive approach to enabling the child to meet his needs and function appropriately in his or her environment was given priority over targeting "problem behaviors." Inclusion of the family as active team members was emphasized.*[9] (emphasis added).

According to Jocelyn et al., these child care workers attended only a total of *"five weekly 3-hour classes."*[10] Despite this, Office analysts have defined the above preschool as an *"intensive community-based integrated treatment program."*[11] Such misleading and inappropriate use of the term "intensive" can only be attributed either to a profound lack of knowledge regarding psychosocial treatment, or a deliberate attempt to mislead the reader about the true nature of work conducted by Jocelyn et al.

The intervention reported by Jocelyn et. al, can in no way be regarded as "intensive," nor can it be described as "treatment" because the intervention was *"directed primarily at the parents and day-care staff* ***rather than the child."***[12] (emphasis added). Moreover, after spending 15 hours learning about various topics relevant to autism, a child-care worker hardly qualifies to deliver science-based treatment for a complex neurological disorder. It is central to note that *nowhere does the BCOHTA report describe exactly what child-care workers did with the children (from a specific operational standpoint) that could constitute "treatment" in the Jocelyn et al. study.*

In short, the BCOHTA elevates the Jocelyn et al. study to a level of importance that is *clearly* not warranted by the insignificant outcome achieved in the study.

In addition, the BCOHTA researchers appear to take on the role of apologists for the Jocelyn et al. study which they consider "ground-breaking." *Jocelyn et al. has virtually no statistically significant child outcome results* aside from a statistically significant language improvement (5.3 months acquisition of language in 3 months — a 2.3 month improvement). A well-designed study would presumably have used outcome measures with sufficient sensitivity to detect improvement in the other six areas that were measured. In contrast, every program in the Lovaas treatment protocol uses data collection techniques which enable progress to be observed daily.

In short, the BCOHTA elevates the Jocelyn et al. study to a level of importance that is *clearly* not warranted by the insignificant outcome achieved in the study.

Do We Need to Ration Autism Diagnoses?

BCOHTA researchers introduce a discussion regarding the costs and benefits of early screening. They then describe Lord (1995), Cox et al. (1999) and Stone et al. (1999) who test early diagnostic tools. Based on this discussion, they conclude:

> *Support for "early" therapy should therefore be directed toward early treatment of children known to have autism, and not toward therapy of children receiving an "early" diagnosis.*[13]

The BCOHTA further state:

> *The published effectiveness evidence does not include any studies which examined overall outcome following early diagnosis using a screening manoeuvre. That is, studies to date have not followed a population of children diagnosed "early" in the natural history of the condition to determine both the benefits from early treatment and the costs associated with false positive and false negative diagnostic labelling.*[14]

The Office takes Rogers' quote out of context. Dr. Rogers' point is that reports of increased treatment success with younger children have significant *treatment* implications.

Office analysts claim Rogers has come to a similar conclusion:

> *Rogers* ***similarly concludes****, "The hypothesis that age at start of treatment is an important variable in determining outcome has tremendous implications for the field and needs to be tested with methodologically rigorous designs."*[15] (emphasis added).

However, the Office takes Rogers' quote out of context. Dr. Rogers' point is that reports of increased treatment success with younger children have significant *treatment* implications.

Rogers states:

> *Whereas there were a variety of methodological problems in this study [Fenske et al., 1995], other converging evidence also speaks to the potential importance of the age variable.*[16]

BCOHTA's focus on false positive or negative diagnostic labeling may be explained by its cost-savings implications; however, Lord (1995), Cox et al. (1999) and Stone et al. (1999) are not concerned with cost savings by diagnosing children late. The opposite is true. These researchers are finding that, on the whole, *a diagnosis at two years of age is quite reliable.*

Stone et al. state:

> *Taken together, these results suggest two conclusions: (1) the identification of an autism spectrum disorder can be made*

> *reliably in children below the age of 3; and (2) the specific diagnosis of autism can be made reliably in children under 3 years, as long as the diagnosticians have experience evaluating young children.*[17]

Unlike Office analysts, the researchers cited above are concerned about false negatives, *i.e.*, they strive *not to miss* a diagnosis of an Autism Spectrum Disorder in a young child. However, the BCOHTA appears to be concerned about false positives that may cost the government money.

The BCOHTA appears to be concerned about false positives that may cost the government money.

Questionable Use of Other Scholars' Research

BCOHTA researchers claim there is a lack of support for Lovaas treatment effectiveness claims in the literature.

For example, BCOHTA researchers quote Rogers:

> *(Studies) did not demonstrate the level of improvement in multiple areas of functioning or the sustained long-term effects of the treatment that Lovaas reported. The field awaits a full, independent replication of the Lovaas study 26 (p. 176).*[18]

However, Rogers *also* states:

> *There are several methodological strengths of this study [the Lovaas study]. Group sizes, although not large, were* ***not unduly small****.* ***There was a treatment manual*** *that outlined both the treatment techniques and the actual content of the treatment. Treatment givers were all trained by the core staff and supervised closely. Children were diagnosed by professionals* ***outside*** *of the treatment team prior to referral and the first set of follow-up data were gathered by outside professionals blind to treatment status. Interrater reliability was reported for pretreatment behavioral measures. Outcome variables at second follow-up included several different kinds of measures,* ***well chosen to document current levels of functioning in areas that are generally significantly affected***

> ***by autism:*** *IQ, adaptive behavior measures, school placement, and behavioral measures. Follow-up was carried out for many years after the treatment was delivered, so that long-term effect of the treatment could be examined. The two control groups allowed for examination of two different treatment conditions, one of which represented* ***typical community programs*** *and the other representing both typical community treatment and some level of* ***behavioral interventions.*** *Thus, one control group could be considered to be allowing for comparison with nonspecific treatment. A very important finding was that in the treated group, outcome was predicted by pre-treatment mental ages*[19] (emphasis added).

It is apparent the U.S. Surgeon General's view regarding the quality and implication of the Lovaas study stands in marked contrast to the view espoused by BCOHTA researchers.

Rogers makes a valid point, as does Lovaas, that Lovaas' study should be replicated and that there is always room to improve. No scholar would deny that; indeed, Lovaas has received considerable grant resources from the U.S. National Institutes of Health and has had a multi-site replication study in progress for more than a decade (150 children across 14 sites).

The BCOHTA report makes *no* mention of the U.S. Surgeon General's report on mental health. U.S. Surgeon General's report states:

> *Thirty years of research demonstrated the efficacy of applied behaviour analysis methods in reducing inappropriate behavior and increasing communication, learning, and appropriate social behavior.* ***A well designed study of a psychosocial intervention was carried out by Lovaas and Colleagues*** *(Lovaas, 1987; McEachin et al., 1993)*[20] (emphasis added).

It is apparent the U.S. Surgeon General's view regarding the quality and implication of the Lovaas study stands in marked contrast to the view espoused by BCOHTA researchers.

BCOHTA and the American Psychological Association

With respect to the American Psychological Association Task Force, the BCOHTA select the following citation to make it appear as though the APA does not support the concept of therapy for children with autism. The BCOHTA says that the American Psychological Association Task Force has stated:

> *With regarding [sic] Lovaas therapy, they state that this program of therapy has not been established as efficacious according to their [APA] criteria. "To date, no comprehensive integrated intervention for autism has sufficient support to achieve either well-established or probably efficacious status partially because of concerns and problems with conducting randomized assignment group designs and a lack of strong replication studies."*[21]

The Office displays an astonishing degree of elitism when it completely dismisses clinical guideline experts and clinicians as unable to establish recommendations consistent with research evidence.

BCOHTA researchers contend the APA citation is *"With regarding [sic] Lovaas therapy..."* . This is not the case — the citation is not specific to Lovaas but applies to all top comprehensive treatment packages. More importantly, BCOHTA researchers strategically exclude the APA position regarding "best practices." The APA Task Force grapples with the dilemma of withholding treatment for patients until the research is flawless.

The APA states:

> *"The existing treatment outcome literature [regarding psychosocial intervention], despite its flaws,* ***does provide guidance for how to proceed with clinical practice...*** *Given the choice between using an intervention proven effective for children similar to ones seen in a clinical setting or using a treatment that has not been subject to this test (or worse, demonstrated to be ineffective), it seems that a best guess for effectiveness would be the treatment that works for a related problem or population (e.g., a less severe manifestation of the disorder or problem)*[22] (emphasis added).

Dr. Ken Bassett, first author of the BCOHTA report, in an article originally authored for colleagues in the Health Technology Assessment field, states: *"...avoid CPG [Clinical Practice Guidelines] like swampland — they are!"*[26]

In short, doing nothing about autism treatment is a policy that is clearly *not* supported by the American Psychological Association, regardless of the Office analysts' interpretation to the contrary.

Moreover, the citation above indicates the APA does not share the BCOHTA's opinion regarding the entire clinical guideline movement. The Office displays an astonishing degree of elitism when it completely dismisses clinical guideline experts and clinicians as unable to establish recommendations consistent with research evidence. The BCOHTA Report states:

> *while acknowledging the limitations of the clinical effectiveness evidence, they tend to make recommendations that extend far beyond what that evidence will support.*[23]

It could be argued that members of the B.C. Guidelines and Protocols Advisory Committee, under Medical Services Commission, likely take a different view regarding clinical practice guidelines, especially since they have issued 28 clinical practice guidelines currently in place for British Columbia.[24]

The New York Autism Clinical Guidelines were based upon the recommendations of an impressive "best in class" group of autism academics who recommended Early Intensive Behavioral Intervention, and relied very heavily on the landmark research of Lovaas and colleagues to establish those guidelines. Perhaps the BCOHTA had to dismiss the clinical guideline movement in order to minimize the impact of the New York Guidelines in the litigation. However, the APA task force, which Office analysts rely upon, supports the use of clinical guidelines for autism treatment.

The wholesale discounting of clinical practice guidelines is not unique to this analysis. The BCOHTA may see clinical guidelines as a threat to its ability to identify treatments as experimental. Dr. Ken Bassett, first author of the BCOHTA report, in an article originally authored for colleagues in the Health Technology Assessment field, states: *"...avoid CPG [Clinical Practice Guidelines] like swampland — they are!"*[25] Dr. Bassett is referring to the "damage" Clinical Practice Guidelines cause the Health Technology Assessment movement's battle against drug companies. However, the point is the same; clinical practice guidelines tend to compete with the power and authority of the Health Technology Assessment movement including the BCOHTA.

A dangerous implication of the highly selective and deceptive use of citations is the fact that it is both difficult and time consuming to uncover and expose the bias. However, the biased BCOHTA report on Lovaas Treatment is a clear illustration of how crucial it is that references and scholarly citations used by this group of health technology academics be thoroughly investigated by outside and independent scholars.

Chapter 5

BCOHTA and Provincial Policy

In This Chapter

- Parents and Daycare Workers as Autism Therapists?
- Diagnosis Control
- Are Generic Supports Effective for Autism?
- Are Parents Naive Consumers?
- Lovaas Labelled as Experimental

The BCOHTA analysis of Lovaas Treatment presents several arguments that provide academic legitimacy for, and support of, provincial special needs policies for young children with autism. This section's purpose is to take a closer look at the relationship between current provincial autism policy and the BCOHTA analysis.

Specifically, there are five recurring themes in the provincial policy agenda: parents and daycare workers as autism therapists; diagnosis control; generic supports; naive consumers; experimental nature of Lovaas.

What occurred at the preschool — minimally trained child care workers interacting with children — would not be considered "treatment" by any definition recognized by impartial psychologists with expertise in psychosocial treatment.

Parents and Daycare Workers as Autism Therapists?

The provincial autism policy has emphasized the role of parents (as opposed to highly qualified professionals) in administering "treatment" to their own autistic children. Indeed, government contractors did not work directly with children. Instead, the task appears to have been to help parents cope with their disabled child.

Office analysts appear to use autism literature to support this provincial policy. The reliance on the Jocelyn et al. (1998) report has already been noted.

BCOHTA researchers state:

> *This study, [Jocelyn et al., 1998] although only 12 weeks in duration, is particularly* ***relevant*** *because it shows randomization is suitable for empirical validation of an early (24-72 months),* ***intensive*** *community-based integrated* ***treatment*** *program.*[1] (emphasis added).

As stated previously, work conducted with autistic children in Jocelyn, et al. (1998) can hardly be viewed as "intensive." What occurred at the preschool — minimally trained child care workers interacting with children — would not be considered "treatment" by any definition recognized by impartial psychologists with expertise in psychosocial treatment.

Over a 15-hour training period, the Jocelyn et al. study delivered small amounts of education to parents and child-care workers regarding autism. Although certainly of some value, psychologists would not consider the extent of Jocelyn et al.'s supposed "autism training" to equal a formal university education and experience in psychosocial treatment. Yet it is precisely this caliber of professional credentials autistic children require if the terms "intensive autism treatment" are to be used legitimately.

In the Jocelyn et al. study, a child-care worker with 15 hours of "training" accompanied an autistic child to a half-day of preschool. The study results showed that the children with autism in the special program *did not significantly improve,* relative to the children with autism who were not accompanied with a child-care worker with 15 hours training. Despite the lack of significant successful outcome data, as described above, BCOHTA researchers support Jocelyn et al., not because children with autism received quality treatment, but because *Jocelyn et al. supports the policy that parents and support workers could somehow be trained to purportedly "do" early intervention.* Training unqualified amateurs is far less costly than funding bona fide, one-on-one, intensive behavioural treatment delivered by competent and credentialed autism treatment professionals.

Training unqualified amateurs is far less costly than funding bona fide, one-on-one, intensive behavioural treatment delivered by competent and credentialed autism treatment professionals.

In short, an important component of the provincial special needs policy therefore appears to be to utilize existing "community-based" resources to administer generic early intervention.

BCOHTA's analysis supports provincial policy described above with the following assertion:

> *But this therapeutic approach, in contrast to behavioural modification, is regarded as requiring intensive training by specialist therapists. Behavioural therapy on the other hand is more adapted for training parents and teachers to be part,* ***often the primary providers****, of the therapy itself*[2] (emphasis added).

However, the BCOHTA report does not discuss whether it is reasonable to expect parents to somehow become autism intervention specialists, with only a perfunctory introduction to autism? Office analysts fail to provide compelling research evidence that parents are qualified to deliver bona fide treatment for the highly complex neurological disorder of autism.

The vast majority of parents have no formal autism treatment qualifications, yet BCOHTA views parents as candidates for "primary providers" of autism therapy.

Instead, researchers at the BCOHTA appear to believe that autism can be adequately treated by parents and paraprofessionals. The vast majority of parents have no formal autism treatment qualifications, yet BCOHTA *inferred that minimal training and qualifications are all that is required to deliver effective treatment for autism.* In a perplexing determination, BCOHTA views behaviour therapy as *"more adapted for training parents..."*[3] rather than a therapy to be delivered to the children themselves.

Some U.S. jurisdictions take a very different view. For example, California and Florida have certification laws for behavioural consultants and therapists. Rigorous criteria are set out for behavioral consultants and therapists before they may legally "treat" children who suffer from autism. Had BCOHTA researchers reviewed these U.S. certification laws in the course of their exhaustive literature search, perhaps they would have come to the conclusion that parents and daycare workers (e.g., Jocelyn et al.) do not meet the minimum standards for even *junior* therapist classification in Florida or California.

It is apparent that these U.S. jurisdictions deem behavioural therapy as a bona fide, powerful treatment that must be regulated to protect patients afflicted with autism. These U.S. state legislatures have taken steps to ensure that high standards of health care are delivered.

The Office further supports the policy of classifying "parents as therapists," when they cite 271 published studies from academic literature regarding behavioral therapy (Applied Behavior Analysis) in the following manner:

> *It may be noted that among the techniques included is home-based, parent-mediated therapy - of particular interest here as one of a variety of parent-mediated therapies.*[4]

However, none of this research is subjected to the BCOHTA's validity analysis that was applied to Lovaas' research.

Perhaps in order to further support the policy of "parents as therapists," BCOHTA suggests that the Lovaas protocol relies on parents as therapists.

BCOHTA states:

> *The initial phase of treatment was delivered largely in the homes, with parents also trained and carrying out the treatment.*[5]

Although parents are trained in some aspects of the Lovaas treatment protocol, and are usually in-home supervisors of their child's treatment program, they do not typically function as the primary therapists. They are, however, expected to "follow through" with Lovaas protocol techniques to provide continuity during their child's every waking hour. Lovaas discusses the problems with parents doing therapy. He states:

Parents' job is to follow through when the therapists leave, or when the child no longer requires intensive therapy.

> *Not all parents of autistic children can be taught to become effective teachers or therapists for their children. This is true in cases where the parents are divorced and the mother has to work for financial reasons...*[6]

Lovaas further elaborates on the role of parents as part of the therapy team:

> *In the introduction to this paper we discussed that the primary reason for involving the parents of the autistic child in the treatment program as explicitly trained cotherapists concerned efforts to generalize the treatment gains to all of the child's environments, and to protect his gains from relapse once formal therapy is terminated. It was also pointed out that since autistic children have such a profound deficiency, nothing short of a major therapeutic-educational effort, necessitating one-to-one treatment on an* ***all-day*** *basis, could be considered sufficient. For all practical purposes such a plan must involve the child's parents*[7] (emphasis added).

The central point is that parents must be as involved as possible; however, Lovaas at no time suggests that the parents perform the primary treatment function. Their job is to follow through when the therapists leave, or when the child no longer requires intensive therapy.

Office analysts also evaluate an alternative home-based therapy to Lovaas, developed out of the TEACCH program. TEACCH may have been selected because it is considered "cost-effective" and because parents perform the therapy. BCOHTA states:

> *The home program involved 10 treatment sessions, in the clinic and home, designed to assist parents in becoming co-therapists.*[8]

BCOHTA goes on to state:

Once again, the BCOHTA researchers apply inconsistent application of evaluative standards.

> *The BCOHTA authors agreed that this study is worth considering because, although the intervention period is only 10 - 12 weeks and it suffers from many methodological flaws, it is a prospective controlled trial using overall outcomes that studied an intensive, home-based treatment alternative to Lovaas therapy.*[9]

Once again, the BCOHTA researchers apply inconsistent application of evaluative standards. They evaluate the TEACCH home program applying the NIH criteria leniently, as opposed to a far more aggressive application of standards to evaluate Lovaas' study using the same NIH criteria. The BCOHTA actually views TEACCH as a viable alternative to Lovaas, despite TEACCH research violating the NIH criteria.

BCOHTA states:

> *The controlled study by Ozonoff, although short and small-scale, provides at least some evidence that alternate, home-based programs, in this instance* ***emphasizing parent teaching*** *as opposed to applied behavioral analysis, need further evaluation both independently and in comparison with Lovaas treatment.*[10] (emphasis added).

Competent delivery of best practices health care for a very complex disorder, such as autism, cannot be delivered by unqualified, under qualified or poorly trained personnel, no matter how loving and caring the workers. It was the failure to fund effective treatment that led to the conclusion that the provincial government had discriminated against the children in the landmark Auton lawsuit.

Diagnosis Control

The BCOHTA report also discusses diagnosis of autism although this does not seem to fall within the stated research question.

BCOHTA imply that parents and professionals may have been "massaging" the system in order to receive government benefits.

BCOHTA states:

> *A more recent problem has emerged in relation to estimates of the incidence of autism. It appears that, at least in the BC context, problems with the diagnosis of autism may not simply be due to problems in the application of validated diagnostic criteria. The possibility arises that children with other pervasive development disorders may nonetheless be diagnosed with autism in order to gain access to services linked to that diagnosis. The extent of this phenomenon or its influence on incidence estimates remains unknown.*[11]

In the above citation, Office analysts support the tight definition of autism to separate it from *"other pervasive development disorders."*[12] In addition, they imply that parents and professionals may have been "massaging" the system in order to receive government benefits for children who would otherwise be ineligible. This is not only offensive, it is also inaccurate:

> (1) at the time of the BCOHTA report, there were no bona fide autism treatment services universally available for children with autism in B.C. so there was little utility in obtaining a diagnosis
>
> (2) The U.S. National Institutes of Health (NIH), views the widespread increase in autism diagnoses as genuine. Dr. Marie Bristol-Power, of the National Institute of Child Health and Human Development and coordinator of autism research at the NIH, states with respect to increases in diagnoses: "I don't think it's just better diagnosis, or that autism or PDD is the disease du jour... there is something else going on, and we are hoping to solve this problem."[13]

By contrast, the BCOHTA supports the hypothesis that no genuine increase in the incidence of autism exists.

BCOHTA states:

> *Support for "early" therapy should therefore be directed toward early treatment of children known to have autism, and not toward therapy of children receiving an "early" diagnosis.*[14]

The BCOHTA apparently does not wish to acknowledge that children with pervasive developmental disorder not otherwise specified (PDD-NOS) need therapy in the same manner as do children with so called "full-blown" autism.

Another indication that Office analysts do not have a firm grasp on autism issues is exemplified by their implicit, and perplexing, rejection of the Autism Spectrum Disorder classification.

BCOHTA states:

> *For example, there may be significant problems associated with labeling children specifically with a diagnosis of autism, as opposed to other pervasive development disorders. Children so labeled may have preferential service access not available to those with other diagnoses, thereby raising potential for an exaggerated incidence of autism diagnosis (see 1.6 below) [The Autism Action Plan]."*[15]

The BCOHTA apparently does not wish to acknowledge that children with pervasive developmental disorder not otherwise specified (PDD-NOS) need therapy in the same manner as do children with so called "full-blown" autism. Lovaas treatment is vital for a range of children on the autism spectrum, not just children with classic autism.

Are Generic Supports Effective for Autism?

Office analysts appear to support the provision of generic supports for children with autism. However, they fail to provide any research evidence from the literature to support the claim that generic special needs services result in successful outcomes for children with autism.

BCOHTA states:

> *Also not examined are the challenges of sustaining standardized services across widely-dispersed geographic areas, such as the province of British Columbia, other than to acknowledge, as the involvement of three government ministries in developing an Autism Action Plan suggests, that a wide range of specialists and special services are required in this field; and that the demands placed on these resources are likely to be increased by the need to integrate the Autism Action Plan with government commitments to other special needs children and their families.*[16]

These health policy technocrats portray parents as naive consumers, somehow duped by media hype, into spending significant sums of money on a treatment that BCOHTA claims is suspect.

BCOHTA also states:

> *Specific behavioural therapies, shown effective, need to be matched to local needs and the abilities of local therapists.*[17]

Are Parents Naive Consumers?

Parents across Canada are currently funding Lovaas Treatment for their children at considerable personal financial cost. These parents are portrayed as "naive consumers" by a paternalistic BCOHTA.

BCOHTA states:

> *In the case of autism, the human drama of the popular press can be especially compelling. If a specific therapy or program holding out hope of 'cure' is presented to families facing daunting challenges, the impact on them is likely to be significant.*[18]

It is unquestionably true that parents are confronted, on a regular basis, with unsubstantiated autism intervention options that claim to improve or "cure" autism. Parents of newly diagnosed children have much to sort through. However, it is unfair and unjustified to suggest that parents are so naive as to solely base treatment strategy for their children on mass media information. There are many other opinions parents consider before taking such an important decision. In particular, they consider the professional opinions of psychiatrists, psychologists and pediatricians. Interestingly, while the BCOHTA report refers to media reports, it does not discuss the impact of court decisions granting parents the right to publicly funded Lovaas Treatment.

Instead, the BCOHTA maintains a remarkably elitist stance:

> *Perhaps the most striking feature of the published literature on the treatment of autism is its power, on so small a basis in evidence to sway a section of the professional community, parents and payment agencies toward the Lovaas form of therapy. Seldom can so much importance have been assigned to such extraordinary effectiveness claims from such a small, quasi-experimental study uncorroborated through independent research.*[19]

To suggest that the professional community of mental health and developmental clinicians has failed to "see the light" concerning Lovaas Treatment, shows striking evidence of intellectual elitism amongst a self-anointed cadre of social engineers.

This paragraph is entirely consistent with the provincial policy in that it supports the view that Lovaas Treatment is "experimental." The BCOHTA goes further to imply that psychiatrists, pediatricians and psychologists are simply not as well informed as BCOHTA researchers because these professionals have been swayed by Lovaas' research.[20]

Put simply, in producing advocacy research in the context of litigation, BCOHTA researchers have attempted to:

1) discredit the science behind decades of Dr. Lovaas' research,
2) discount the exhaustive review and analysis of the New York State Department of Health Report on "best practices," and
3) strategically exclude the U.S. Surgeon General's Report on Mental Health from their purportedly "exhaustive" literature search.

Lovaas Labelled as Experimental

The BCOHTA concluded that Lovaas is "experimental." The BCOHTA states:

> *A scientific claim of effectiveness is being used to force action, but the same scientific evidence is inadequate to provide any guidance on how to proceed.*[21]

The BCOHTA further states:

> *Because of the major methodological flaws, however, the findings of these researchers cannot be regarded as conclusive. Rather, their contribution might have been expected to fuel further hypothesis generation. While this has occurred to some degree, the work has not been sufficient to bring the science to what might be described as an authoritative level.*[22]

According to Office analysts, if parents are satisfied with an intervention but no quantifiable improvement shows in the child's condition, that is valid outcome for BCOHTA researchers.

Yet, the BCOHTA report also appears to embrace measures insignificant to autism treatment. For example, it relies on parental satisfaction as a relevant measure for the Jocelyn study.

In connection with *this* study, BCOHTA analysts state:

> *Effectiveness need not be measured in terms of measurable changes on rigorously administered IQ tests.* ***Equally valid*** *are a whole range of effects including parent involvement, satisfaction and quality of life*[23] (emphasis added).

In other words, if parents are satisfied with an intervention but no quantifiable improvement shows in the child's condition, that is valid outcome for the BCOHTA.

Further inconsistency in evaluation standards, in terms of research efficacy, is demonstrated by the ever changing standards of evaluation. An example is the Report's recommendation of treatment programs reviewed by Dawson and Osterling (aside from the Lovaas' study). The BCOHTA-recommended programs a) have much less rigorous standards relative to the Lovaas study design and protocol, and b) simply do not exist in British Columbia.

BCOHTA analysts state:

> *Based on expert opinion and survey results they identify several key elements shared by all "nationally known models or programs" as "earliest possible start to intervention; individualization of services for children and families; systematic playful teaching, specialized curriculum; intensity of engagement; and family involvement.*[24]

However, reliance on Dawson and Osterling (1997) is problematic. Most of the programs Dawson and Osterling review do not meet the NIH criteria upon which Office analysts base their analysis of Lovaas. Dawson and Osterling find that the early intervention program with the best results from one of the most rigorously designed and implemented program, is the Lovaas Autism Treatment protocol. None of the other treatment programs reviewed by Dawson and Osterling have experimental and control groups; nor do they use comparable, rigorous outcome measures as used by Lovaas. Yet, the BCOHTA apparently perceive no conflict in accepting features which the majority of the Dawson and Osterling (1997) programs seem to share.

What BCOHTA researchers exclude from their analysis is that of the eight programs reviewed by Dawson and Osterling, three are *intensive behavioural intervention* programs.

The BCOHTA researchers state:

> *Ultimately, new programs may contain many of the features of US programs described by Dawson and Osterling. They note that regardless of divergent philosophies of therapy, eight independent programs have developed around a common model of early, intensive therapy for children with autism, which include* ***parental involvement.*** *These 'elements of effective programs' were further defined and described in a prospective study, funded by the Office of Special Education, U.S. Department of Education.*[25] (emphasis added).

What BCOHTA researchers exclude from their analysis is that of the eight programs reviewed by Dawson and Osterling, three are *intensive behavioural intervention* programs: the UCLA Young Autism Project, the Princeton Child Development Institute, and the Douglas Developmental Center. *However, of particular significance to children with autism in British Columbia is the fact that, at the time of the report, there was no provincial funding for any specifically named autism treatment.*

Chapter 6

Clinicians vs. Health Policy Technocrats: In Defence of the New York Department of Health

In This Chapter

- BCOHTA's Selective Analysis of the New York State Autism Report
- Natural Competitors? Health Technolgy Assessment vs. Clinical Guidelines

Although B.C. Office of Health Technology Assessment researchers lack training and education in psychology, psychiatry or autism treatment, they nonetheless appear to believe they have academic competence to discount the collective opinion of the community of mental health professionals. These clinicians are charged with the task to contend with the severe, chronic developmental disorder of autism, which results in significant lifelong disability.

The growing consensus in the community of professionals referenced above is that intensive behavioural intervention based on the work of psychologist O.I. Lovaas currently constitutes "best practice" in the treatment of Autism Spectrum Disorder. Prominent examples of this consensus amongst experts and professionals are:

1) the report issued by the New York State Department of Health on autism clinical practice guidelines;
2) the Mental Health report of the U.S. Surgeon General, and
3) in British Columbia, Canada, Sixty-Three Licensed Psychiatrists have formally endorsed Lovaas Treatment as medically necessary.

The BCOHTA appear to believe they have academic competence to discount the collective opinion of the community of mental health professionals.

However, despite the depth and breadth of education, expertise and experience of clinicians in the management and treatment of autism, Office analysts severely discount the collective opinion of clinicians regarding the effectiveness of Lovaas Treatment as a "best practice" autism treatment.

BCOHTA states:

> *Perhaps the most striking feature of the published literature on the treatment of autism is its power, on so small a basis in evidence, to sway a section of the professional community...*[1]

The BCOHTA Report goes on to discount the New York report and the general concept of clinical guidelines:

> *This is not to direct particular criticism at the NY Clinical Practice Guidelines. In fact, they are similar to most guidelines developed by clinical experts, in that while acknowledging the limitations of the clinical effectiveness evidence, they tend to make recommendations that extend far beyond what that evidence will support.*[2]

This section addresses the BCOHTA criticisms regarding the New York Report and relationship of the BCOHTA to the Clinical Guideline Movement.

Selective Analysis of the New York Autism Report

The New York State Department of Health report is academically rigorous and strictly adheres to science-based evaluation of *all major* autism treatment options. Despite this, Office analysts describe the New York report as uncritical in its evaluation of autism treatments.

In marked contrast to the report presented in B.C. Supreme Court by BCOHTA analysts, the New York Report is not a product of a closed-door, court-based process.

BCOHTA analysts state:

> *Shortcomings of planning decisions made on this basis are exemplified by the New York State Department of Health, Clinical Practice Guidelines, which show how readily the dilemma may be worsened by a consensus process that uncritically applies effectiveness claims.*[3]

Researchers and academics who authored the New York report did, in fact, use an evidence-based scientific process. A panel of sixty-two (62) peer reviewers, who are experts in autism, were enlisted to ensure an objective and meaningful analysis of current autism treatments. In marked contrast to the report presented in B.C. Supreme Court by BCOHTA analysts, the New York Report is not a product of a closed-door, court-based process. Unlike the BCOHTA analysis, the New York Report was produced in a transparent fashion, according to recognized principles of clinical practice guidelines development. A large number of experts in the field of autism oversaw this report.

Authors of the New York Report state:

> *This guideline was developed by an independent multidisciplinary panel convened by the New York Department of Health (DOH) under the direction of the Early Intervention Program.* ***The panel employed a systematic process to review the scientific evidence****, where evidence was available, and combined this with expert clinical judgment to develop*

> *evidence-based guideline recommendations on assessment and intervention of young children with autism*[4] (emphasis added).

The New York Report further states:

> *The key elements of the guideline development approach selected by the DOH include: a.* ***Using a scientific process that is evidence-based****, b. Ensuring a multidisciplinary approach, c. Developing a guideline that is valid, objective, and credible*[5] (emphasis added).

The New York report relied upon the methodology used by the Agency of Health Care Policy and Research (AHCPR), a research protocol otherwise embraced by the BCOHTA.

The New York report relied upon a standard methodology for developing clinical practice guidelines, namely the methodology used by the Agency of Health Care Policy and Research (AHCPR), a research protocol otherwise embraced by the BCOHTA.

According to the New York Report:

> *The AHCPR guideline methodology was derived from the work of many experts in health services research and incorporated the principles for developing high-quality practice guidelines set forth by the U.S. Institute of Medicine (1992)... Many health services researchers consider the AHCPR methodology to be the standard for developing evidence-based clinical practice guidelines.*[6]

In 1997, the BCOHTA conducted a systematic review of several clinical practice guidelines for the testing of cholesterol, entitled, *"Supporting Clinical Practice Guidelines Development: An appraisal of existing cholesterol testing guidelines.*[7] In this work, BCOHTA researchers used criteria derived from *exactly* the same AHCPR methodology employed by the New York State Department of Health in development of their autism treatment clinical guidelines.

BCOHTA then stated:

> *To review and evaluate the process used in developing clinical practice guidelines, and to determine the extent to which the*

guidelines were "evidence-based", BCOHTA used a set of 15 appraisal criteria derived from work done by the Institute of Medicine and the Agency for Health Care Policy and Research. comprehensive list of these criteria is presented in Table 1.[8]

Natural Competitors? Health Technology Assessments versus Clinical Guidelines

Although Office analysts have used clinical guidelines in the past, *i.e.*, for cholesterol screening, the BCOHTA severely discounts the general concept of clinical practice guidelines:

> *...unsubstantiated extrapolation from limited clinical effectiveness evidence is the major drawback of the clinical practice guideline movement.*[9]

The BCOHTA selectively uses Clinical Guidelines when it is convenient, but discounts the entire clinical guideline movement when it hurts their argument.

BCOHTA researchers level general criticism at the New York Report for its reliance upon research the BCOHTA claims is "quasi-experimental," However, the BCOHTA fails to do a systematic review of the process used to develop the New York Report. This is in marked contrast to the systematic BCOHTA review (1997) of cholesterol testing clinical practice guidelines.

The *"...15 appraisal criteria derived from work done by the Institute of Medicine and the Agency for Health Care Policy,"* were conspicuously not used by the BCOHTA to evaluate the New York report. If the evaluation were applied to the New York Clinical Guidelines, the Guidelines would have rated highly.

Following are BCOHTA evaluation criteria for Clinical Guidelines reproduced from the BCOHTA appraisal of cholesterol testing clinical guidelines. In the context of the New York Report on clinical practice guidelines for autism, BCOHTA neglected to use its very *own* clinical assessment guidelines, even though they were readily available.[10] The BCOHTA selectively uses Clinical Guidelines when it is convenient, but discounts the entire clinical guideline movement when it is not.

Table 1: Criteria for appraising clinical practice guidelines

1. How was the panel constituted?	
a) selected by contracting agency or requesting agency?	Yes/No-Describe
b) nominated by professional or clinical organization?	Yes/No-Describe
c) multi-disciplinary? (>1 health / health-related discipline)	Yes/No-Describe
d) were selection criteria established? Were they assessed by interview of the candidate and nominating organizations? Did they incude:	
-possession of outstanding clinical and academic credentials?	Yes/No-Describe
-willingness to consider alternative opinions?	Yes/No-Describe
-possession of an open mind about clinical guidelines?	Yes/No-Describe
-ability to work well in group (as judged by peers)?	Yes/No-Describe
e) was a balance achieved between:	
-academia vs. clinical-based practice?	Yes/No-Describe
-geography?	Yes/No-Describe
-gender?	Yes/No-Describe
-ethnicity?	Yes/No-Describe
-practice style (those who do and do not refer for cholesterol testing)?	Yes/No-Describe
f) was one chair or 2 co-chairs appointed?	Yes/No-Describe
2. How were the key methods and procedural issues handled?	
a) were the topic and population to be targeted by clinical guidelines delineated? What were they?	Yes/No-Describe
b) were criteria for deciding on what to include as scientific evidence established? What were they?	Yes/No-Describe
c) was a rating scheme adopted to report on the strength of the evidence underlying a recommendation? Which one?	Yes/No-Describe
3. What process was used to conduct the literature search and to identify the research evidence to be included?	
a) was a search conducted? By who?	Yes/No-Describe
b) was a search strategy elaborated? What was it?	Yes/No-Describe
c) were inclusion / exclusion criteria defined? What were they?	Yes/No-Describe
d) was a time frame determined? What was it?	Yes/No-Describe
4. How was the strength of the research evidence assessed?	
a) was an appraisal conducted? By who?	Yes/No-Describe
b) were appraisal criteria used? Which ones?	Yes/No-Describe

...continued

Table 1 (continued)

5. What research evidence was provided or was missing regarding: **The ability of the lipid tests to discriminate between those who will or will not develop CHD?** a) prevalence b) sensitivity c) specificity d) false positive e) false negative f) positive predictive value g) negative predictive value	Discussed/Not Discussed and Describe " " " " "
Whether knowledge of cholesterol level will change patient management beyond lifestyle modifications?	Discussed/Not Discussed and Describe
Whether the change in management will improve health outcomes? a) incidence of angina and non-fatal MI b) mortality by CHD c) all-causes mortality	Discussed/Not Discussed and Describe "
6. What was done when research evidence was missing? a) were population sub-groups considered? Which ones? b) was an expert panel used? How was it composed? c) was panel consensus achieved on management or range of management strategies for all sub-groups? How was it achieved?	 Yes/No-Describe Yes/No-Describe Yes/No-Describe
7. What was the link between the research evidence and the recommendations? i.e., Were the recommendations supported by research evidence or by the group's conclusion on the research evidence?	Yes/No-Describe
8. Was a clinical algorithm used to present the recommendations?	Yes/No-Describe
9. Were peer reviews to address the scientific validity of the guidelines: a) done? When? How often? b) done while reviewers maintained strict confidentiality? How? c) done first by an "inner circle" of experts? How were the experts nominated? d) done second by an "external circle" of experts? How were the experts nominated?	 Yes/No -Describe Yes/No-Describe Yes/No-Describe Yes/No-Describe

...continued

Table 1 (continued)

10. Was a pilot review conducted to assess:	
a) the clarity of the guidelines? How was that done?	Yes/No-Describe
b) the feasibility of applying the guidelines in practice? How was that done?	Yes/No-Describe
c) the "user friendliness" of the guidelines? How was that done?	Yes/No-Describe
d) the utility of the guidelines in the clinical setting? How was that done?	Yes/No-Describe
e) whether all the exceptions to the guidelines were mentioned? How was that done?	Yes/No-Describe
11. Was a contracting agency involved in the development of the clinical guidelines? Which one?	Yes/No-Describe
12. How was the labour divided between the requesting and contracting agencies?	Describe
13. Were future updates of the clinical guidelines planned? When?	Yes/No-Describe
14. Was the description of projected health outcomes to be achieved by guidelines included? How were those projections estimated?	Yes/No-Describe
15. Was the description of projected health costs / savings to be achieved by clinical guidelines included? How were those projections estimated?	Yes/No-Describe

Chapter 7

Academic Rivalry in the Field of Autism Research

In This Chapter

- Dr. Sally Rogers
- Drs. Schopler and Mesibov
- BCOHTA Reliance on Dr. Gresham

From the considerable number of academics in the field of autism research and treatment, the BCOHTA selected literature from a minority who are critical of research conducted by Lovaas. The views of comparatively pro-Lovaas or neutral researchers that were included in the report were cited selectively to leave the impression that they were critical of Lovaas' work. In this section, the background and area of research of these BCOHTA selected academics is discussed.

Dr. Sally Rogers

Dr. Rogers considers Lovaas' design the *"strongest scientific design"* even in comparison to her own study.

BCOHTA researchers portray Dr. Rogers as very critical of Lovaas' work. The treatment philosophy that has guided Rogers' model (primarily developmental) is very different to Lovaas' work (largely behavioral); however, her comments have been taken out of context in the Office report.

Rogers conducted a systematic review of all comprehensive treatment programs for children with autism and selected eight studies which she then reviewed. Four of the eight studies were Lovaas' studies or replications, and two of the studies were behavioral, relying on a variety of behavioral techniques including discrete-trial-training. Dr. Rogers considers Lovaas' design the *"strongest scientific design"* even in comparison to her own study. Rogers' research is philosophically very different to Lovaas' work. Rogers describes her model as follows:

> *The model was developmentally based and heavily influenced by Piaget's theory of cognitive development, pragmatics theory of language development, and Mahler's theory of development of interpersonal relationships.*[1]

Rogers' study compares the progress of a group of children with autism or related disorders to a group of children with other emotional/behavioral and developmental disorders. Significantly, Rogers' study does not use a design with a randomly assigned experimental and control group; rather, this design has no control group since both groups of children receive the same treatment. Her results are not as promising as the results reported by Lovaas; however, they are positive. Roger et al. report:

> *... first hypothesis that both groups would make greater cognitive and language gains than expected by maturation alone was supported.*[2]

However, this finding is not as impressive as outcomes reported by Lovaas. Rogers' analysis and critique of Lovaas' research is more balanced then as presented by the Report.

Drs. Schopler and Mesibov

In general, when school districts have pitted their TEACCH programs against the Lovaas protocol desired by parents, many courts have ruled in favor of the Lovaas method.

Schopler and Mesibov are two researchers affiliated with a program called Treatment and Education of Autistic and Related Communication Handicapped Children (TEACCH). Ozonoff and Cathcart (whose home-based TEACCH program was evaluated by the BCOHTA researchers) describe the history of the TEACCH program:

> *In 1966, a treatment program for individuals with autism was established at the University of North Carolina (Schopler & Reichler, 1971). This program was focused on the Treatment and Education of Autistic and related Communication handicapped Children and has come to be known by its acronym, Division TEACCH. In the 1960s, there were a number of ways in which this program was highly novel.*[3]

Schopler was largely responsible for establishing North Carolina's model for teaching autistic children (Schopler, 1987). At the time, his ideas were considered revolutionary and were adopted by school districts all over the United States. Lovaas' protocol was still being developed. With the growing popularity of Lovaas' protocol amongst both the professional community and with parents, the TEACCH methodology began to lose favour with many parents and professionals. Despite the lack of support for TEACCH amongst many parents and professionals, overall, school districts still want to continue with the TEACCH methodology, because, compared to the Lovaas protocol, it is comparatively inexpensive to implement. Likely as a result of school districts' affinity for TEACCH, there has been a marked trend toward legal action against U.S. school districts by parents attempting to access Lovaas treatment for their children, because many view it as a superior, although more costly, intervention.

In general, when school districts have pitted their TEACCH programs against the Lovaas protocol desired by parents, many courts have ruled in favor of the Lovaas method. In 1998, Schopler published an advocacy piece urging parents to avoid the use of the courts.

Schopler states:

> *There are considerable negative consequences to having research claims judged in the courts. Individual children may be denied the most appropriate intervention, other than the Lovaas method. An adversarial and distrustful environment is created, loss of public credibility for professionals is increased, a backlash against special needs programs is encouraged...*[4]

It is noteworthy that the BCOHTA does not always disclose its reliance on Dr. Gresham's work.

Schopler further states:

> *I can understand why some parents may choose to try the Lovaas method, but at this time, in the interests of their children, I urge them to oppose it as social policy in the form of entitlement under IDEA, Part H.*[5]

Schopler's position regarding parents' attempts to access Lovaas Treatment through the Individuals with Disabilities Education Act is understandable, insofar as the comparably more popular Lovaas protocol could supplant Schopler and Mesibov's TEACCH protocol. The BCOHTA presents the views of Schopler and Mesibov without informing the reader that, potentially, these academics have something to lose in the TEACCH versus Lovaas competition.

BCOHTA Reliance on Dr. Gresham

The BCOHTA analysts relied extensively on Dr. Gresham's 1999 article to support their own analysis of Lovaas' research. This may not be surprising given that Dr. Gresham is a well known critic of Dr. Lovaas. However, it is noteworthy that the BCOHTA does not always disclose this reliance on Dr. Gresham's work. Indeed, Gresham et al. (1999) is not even included among the BCOHTA references (refer to the last page of Chapter 7 for a comparison of the Gresham and BCOHTA papers).

Gresham further expresses his outrage regarding parents asserting the rights of their children to receive Lovaas Treatment.

In his 1999 article, Gresham reviews most of the same programs as does Rogers, but makes no conclusion as to which study has the best design. He attacks Lovaas' study more strongly than the others; however, his conclusions are similar. According to Gresham, none of the comprehensive autism treatment programs he reviews meet National Institute of Health standards.

Gresham states:

> *We note that school psychologists have been and might be asked to testify in fair hearings called by parents requesting certain treatment programs for their children with autism. Almost exclusively in recent years, these fair hearings have been called by parents requesting a "Lovaas-type program" or, more specifically, 40 hours of in-home discrete trial training. Unfortunately, parents, fair hearing officers, and/or administrative law judges are often unable to analyze critically the strength of research supporting these programs. It is clear that school districts cannot rely on all persons to use fundamental logic of research methodology and experimental validity to evaluate the efficacy or effectiveness of treatment programs for autism.*[6]

Gresham makes it quite clear that he disagrees with the judiciary's rulings on public spending for Lovaas Treatment. His concerns appear related to the impact of court rulings on government special needs expenditures.

Gresham states:

> *The stakes are high as these exchanges are not mere academic exercises; rather, families of children with autism deserve critical analysis as do taxpayers who will be asked to finance the estimated $60,000 per child per year and other school children receiving special education and general education services as limited financial resources are frequently diverted into attorney's fees and high cost programs such as EIP.*[7]

Gresham further expresses his outrage regarding parents asserting the rights of their children to receive Lovaas Treatment:

> *An analysis by Feinberg and Beyer (1997) indicated that the number of so-called "Lovaas disputes" more than doubled in 1996 and that attorneys expect even more litigation in the coming years. If anything positive has accrued from these disputes it only may be the gainful employment of attorneys who appear more than willing to take these cases to fair hearings and/or the courts.*[8]

Gresham further states:

> *In these times of precious economic resources for education, the "added benefit" of the Lovaas program, given the high cost, should be examined.*[9]

Gresham's justification of resource allocation argument is echoed by BCOHTA. It appears as if the rationing of health care for children with autism is not confined to the BCOHTA alone.

Evidence of BCOHTA's uncredited use of the Gresham et al. paper on Lovaas Autism Treatment:

This graphic represents an analysis that reveals off-the-books 'borrowing of others' academic work. It shows BCOHTA's use of Gresham et al. (1999) in the production of the BCOHTA Lovaas Treatment report for government's defense in B.C. Supreme Court. Noteworthy is that of the many articles BCOHTA cites as references in it's "exhaustive" review of the literature, Gresham's anti-Lovaas publication-a work relied upon heavily by the Office-is the *one* paper conspicuously omitted fronm the bibliography of the BCOHTA Lovaas Treatment report.

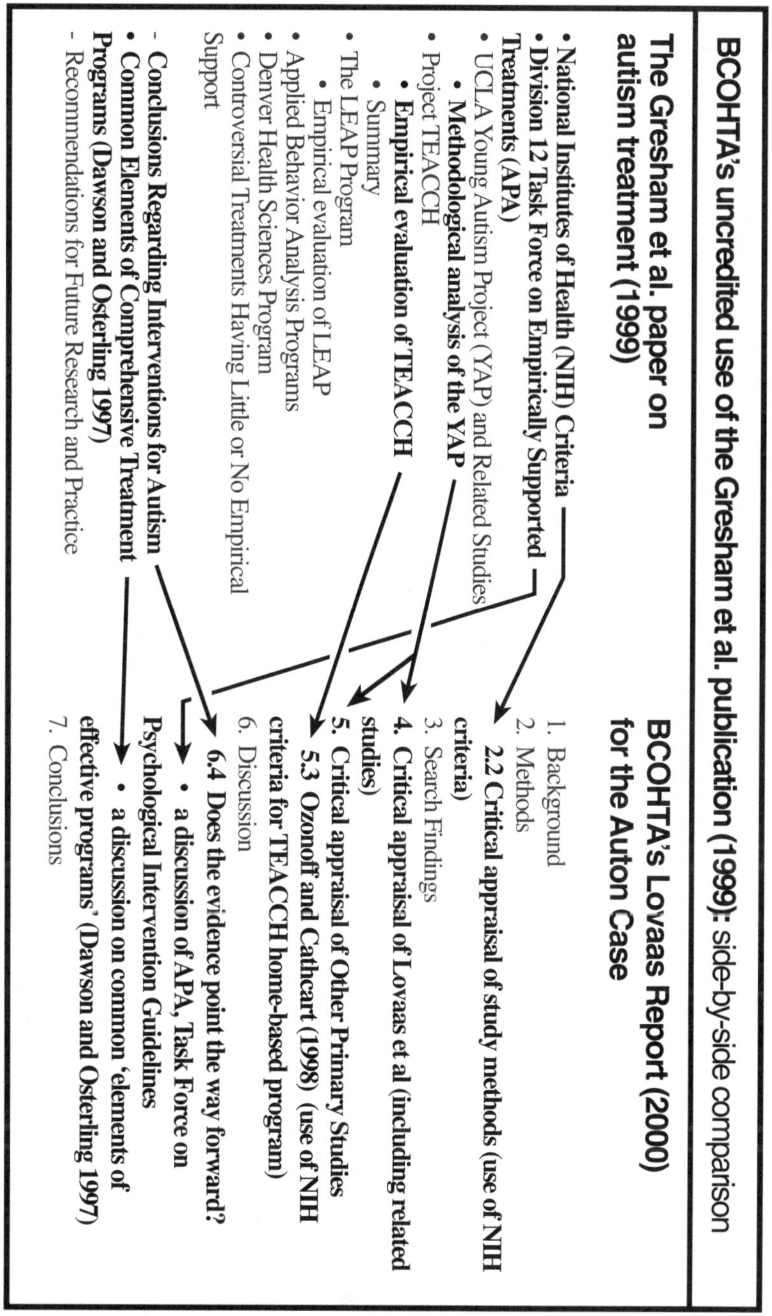

Part II

What Happened in the Supreme Court of British Columbia

Chapters in Part II

Part II reports on what happened in the Supreme Court of British Columbia during the landmark Auton case (Auton et al. v. the Attorney General et al.). Specifically, a discussion of the Judge's ruling regarding the case and the role of the British Columbia Office of Health Technology Assessment's Lovaas report is presented here. Significantly, testimony given during a cross-examination of the lead author of the BCOHTA report, Dr. Ken Bassett, is discussed, as well as how this BCOHTA testimony supports the analysis of the BCOHTA report presented in Part I.

Once again, using a thematic approach, this section ties in information from BCOHTA cross-examination in the court case and serves as further evidence supporting the allegation that the BCOHTA engaged in agenda-based research to support the B.C. Government effort to discredit Lovaas Autism Treatment as "experimental."

Chapter 8

B.C. Supreme Court's Landmark Ruling

In This Chapter

- Highlights of Justice Allan's Judgment on Autism Treatment

Highlights of Justice Allan's Judgment on Autism Treatment

At the end of the day, what *really* happened in the B.C. Supreme Court autism case? The July 2000 ruling constitutes a condemnation of the government's failure to meet its constitutional obligation to ensure equal access to government services, in this case health care for children with autism. Specifically, the court declared that Early Intensive Behavioral Treatment is a *"medically necessary"* service that must be funded by government. Justice Allan states:

> *[102] The Crown's narrow definition of a "medically necessary service" as one that must be provided by a health care practitioner presently scheduled by the MSC precludes delivery of Lovaas Autism Treatment or ABA or any intensive behavioural therapy as a benefit. However, as Dr. Baer suggests, a more accurate definition of medical treatment is whatever cures or ameliorates illness. On the basis of the expert evidence introduced by both parties, I find that* ***early intensive behavioural treatment is a medically necessary service***[1] (emphasis added).

"On the basis of the expert evidence introduced by both parties, I find that early intensive behavioural treatment is a medically necessary service.

The petitioners are the victims of... direct discrimination."

In addition, the court ruled that *the government is in violation of the constitutional rights of autistic children by not providing medically necessary treatment for their condition.* The judge went further to rule that this breach is *direct* discrimination as defined by the Canadian Charter of Rights and Freedoms. Justice Allan goes on to state in the ruling:

> *[132] In my opinion, there is no need to consider adverse effects discrimination. The petitioners are the victims of the government's failure to accommodate them by failing to provide treatment to ameliorate their mental disability.* ***That failure constitutes direct discrimination.*** *Further, the petitioners' disadvantaged position stems from the government's failure to provide effective health treatment to them, not from the fact that their autistic condition is characterized, in part, by an inability to communicate effectively or at all*[2] (emphasis added).

In paragraphs 134 and 135, the Judgment rejected government's argument that children with autism are *already* part of the health care system because, for example, if an autistic child were afflicted with cancer, Medicare would cover the cost of cancer treatment.

> *[134] ... the Crown submits that if an autistic child gets cancer, he or she will receive treatment for cancer. That justification is misguided as well as unfortunate. It ignores the fact that* ***autism is a medical disability just as cancer is and that both require treatment.*** *As the petitioners point out, autism is a disability so severe and comprehensive that it affects all aspects of their lives. They require treatment for that condition, as well as any other conditions that they may be unfortunate enough to incur additionally*[3] (emphasis added).

"...autism is a medical disability just as cancer is and both require treatment."

> *[135] Autism* **is** *the disorder or illness that requires treatment. It is of little assistance to reassure people suffering from debilitating illnesses that although the state will not provide treatment for that illness, should they break a leg or develop pneumonia, they will be treated for those conditions. While one of the effects of autism may be an inability to communicate and obtain government services which are universally available, the gravamen of the government's omission is its* ***failure to provide treatment for the underlying disability, not its willingness to ensure access to other benefits*** [4] (emphasis added).

What is highly significant here — and should be very disturbing to the Health Technology Movement along with universities that host them — is that Justice Allan ruled that *the BCOHTA report is obviously biased and of minimal value,* in support of the government's defence against the families' legal action. Despite their best efforts to support the B.C. Government and its Ministry of Health in court, researchers at the BCOHTA failed to persuade the B.C. Supreme Court that their health technology research is the impartial, disinterested work of university academics.

> *[41] Dr. Bassett is a Senior Medical Consultant with the B.C. Office of Health Technology Assessment Centre for Health Services and Policy Research ("BCOHTA") at U.B.C. BCOHTA is* ***funded by the Provincial Government*** *for the purpose of "promoting and encouraging the use of assessment*

> *research in policy, planning and utilization decisions by government, health care executives and practitioners." BCHOTA [sic] was asked by the Crown to provide "an assessment of the effectiveness evidence" regarding Lovaas Autism Treatment for pre-school children with autism*[5] (emphasis added).

In the paragraph below, the Supreme Court noted that the BCOHTA attempted to "pass off" its report as having been externally reviewed and completed for submission to the court when, in fact, it was not. In truth, only *one* external reviewer had offered comments to that point and he is a government employee. Clearly this attempt to mislead was not lost upon Justice Allan:

> **"The Supreme Court noted that the BCOHTA attempted to "pass off" its report as having been externally reviewed and completed for submission to the court when, in fact, it was not."**

> *[42] Drs. Bassett, Green, and Kasanjian prepared the report entitled "autism and Lovaas treatment: A systematic review of effectiveness evidence" (the "BCOHTA Report"). The foreword to that report describes the methodology utilized in BCOHTA projects generally. It states that "reports are reviewed internally, and then sent for external review to experts from a variety of academic or clinical disciplines. Comments and suggestions are considered before a final document is produced."* ***That statement clearly implies that the BCOHTA Report, which was prepared for the purpose of this litigation, was subjected to external peer review before it was filed*** *as an exhibit in these proceedings. However, Dr. Bassett testified that, as at the date of the hearing, the BCOHTA Report was out for external review and only one response had been received.* ***He described the BCOHTA Report as the final document for these proceedings but not the final document for the purpose of publication*** [6] (emphasis added).

Significantly, in paragraph 43 of the Auton ruling, Justice Allan noted that the "external review" process is not itself without bias since the BCOHTA elected to forgo consulting with *any* professionals who had favourable opinions regarding the work of Dr. Lovaas or the UCLA treatment protocol in general.

> *[43] Dr. Bassett and his colleagues did not consult with any psychiatrists or clinicians who are known to support Lovaas*

Autism Treatment. ***They spoke with only one external medical consultant, Dr. Miller****, who commented that the incidence of autism might appear higher than it actually is because of a tendency to label a child with autism or ASD to obtain access to services. On the basis of that single anecdotal comment, the BCHOTA [sic] Report states:*

> *"A more recent problem has emerged in relation to estimates of the incidence of autism. It appears that, at least in the BC context, problems with the diagnosis of autism may not simply be due to problems in the application of validated diagnostic criteria. The possibility arises that children with other pervasive development disorders may nonetheless be diagnosed with autism in order to gain access to services linked to that diagnosis"*[7] (emphasis added).

"Dr. Bassett and his colleagues did not consult with any psychiatrists or clinicians who are known to support Lovaas Autism Treatment."

It should be disturbing to health technology professionals in Canada, the U.S. and beyond, that so serious an allegation can be leveled against parents based on so little.

In paragraphs 44 and 45, the B.C. Supreme Court makes the point that the BCOHTA's agenda of evaluating whether Lovaas Treatment "cures" autism was simply their own agenda, insofar as the researchers involved in Lovaas' autism treatment research have never made a curative claim in the decades of research that have gone into developing the uniquely effective treatment protocol.

[44] The Executive Summary of the BCOHTA Report begins with the following statement:

> *"This systematic review examined whether early intensive behavioural therapy for children with autism results in normal functioning, or essentially a cure. The scientific validity of this curative claim is*

central both to legal proceedings brought on behalf of several children in British Columbia against the Province seeking an intensive behavioural program; and to cost-benefit analyses and clinical guidelines used for planning autism treatment programs."[8]

The B.C. Supreme court explicitly nullifies the central assumption that constitutes the foundation of the BCOHTA Lovaas report:

> *[45] The BCHOTA Report reiterates that Drs. Lovaas and McEachin claim that their treatment "normalized or cured children with autism." As noted earlier,* ***neither Dr. Lovaas nor Dr. McEachin — nor the petitioners — assert such a claim*** [9] (emphasis added).

"The BCOHTA Report reiterates that Drs. Lovaas and McEachin claim that their treatment "normalized or cured children with autism." As noted earlier, neither Dr. Lovaas nor Dr. McEachin - nor the petitioners - assert such a claim."

Significantly, the Supreme Court rejected the government's argument that Lovaas selectively chose only "best case" scenario children. The lead author of the BCOHTA report could not provide the court with any suggestions as to *how* a researcher would be able to select children in this manner. Moreover, an expert witness testified that this would be a very difficult exercise.

> *[46] The BCOHTA Report criticizes the Lovaas study because it used a small number of children and further suggests that the reported findings of benefits may have been achieved by assembling a high-functioning group of autistic children. Dr. Bassett was unable to suggest how one would assemble a high functioning group and agreed, in cross-examination, that he was unaware of any evidence to contradict Dr. Baer's opinion that such a selection could not be made.*[10]

In paragraph 47, the court dismissed the entire BCOHTA Report by acknowledging its lack of value in shedding any light on this academic debate.

> *[47] While the BCHOTA [sic] Report criticizes the methodology of the Lovaas and McEachin studies and the absence of replication at length, it adds little if anything to the existing debate in the scientific journals on the subject.*[11]

British Columbia's Supreme Court discredited and rejected the *entire* BCOHTA report on Lovaas effectiveness. Such wholesale dismissal of a Health Technology report should be cause for great concern, since Health Technology analysts are relied upon to create health policy throughout the industrialized world. However, that discussion is beyond the scope of this book. The court goes on to say,

> *[48] **The BCOHTA Report exhibits an obvious bias towards supporting the Crown's position in this litigation. That detracts significantly from its usefulness***[12] (emphasis added).

> *[49] The BCOHTA Report does acknowledge the fact that behaviour therapy, or ABA, is accepted as a benefit to children with autism. Its authors agree that early intervention with behavioural treatment can help to alleviate autistic symptoms in many if not most autistic children. Dr. Bassett testified that he was unaware of any government-funded programme in B.C. that provided behavioural therapy.*[13]

"While the BCOHTA Report criticizes the methodology of the Lovaas and McEachin studies and the absence of replication at length, it adds little if anything to the existing debate in the scientific journals on the subject."

Although the BCOHTA report is a sophisticated example of "science for sale," the B.C. Supreme Court Justice was not convinced by the report's presentation of "scientific evidence" underlying the efficacy of Lovaas-type Autism Treatment, or "EIBI" or ABA (all synonymous). The court supported families' claims that the issue of Autism Treatment is one of health care and not social services or education. Justice Allan states:

> *[153] The infant petitioners suffer from a serious mental disability for which effective treatment in the form of ABA is available. **The inability of the petitioners to access that treatment is primarily an issue of health care**, not education or social services*[14] (emphasis added).

The judge further commented upon how the Ministry of Health could easily incorporate autism treatment into its ministry if it chose to do so. The Justice Allan states:

> *[154] **The Crown, and specifically the Ministry of Health, provides no effective treatment for the medical disability of autism.** The respondents' argument that they are unable to*

> *provide effective treatment for autism because of constraints in the legislation governing medicare* ***attempts to erect a false barrier.*** *Early intensive behavioral treatment could be provided by MOH in one of two ways. MSC may determine that behavioural therapy merits funding according to the criteria set out under the Medical Services Plan and add behavioural therapists to the scheduled list of health care providers by regulation. Alternatively,* ***MOH could pay for the treatment through block funding as it has done to pay for interpreters for the deaf to comply with the decision in Eldridge, supra****. It is for the Crown to determine the measures it will take to comply with its constitutional obligations*[15] (emphasis added).

"The BCOHTA Report exhibits an obvious bias towards supporting the Crown's position in this litigation. That detracts significantly from its usefulness."

In addition, Madame Justice Allan quoted Dr. Thomas Barnett [sic] who described the involvement of the social services-based, Ministry of Children and Families' attempt to deliver qualified mental health care to children as an abysmal failure and "an experiment gone wrong."

The judge states:

> *[58] Dr. Thomas Barnett, who is the child psychiatry representative on the B.C. Psychiatric Association, described the transfer of child and youth mental health programmes from MOH to MCF in 1997 as "an expensive experiment gone wrong." At the community level, he sees no benefits resulting from the transfer, in large part because* ***the individuals who make policy within MCF and determine what services are available for autistic children lack training in psychiatry, psychology or behavioural intervention"***[16] (emphasis added).

In terms of the government's key expert witness, Dr. Frank Gresham, Justice Allan states:

> *[52] Current research has established, with some certainty, the efficacy of early intervention in assisting many children to achieve significant social and educational gains. The expert witnesses agree that* ***the most effective behavioural therapies are those based on principles of ABA. There are no effective***

> ***competing treatments. As Dr. Gresham stated, "there is no question that ABA is the treatment of choice for children presenting with autistic disorder based on over 35 years of research in the field."*** *He emphasized the fact that although replication of the Lovaas study was necessary, treatment should not be delayed awaiting the outcome*[17] (emphasis added).
>
> *[66] It is ironic that the very limited treatment services provided by the Crown not only fail to meet the gold standard of scientific methodology; they are positively discredited by one of the Crown's own expert witnesses.*[18]

"Early intensive behavioral treatment could be provided by ... the Medical Services Plan... [or] ... through block funding as it has done to pay for interpreters for the deaf to comply with the decision in Eldridge, supra."

The B.C. Government, with its BCOHTA academic "hired guns", was not able to convince B.C. Supreme Court that Lovaas treatment is "experimental," and that children with autism are somehow *already* included in the health care system. Finally, for the first time in the history of this vexing disorder, autism treatment has been declared by the courts as a "medically necessary" service, as opposed to a social services support issue. The implication of this ruling is that responsibility for funding bona fide, science-based autism treatment rests with the publicly funded Canadian Health Care system. In practical terms, this means government has an obligation to fund autism treatment in the same terms as physical illness. Most importantly, this means all children must have access to effective autism treatment regardless of ability to pay. Although the "autism wars" are far from over, the battle in B.C. Supreme Court was won.

How did the B.C. Supreme Court Judge arrive at a ruling that the British Columbia Office of Health Technology Assessment report was an obviously biased work that supports the governments position, thereby detracting significantly from its usefulness? First, several expert witnesses provided testimony opposing the BCOHTA report and its assertions. Second, the lead author, Dr. Ken Bassett, was required to defend the BCOHTA report in court during a five hour cross-examination, under oath and on the stand. During this cross-examination of the senior author, the court uncovered the most compelling evidence confirming the biased nature of the BCOHTA's report, "Autism and Lovaas treatment: A systematic review of effectiveness evidence." Chapter nine has key parts of the testimony given by Dr. Bassett. This cross-examination is set out in considerable detail to afford readers the opportunity to arrive at their own conclusions about the BCOHTA.

Chapter 9

BCOHTA On the Stand

In This Chapter

- The Office of Health Technology On the Stand
- BCOHTA's Government Links
- BCOHTA Selected "Yes Men" for Autism Consultation
- BCOHTA's "Made for Court" Advocacy Analysis
- BCOHTA Embraces Unsubstantiated Autism Programs and Research
- Double Standard: Lovaas Studies Meet BCOHTA Criteria for Attack
- BCOHTA Report Excludes Relevant Articles That Support Lovaas Treatment
- Analysis of BCOHTA Critique of Lovaas Treatment Research
- What Happened After BCOHTA Report Ruled Biased?

The Office of Health Technology On the Stand

Chapter 9 takes us into the court room, "front and center" at the cross-examination of BCOHTA head, Dr. Ken Bassett, before a B.C. Supreme Court judge during the Auton hearings in February 2000. The chapter presents, in some detail, the back and forth of the cross-examination, pointing out the significance of each exchange between Dr. Bassett and the lawyer for the families.

BCOHTA's Government Links

Dr. Ken Bassett:

"In fact, we've almost lost our funding, I think, a couple of times because we developed and published reports that were contrary to government policy."

BCOHTA's economic reliance on the provincial Ministry of Health has already been noted. This issue was canvassed in the B.C. court case.

Government Counsel:

> "Now, has BCOHTA ever produced a report that you consider unfavourable to the position of the Ministry of Health?"

Dr. Bassett (Director of the BCOHTA):

> "Oh, most definitely. We're considered the watch dogs on evidence. And the use of claims of scientific validity are problematic both by clinicians and by policy makers. So we've almost as often been in a position to criticize assumptions of scientific validity by government and government policy makers as we have by clinicians who are uncomfortable with having the state of evidence clarified. In fact, we've almost lost our funding, I think, a couple of times because we developed and published reports that were contrary to government policy. And it ended up, in fact, as a news item and then the national news because it was quite problematic" (emphasis added).

Government Counsel:

> "Now, do you feel vulnerable now when you produce a report at the request of government?"

Dr. Bassett:

> "Vulnerable? I think that this is a very uncomfortable role for anyone to be in."

Academic Conflict of Interest?

In the following excerpt, Dr. Bassett is asked to address the issue of conflict of interest. Specifically, at issue is the fact that the Government of British Columbia, in an effort to defeat an autism lawsuit, commissioned a BCOHTA study to support an argument that Lovaas Treatment is "experimental" and therefore, not eligible for public health care funding.

Family Counsel:

" ... the B.C. Office of Health and Technology Assessment receives significant funding from the provincial government; is that right?"

Dr. Bassett:

"Yes."

Family Counsel:

> " ... the B.C. Office of Health and Technology Assessment receives significant funding from the provincial government; is that right?"

Dr. Bassett:

> "Yes."

Family Counsel:

> "And the funding is provided through the — that is to the B.C. Office of Health Technology Assessment — through the Centre for Health Sciences and Policy Research?"

Dr. Bassett:

> "Yes, that's right."

Family Counsel:

> "And that latter body in 1998, '99 was funded to the tune of $7,952,101 from the Ministry of Health?"

> **Family Counsel:**
>
> **"In fact, it wasn't until these proceedings were begun that you were asked to provide any information at all to the government; is that right?"**
>
> **Dr. Bassett:**
>
> **"That's correct."**

Dr. Bassett:

> "I'm not sure of the exact amount. That would be for five years. That sounds about right."

Family Counsel:

> "And then they, in turn, pass funding along to your group?"

Dr. Bassett:

> "Yes."

Family Counsel:

> "Now, the Ministry of Health is one of the defendants in these proceedings; you understand that?"

Dr. Bassett:

> "Yes."

Family Counsel:

> "In fact, it wasn't until these proceedings were begun that you were asked to provide any information at all to the government; is that right?"

Dr. Bassett:

> "That's correct."

Family Counsel:

> "So, there was never any effort on the part of the Ministry of Health or any other ministry of the provincial government of British Columbia to provide any assessment of Applied Behavior Analysis therapy prior to your recent effort; is that fair?"

Dr. Bassett:

> "That's correct."

The above exchange shows that in its Lovaas Treatment report, the BCOHTA, was recruited in the context of litigation where the provincial government, including the Ministry of Health, was alleged to be discriminating against children with autism by failing to provide Lovaas Treatment.

University of British Columbia Ethics Guidelines

> **Family Counsel:**
>
> **"...Our grant goes to the university and it is administered through the university, where we're subject to their rules of research, conduct, ethical behavior."**

Family Counsel:

> "And is it fair to say that the B.C. Office of Health Technology Assessment is in any way affiliated with the University of British Columbia?"

Dr. Bassett:

> "We're centered in the University of British Columbia. Our grant goes to the university and it is administered through the university, where we're subject to their rules of research, conduct, ethical behavior."

Family Counsel:

> "And, in fact, one of the University of British Columbia policies is that groups such as yours are not to advocate for vested interests?"

Dr. Bassett:

> "True."

Family Counsel:

> "You don't see any vested interest in that your funding comes from one of the defendants in these proceedings?"

Dr. Bassett:

> "Our funding comes to our office the same as any other part of the medical school, any other part of the university."

Family Counsel:

> "You don't see it as a problem that you're offering an opinion where the interests of the Ministry of Health are at stake in these proceedings?"

Family Counsel:

"You wrote this for this lawsuit, I thought you told us?"

Dr. Bassett:

"The central question is for the lawsuit."

Dr. Bassett:

> "No."

Family Counsel:

> "Isn't that directly contrary to UBC policy?"

Dr. Bassett:

> "I don't see how it would be."

Family Counsel:

> "You wrote this for this lawsuit, I thought you told us?"

Dr. Bassett:

> "The central question is for the lawsuit."

To comply with University of British Columbia ethics guidelines, Office research must be disinterested. In other words, they are not permitted to publish advocacy research for their source of funding. If it were a drug company that funded the BCOHTA and that company were on trial, it would be a clear breach of the university's rules of research, conduct and ethical behavior for BCOHTA to issue a report in defense of that drug company. The fact that in this case the source of the conflict of interest is a provincial government should not confer preferential immunity from the universities ethics rules.

No Expertise in Autism

It has already been argued that the BCOHTA researchers have no experience with autism nor any expertise in its treatment. Nevertheless, despite a lack of knowledge and training in the field, the Office embarked on an analysis of the preeminent treatment protocol in the field of autism treatment.

Family Counsel:

"In fact, you've never been involved in research or treatment of autism, have you?"

Dr. Bassett:

"Right."

Family Counsel:

> "You weren't involved in research or treatment of autism?"

Dr. Bassett:

> "No."

Family Counsel:

> "In fact, you've never been involved in research or treatment of autism, have you?"

Dr. Bassett:

> "Right."

The matter went further.

Family Counsel:

> "Now, the merits of the various tests of psychosocial development are not within the expertise of the B.C. Office of Health Technology Assessment, are they?"

Dr. Bassett:

> "No, they are not."

Family Counsel:

> "And the B.C. Office of Health Technology Assessment have never undertaken any analysis of neurologic disorders?"

Dr. Bassett:

> "Not that I can remember."
>
> [...]
>
> "Whenever there is a technical issue such as this in a particular subfield like autism where someone such as Dr. Lovaas and Drs. Gresham and McMillan are arguing over particular characteristics and we cite the argument and we cite both sides of the argument as best we can..."

Family Counsel:

"And the B.C. Office of Health Technology Assessment have never undertaken any analysis of neurologic disorders?"

Dr. Bassett:

"Not that I can remember."

Family Counsel:

> "And your researchers don't have the training or wherewithal to interpret the validity of that debate, or positions?"

Dr. Bassett:

> "In this particular incident to do with prorated mental age, we thought it was inappropriate to raise this as a major issue or to get involved in that debate."

Here Dr. Bassett admits that his office thought it inappropriate to wade into this issue; however, he contradicts this point by admitting that they did cite the argument as best they could. It would appear that BCOHTA was only too willing to highlight criticisms of Lovaas without providing equal space to the responses.

BCOHTA Selected "Yes Men" for Autism Consultation

Counsel for the families also pointed out that an entire class of professionals who support Lovaas therapy were not consulted by the BCOHTA.

Family Counsel:

> "Did you consult with any of the 63 psychiatrists in the province who are on record of supporting Lovaas therapy, even one of them?"

Dr. Bassett:

> "We haven't consulted with any psychiatrists."

Family Counsel:

> "Did you consult with any clinicians at all who are in favour of Lovaas therapy?"

Dr. Bassett:

> "We didn't, no."

This omission is significant because in British Columbia, sixty-three (63) licensed psychiatrists signed a petition strongly endorsing Lovaas Treatment. The petition follows:

> I agree that Lovaas type behavioural autism treatment, a form of Applied Behavior Analysis, is a highly effective treatment for children with autism and is the most effective treatment currently available for this neurological condition. Insofar as it significantly improves the condition of autistic children, I am of the opinion that it is medically necessary treatment that should be widely available upon diagnosis and funded under the Provincial Medical Services Plan or by the Ministry of Health, or both. (Signed: Sixty-three (63) licensed BC psychiatrists; petition on file with FEAT of B.C.)

Family Counsel:

"Did you consult with any of the 63 psychiatrists in the province who are on record of supporting Lovaas therapy, even one of them?"

Dr. Bassett:

"We haven't consulted with any psychiatrists."

However, BCOHTA was prepared to rely on the opinion of Dr. Miller, a pediatrician.

Family Counsel:

> "If you look at page 3 of your paper, you say:
>
> A more recent problem has emerged in relation to estimates of the incidence of autism. It appears that at least in the B.C. context, problems with diagnosis of autism may not simply be due to problems in the application of a validated diagnostic criteria. The possibility arises that children with other pervasive development disorders may nonetheless be diagnosed with autism in order to gain access to the services linked to that diagnosis.'
>
> Now, That's based on the say so of Dr. Miller alone?"

Dr. Bassett:

> "Yes."

Family Counsel:

> "And you have been critical of Dr. Lovaas, who has done follow-up research, and said it isn't good enough, but you're prepared to rely on the say so, untested, of Dr. Miller in this regard, are you?"

Family Counsel:

"And you have been critical of Dr. Lovaas, who has done follow-up research, and said it isn't good enough, but you're prepared to rely on the say so, untested, of Dr. Miller in this regard, are you?"

Dr. Bassett:

> "In the background section. We're not making a substantive claim based on this. We're raising it as an issue and pointing out the source... We only raise it as a possibility."

Questionable Academic Review Process

The BCOHTA attempts to garner legitimacy for its advocacy research by using an "external review" process that substitutes for the rigorous peer review process characteristic in the publication of academic papers. The process the BCOHTA uses is questionable because it is the office itself that chooses who should review its documents. In addition, in this case the two external reviewers selected to review the BCOHTA Lovaas Report were themselves employees of one Ministry defending itself in the Auton legal action — The Ministry of Health.

The BCOHTA attempts to garner legitimacy for its advocacy research by using an "external review" process that substitutes for the rigorous peer review process characteristic in the publication of academic papers.

Even more troubling is the fact that the BCOHTA did not complete even this limited review process before submitting its report to the court. Comments of their external reviewers had not all come back yet; however, the BCOHTA report suggested the review process had been completed.

Family Counsel:

> "... in the fourth paragraph you say...:
>
> > 'Reports are reviewed internally and then sent for external review to experts from a variety of academic of clinical disciplines.'
>
> To whom was this report sent for external review?"

Dr. Bassett:

> "I can bring the list. It is out for external review right now."

Family Counsel:

> "You haven't got the results back?"

Dr. Bassett:

> "We have one result back."

> **Family Counsel:**
>
> **"Well, do you think it is fair, Doctor, to suggest, as you have in this foreword, that there has been external review of your report when you have got one response back?"**
>
> **Dr. Bassett:**
>
> **"This is the process that we go through."**

Family Counsel:

"Well, do you think it is fair, Doctor, to suggest, as you have in this foreword, that there has been external review of your report when you have got one response back?"

Dr. Bassett:

"This is the process that we go through."

Family Counsel:

"So it didn't apply to this particular report; it is a process you normally go through, but you didn't go through in this case?"

Dr. Bassett:

"It is exactly what we're going through right now."

Family Counsel:

"But you haven't been through it, have you?"

Dr. Bassett:

"We had Dr. Miller review the draft prior to submission here and it is now going through the exact process described here."

Family Counsel:

"It hasn't gone through the process yet?"

Dr. Bassett:

"For publication, yes, that's what it is going through."

Family Counsel:

> "Well, you only have one external review as comments, don't you?"

Dr. Bassett:

> "One back, you. Counting Dr. Miller that would be two."

Family Counsel:

Family Counsel:

"Well, you only have one external review as comments, don't you?"

Dr. Bassett:

"One back, you. Counting Dr. Miller that would be two."

> "Well, who is the other one?"

Dr. Bassett:

> "I've got it here in the pile."

Family Counsel:

> "Go ahead..."

The Judge:

> "Excuse me, before you go on, is it safe to say this is not the final document?"

Dr. Bassett:

> "This is the final document that we submitted but what we plan to do is publish because that's our mandate, our office is required to produce a report for publication, so the review that's going on now is the broader review for publication."

The Judge:

> "But that's — that isn't suggested in the foreword. That isn't evident. It says,

> 'Comments and suggestions are considered before a final document is produced. Distribution of the report is provided by the — from the office through inclusion on a mailing list. Reports are also available for public distribution.'

It makes it sound as if this is the final report that is available for public distribution."

Dr. Bassett:

"I suspect the problem is that this executive — sorry, this foreword is the standard foreword for all reports. And I think in submitting this report to this judicial review, it was put into this submission, and I think it is because we haven't submitted anything to a judicial review and it was difficult to know how to do that in a timely way and still do our own more formal review as described here. But I think that is misleading."

The Judge:

"But that's — that isn't suggested in the foreword. That isn't evident...

It makes it sound as if this is the final report that is available for public distribution."

Dr. Bassett:

"I suspect the problem is that this executive — sorry, this foreword is the standard foreword for all reports."

BCOHTA's "Made for Court" Advocacy Analysis

Presented here is evidence that the authors of the BCOHTA Report chose to be very selective in the type of analysis done so that the work of Lovaas and colleagues could be discredited in court as being an "experimental" treatment for autism.

This section discusses the six major themes developed by the Office for their selective analysis of Lovaas Autism Treatment: The Curative Claim, Targeting only Lovaas Treatment for Evaluation, ABA Accepted Uncritically, Alternative Autism Programs and Research Accepted Uncritically, Only Lovaas Studies "Acceptable", Several Relevant Articles Excluded.

Curative Claim

The BCOHTA Report sets up a "straw man" argument that Lovaas and colleagues make a curative claim regarding the autism treatment method they developed. The report then sets about knocking down the argument as part of the effort to discredit the treatment protocol in court. In other words, the Office states that Dr. Lovaas claims to have cured autism, instead of stating that Lovaas never made such a claim, but rather, that it is Lovaas' academic rivals who incorrectly level the charge that Lovaas makes a curative claim. The BCOHTA unquestionably adopted as their own, the straw man argument developed by critics of Lovaas Treatment.

Family Counsel:

"You start ...:

'This systematic review examined whether early intensive behavioural therapy for children with autism results in normal functioning or essentially a cure.'

So you were looking in this work to see if Lovaas therapy cured autism?"

Dr. Bassett:

"As defined by him, yes, which is normal functioning."

Family Counsel:

> "You start out at the top of this page saying:
>
> > 'This systematic review examined whether early intensive behavioural therapy for children with autism results in normal functioning or essentially a cure.'
>
> So you were looking in this work to see if Lovaas therapy cured autism?"

Dr. Bassett:

> "As defined by him, yes, which is normal functioning."

Family Counsel:

> "Does Dr. Lovaas ever presume to state that his therapy cures autism?"

Dr. Bassett:

> "He states that it results in normal functioning."

Family Counsel:

"Does he ever suggest anywhere that it is a cure for autism?"

Dr. Bassett:

"No, in fact I think he argues the opposite. I think he argues that it can't necessarily be seen as a cure. He says that it results in what is normal — described as normal functioning by classroom teachers or peers."

Family Counsel:

"Well, Doctor, you have deliberately taken a pejorative and a very charged word and incorporated it into this executive summary knowing full well that Dr. Lovaas and his colleagues deny ever making such a statement, haven't you."

Dr. Bassett:

"I don't see it that way."

Family Counsel:

"Do they ever purport to offer a cure for autism?"

Dr. Bassett:

"They do what I just said, they purport to result in children that are considered to be normally functioning."

Family Counsel:

"You have read the literature and you know that they have specifically said we're not suggesting it is cured, don't you?"

Family Counsel:

"Well, Doctor, you have deliberately taken a pejorative and a very charged word and incorporated it into this executive summary knowing full well that Dr. Lovaas and his colleagues deny ever making such a statement, haven't you."

Dr. Bassett:

"I don't see it that way."

Dr. Bassett:

> "When, pressed that's what they argued, yes, that's what Dr. Lovaas and colleagues argued."

Family Counsel:

> "What do you mean, 'when pressed?' They have never suggested a cure, have they?"

Dr. Bassett:

> "When pressed, what I'm referring to is a debate that they're involved in the literature (sic)."

Family Counsel:

"That's when Dr. Gresham —"

Dr. Bassett:

"Yes."

Family Counsel:

"— accused them of offering a cure, and they said we've done no such thing. That's how it was generated, wasn't it?"

Dr. Bassett:

"Exactly."

Family Counsel:

> "That's when Dr. Gresham..."

Dr. Bassett:

> "Yes."

Family Counsel:

> "— accused them of offering a cure, and they said we've done no such thing. That's how it was generated, wasn't it?"

Dr. Bassett:

> "Exactly."

[...]

Family Counsel:

> "Now, you don't answer the question that you pose at page 10, instead you say at page 44:

> 'the Lovaas et al. (1987) and McEachin (1993) study, while methodologically stronger than published reports of alternative therapies, is inadequate to establish the degree to which this form of therapy results in children achieving normal functioning, however defined.'

That isn't the question you asked for yourselves is it? It doesn't answer the question you asked, does it?"

Family Counsel:

"Well, Doctor, you say you're looking to see if there are improved overall outcomes. And then what you answer is you're not satisfied there is normal functioning. Now, that's a far stricter question than you posed?"

Dr. Bassett:

"The two are synonymous from our research perspective."

Dr. Bassett:

"I think it directly answers it."

Family Counsel:

"Well, Doctor, you say you're looking to see if there are improved overall outcomes. And then what you answer is you're not satisfied there is normal functioning. Now, that's a far stricter question than you posed?"

Dr. Bassett:

"The two are synonymous from our research perspective."

Family Counsel:

"You see normal functioning as synonymous with improved overall outcome."

Dr. Bassett:

"Well, the research question was designed for the search protocol; as it is explained, it is designed to be inclusive, it is designed to look at all intensive behavioural therapies, it's designed to look for evidence of improved overall outcome and it's looking for comparative trials and it would include claims or evidence regarding normal functioning. So it is strictly within the research question. It is exactly what we were assessing, were claims regarding — the scientific validity of claims regarding improved overall outcome which includes the normal functioning."

Family Counsel:

"All right. It includes normal functioning. The only answer you offer is with respect to normal functioning as subset of improved overall outcome, isn't it?"

> **Family Counsel:**
>
> **As far as you can go is to say, well, we can't be sure that it results in children achieving normal function?"**
>
> **Dr. Bassett:**
>
> **"That's what we state."**

Dr. Bassett:

"That's because this hasn't been studied in other treatments and with other options. We explain at length why we've included what we've included and we've not found adequate trials to include to give additional information to more, I think you... you're inferring [sic] is a less strict interpretation of improved overall outcome."

Family Counsel:

"Doctor, the only answer you offer is with respect to whether therapy results in normal functioning. You don't purport to offer any other answer than that, do you?"

Dr. Bassett:

"This is what we can say based on the evidence."

Family Counsel:

"As far as you can go is to say, well, we can't be sure that it results in children achieving normal function?"

Dr. Bassett:

"That's what we state."

Family Counsel:

> "Yah. But you can go so far, Doctor, to suggest, as to say it clearly results in improved functioning - -"

Dr. Bassett:

> "Which is what we stated."

Family Counsel:

> "— and you have chosen not to state that?"

Dr. Bassett:

> "We state that at the very beginning as a premise, before we even get into the details of the systematic review. We accept that these techniques do provide benefit to children and their families."

Finally, Dr. Bassett admits that Lovaas Treatment does ameliorate autism. This contradicts the BCOHTA report which attempts to portray Lovaas treatment as "experimental," and therefore, not worthy of funding.

Finally, Dr. Bassett has no choice but to admit that Lovaas Treatment does indeed ameliorate the condition of autism. This is important because the BCOHTA report attempts to portray the Lovaas treatment protocol as purely "experimental," leading to the conclusion that it is premature to decide the treatment has substantive benefit for children afflicted by the disorder.

Upcoming in the cross-examination is the BCOHTA accusation that Lovaas makes a curative claim.

Family Counsel:

> "Can we look at page 39 of your report. The third paragraph from the bottom, you say:
>
> > 'The absence of corroborative evidence of recovery from autism does not devalue the effectiveness of early intensive and comprehensive treatment programs in

> achieving significant developmental gains. However, Lovaas and his research colleagues have not limited their effectiveness claims to achieving developmental gains. Instead, they have permitted and even fostered the premise that appears throughout the published literature associating their therapy with a notion of achieving normal functioning in as many as half a given population of children with autism.'

Now, I'm going to suggest to you, Doctor, that it isn't Lovaas and his colleagues who have fostered that premise, but rather Gresham, in an effort to detract from Lovaas's work, who accuses Lovaas of claiming he's got a cure. In fact, Lovaas makes no such claim, isn't that —"

Family Counsel:

"Now, I'm going to suggest to you, Doctor, that it isn't Lovaas and his colleagues who have fostered that premise, but rather Gresham, in an effort to detract from Lovaas's work, who accuses Lovaas of claiming he's got a cure. In fact, Lovaas makes no such claim, isn't that —"

Dr. Bassett:

"That's your opinion. I mean ..."

Family Counsel:

"But isn't that really a fair statement of what's gone on in the literature?"

Dr. Bassett:

"It's not for me to say."

Family Counsel:

"Well, you say here that it's Lovaas's colleagues who are fostering this premise. And I'm suggesting to you that that's not true, it's Gresham who is doing that, setting up a straw man."

The cross-examination continues with further discussion of the Straw Man argument made by the BCOHTA that Lovaas Treatment claims to be "curative".

Family Counsel:

> "Well, Doctor, in fairness to Dr. Lovaas, he does more than discuss the 47 percent, the nine children who appear near normal. He's got eight of the remaining ten who show remarkable gains."

Dr. Bassett:

> "M'mm-hmm."

Family Counsel:

"But you choose to categorize them as the fostering of the premise associating the therapy with achieving normal functioning. That's how you summarize it?"

Dr. Bassett:

"Yes, in the sense that I explained."

Family Counsel:

> "So he isn't just pointing to the 47 percent and he isn't claiming that all of the children will achieve normal functioning. What he's doing is reporting what, in fact, is evident from his work, that is, that the improvement rate up to and including apparently normal functioning was remarkable in 17 of the 19 children; wasn't it?"

Dr. Bassett:

> "So he's reporting improvement in the others? Yes. Which is what is expected. We're not denying that he's reporting on his findings."

Family Counsel:

> "But you choose to categorize them as the fostering of the premise associating the therapy with achieving normal functioning. That's how you summarize it?"

Dr. Bassett:

> "Yes, in the sense that I explained."

Although Dr. Bassett is forced to admit that it is Lovaas' critics who foster the premise of normal functioning, he still stands by his analysis that it is Dr. Lovaas who makes the curative claim when he says: "Yes, in the sense that I explained." Under further cross-examination, Dr. Bassett admits there are many diseases for which no cure exists; yet the British Columbia medical system fully covers the cost of what are often very expensive treatments. This admission on the part of BCOHTA spotlights the discriminatory stance of the B.C. Government's refusal to fund science-based autism treatment for children who need it.

Family Counsel:

"All right. And when you talk about treatments, you can't cure Parkinson's disease, can you?"

Dr. Bassett:

"Not that I know of."

Family Counsel:

"So it is ameliorating the condition that is the subject of funding through the Ministry of Health?"

Dr. Bassett:

"Yes..."

Family Counsel:

> "All right. And when you talk about treatments, you can't cure Parkinson's disease, can you?"

Dr. Bassett:

> "Not that I know of."

Family Counsel:

> "So it is ameliorating the condition that is the subject of funding through the Ministry of Health?"

Dr. Bassett:

> "Yes, symptomatic relief of Parkinson's disease..."

Family Counsel:

> "And the same can be said about diabetes, diabetes is a non-curable condition?"

Dr. Bassett:

> "Yes."

Family Counsel:

> "And yet the government funds insulin for it and various other treatment modalities; correct?"

Dr. Bassett:

> "Correct."

Family Counsel:

> "Without a view to curing it but rather with a view to assisting those who have it to function in day-to-day life?"

Dr. Bassett:

> "Yes."

Family Counsel:

"And yet the government funds insulin for it and various other treatment modalities; correct?"

Dr. Bassett:

"Correct."

Family Counsel:

"Without a view to curing it but rather with a view to assisting those who have it to function in day-to-day life?"

Dr. Bassett:

"Yes."

After admitting that a "cure" is not a necessary outcome of science-based treatments, nor a criterion for universally available, publicly funded health care, Dr. Bassett eventually concludes that Lovaas and colleagues have not, in fact, erroneously claimed that Lovaas treatment "cures" children with autism.

Family Counsel:

> "Could you turn to page 37 of your report. You refer towards the bottom to Mesibov?"

Dr. Bassett:

> "Yes."

Family Counsel:

> "'Raises the principal concern with this approach readers might jump to the conclusion that the children might be cured.'
>
> To your knowledge, is the scientific world leaping to that conclusion?"

Dr. Bassett:

> "No."

Dr. Bassett finally admits that the operating assumption of the BCOHTA Lovaas Autism Report is not based in fact. The scientific community does not view Lovaas Treatment as a cure for autism. It is a false question with a predetermined answer that constitutes the foundation of biased research.

BCOHTA Selects Only Lovaas Treatment for Attack

Family Counsel:

"To your knowledge, is the scientific world leaping to that conclusion [that the children might be cured]?."

Dr. Bassett:

"No."

Outside of Lovaas Treatment, the BCOHTA did not evaluate a *single* other autism treatment protocol or intervention in the report used to defend Government in court. This is an important detail since government claimed in court that they provide all manner of services for children with autism. Not one of those services was looked at by BCOHTA. The single published paper that did — Eaves and Ho, 1996 — was excluded from the report. So the question becomes obvious: was BCOHTA asked by government to study the science behind autism treatments, or focus only on discrediting Lovaas treatment to win a lawsuit? If the balance of evidence suggests the latter, then the health technology movement has a serious problem on their hands — believability or lack thereof.

Despite the lack of scrutiny over special needs service programs in BC, many millions of dollars are spent on service providers yearly without criteria or expectations for positive outcomes. In the cross-examination exchange that follows, the attorney for families systematically looks at various Government-funded services available to parents of children with autism in British Columbia, and asks Dr. Bassett whether the Government requested the same type of Office analysis of the various government services providers it currently funds.

Family Counsel:

> "Have you been asked to comment on government funding of therapy described as LEAP, L-E-A-P?"

Dr. Bassett:

> "No."

Family Counsel:

"Giant Steps?"

Dr. Bassett:

"No."

Family Counsel:

"CBI?"

> **Family Counsel:**
>
> **"So what we can take from the Jocelyn work is not that it produces any meaningful or helpful results, but it's a great designed study?"**

Dr. Bassett:

"No."

Family Counsel:

"Gateway?"

Dr. Bassett:

"No."

Family Counsel:

"TEACCH, the acronym T-E-A-C-C-H?"

Dr. Bassett:

"No."

This central BCOHTA admission is important because it confirms that the Government did not commission the Office to evaluate all autism services and treatments in an effort to improve its policies — it wanted BCOHTA to examine only the program sought by the families in the lawsuit, and BCOHTA obliged. Evidence of a double standard is additional confirmation of the irrefutable: the BCOHTA Lovaas report is nothing more than agenda-based, advocacy research targeted at the most vulnerable minority in society, disabled children.

Family Counsel:

> "Well, is that what you were instructed to do, undertake a systemic analysis [of] applied behavioural analysis treatment of autistic children?"

Dr. Bassett:

> "That was the topic that they'd raised, yes."

Family Counsel:

> "You didn't do that, did you?"

Dr. Bassett:

> "Sorry?"

Family Counsel:

> "You didn't do that, did you? All you did was look at Lovaas?"

Dr. Bassett:

> "We did a systematic review of all the evidence for —"

Family Counsel:

> "For or against Lovaas?"

Dr. Bassett:

> "Of all the programs of applied behavioural analysis that had minimum inclusion criteria that we applied, which was a control group, and they're included."

Dr. Bassett:

"Well, it shows that this type of research methodology is not only possible but it has been done and it's ethically feasible in Canada."

Family Counsel:

> "You didn't look at LEAP, you didn't look at Giant Steps, didn't look at CBI, didn't look at TEACCH, didn't look at Gateway. What did you look at other than Lovaas?"

Dr. Bassett:

> "We looked at the other, we looked at the TEACCH, we looked at the one with Ozonoff and their program. What we looked for were any trials of sufficient quality to draw any conclusion about overall benefit to children."

Family Counsel:

> "Did you look at —"

Dr. Bassett:

> "So we didn't include or exclude any particular program. We were looking for a quality of evidence which was defined in our research question."

Family Counsel:

> "Did you look at any of the existing programs in British Columbia where tax dollars are being spent in an effort to determine whether Lovaas would be preferential to those?"

Dr.: Bassett:

> "We looked for that evidence, there wasn't any."

Family Counsel:

"Did you look at any of the existing programs in British Columbia where tax dollars are being spent in an effort to determine whether Lovaas would be preferential to those?"

Dr. Bassett:

"We looked for that evidence, there wasn't any."

It may be convenient for government to avoid a BCOHTA analysis of the effectiveness of government's autism services. However, from a disinterested standpoint, this would be the right comparison to make — Lovaas Treatment versus government contracted services. It is therefore significant in the above admission of Dr. Bassett, that what Government offers children with autism is so poor it does not meet minimum criteria for inclusion in a BCOHTA study. This is a neat tautology insofar as it essentially says, "We can't criticize the B.C. Government's autism policy because what it offers for children with autism is so abysmal it does not even show up on the 'radar screen' of what we can bring ourselves to study." Government autism policy and services don't even qualify as science by BCOHTA standards.

Family Counsel:

> "All right. You go on in paragraph 4 and say:
>
> > 'As requested by the government, BCOHTA has produced a report assessing the effectiveness of Lovaas therapy.'
>
> And that's what your report was about, wasn't it?"

Dr. Bassett:

> "Yes."

Family Counsel:

> "And no more?"

Dr. Bassett:

> "It was also about other evidence for — of sufficient quality to determine the overall effect on children. There wasn't any."

Family Counsel:

> "Of Lovaas therapy?"

Dr. Bassett:

> "No, of alternates as well."

Family Counsel:

"And because of that outcry, you're aware Dr. Lovaas went back to the funding agency, the U.S. National Institute of Mental Health, and obtained their specific approval for the randomization that he did employ? You're aware of that, aren't you?"

Dr. Bassett:

"I'm not aware of that."

Family Counsel:

> "All right. Now, with — was that the specific instruction that you had, the two portions of paragraphs 3 and 4 I read to you after these meetings with the ministries?"

Dr. Bassett:

> "It is a specific question that we developed following meeting them."

Excluded from scrutiny were all other Government services, including the ineffective government services discredited in court as ineffective in the treatment of autism.

Family Counsel:

> "So that's the question you're asking yourself?"

Dr. Bassett:

> "Yes."

The above exchange between the Family Counsel and Dr. Bassett confirms that government requested that health policy analysts at the BCOHTA target Lovaas Treatment exclusively. Excluded from scrutiny were all other Government services, including the ineffective government services discredited in court as ineffective in the treatment of autism. In the following portion of the cross examination, Dr. Bassett confirms that, due to their scientific rigour, studies testing the Lovaas Protocol were the *only* studies accepted for scrutiny by the BCOHTA. This is significant because the Government of British Columbia attempted to make the argument that they were in fact *already* providing a variety of treatments for autism. Clearly the so-called treatments were not scientifically substantiated, even according to the Ministry of Health's own academic analysts.

Family Counsel:

> "Then if you skip down to the fourth paragraph, you say:
>
>> 'Four controlled studies of treatment programs were identified that reported overall outcome for children.'

And you rejected the remaining 146 — Yes?"

Dr. Bassett:

"Yes."

Family Counsel:

"— because they didn't meet standard inclusion criteria?"

Dr. Bassett:

"Yes."

Family Counsel:

"And among the works that you rejected on that basis, included the work of Rogers, the work of Strain, the work of Harris and others, and in particular, the work of Dr. Gresham; correct?"

Dr. Bassett:

"Yes."

Family Counsel:

"And among the works that you rejected on that basis, included the work of Rogers, the work of Strain, the work of Harris and others, and in particular, the work of Dr. Gresham; correct?"

Dr. Bassett:

"Yes."

Here Dr. Bassett admits that the BCOHTA rejected the science behind the LEAP program, which was funded by the B.C. Government. In addition, he admits that the science behind some of Lovaas' most strident critics such as Dr. Gresham, and Dr. Strain did not qualify to even be studied by BCOHTA due to poor study design and lack of scientific rigor.

Family Counsel:

"Well, Dr. Bassett, if there wasn't anything to compare it to at the time, what do you expect of Dr. Lovaas?"

Dr. Bassett:

> "We only put together the list of criteria — the Court should understand that the criteria that we used and that you will see referred to are from the NIH, the National Institute of Medicine (sic) program."
> -
> -

Family Counsel:

> "... But if there's no treatment available to create a group to compare to, surely that's an absolutely impractical suggestion?"

Dr. Bassett:

> "It's not a suggestion. We didn't make that as a suggestion. We applied a criteria. We did not return to that criteria as a critique of Dr. Lovaas's work. In fact, in the discussion, we say quite clearly that we recognize this is in a way at the time ground breaking because — for what you said: The alternative to institutionalization."

Family Counsel:

> "So the reality is there wasn't anything for him to compare it to at the time he was doing it, was there?"

Dr. Bassett:

> "Presumably not."

In the above exchange, Dr. Bassett admits that one of the major criticisms of Lovaas' study — that Dr. Lovaas did not compare his treatment to another treatment — is groundless. This is especially true when one considers that Dr. Lovaas used *two* control groups, one of which was the special education system operating in the Los Angeles school district throughout the duration of the study. In the arid universe of autism research, this approach was genuinely groundbreaking.

Family Counsel:

"... But if there's no treatment available to create a group to compare to, surely that's an absolutely impractical suggestion?"

Dr. Bassett:

"It's not a suggestion. We didn't make that as a suggestion. We applied a criteria.

Ironically, Generic ABA is Accepted by BCOHTA Uncritically

Further along in the cross-examination, Family Counsel points to the double standard used in the BCOHTA report, since it expediently accepts the entire field of Applied Behavioural Analysis, uncritically and on a wholesale basis. Yet the successful application of those same ABA principles in Lovaas Treatment is considered by BCOHTA to be "experimental."

When the Family Counsel points out that the ABA studies generally do not use a control group, Dr. Bassett is not surprised. However, when it came to Lovaas' study in which a control group was used — which creates a more robust experimental design — Lovaas attracted a large amount of criticism from BCOHTA about the purportedly poor quality of the study. This is clearly a hypocritical double standard that supports the contention that BCOHTA's involvement in Lovaas Treatment "research" is tainted by a government dictated agenda in court.

Dr. Bassett admits that one of the major criticisms of Lovaas' study — that Dr. Lovaas did not compare his treatment to another treatment — is groundless. This is especially true when one considers that Dr. Lovaas used two control groups.

Family Counsel:

> "You say on page 6 of your report, in the paragraph beneath the quote, second sentence:
>
> > 'The author describes 271 published studies evaluating behavioural techniques directed at target behaviour which are divided into categories of aberrant behaviour, social skills, language, daily living skills and academic skills.'
>
> Did you look at any of the 271 published studies on ABA?"

Dr. Bassett:

> "No, we did not."

Family Counsel:

> "If I were to suggest to you, sir, that the vast majority of those studies employed no control group, would that surprise you?"

Dr. Bassett:

> "Not at all."

The fact that the BCOHTA did not recognize the above admission as a serious contradiction — accepting ABA studies en masse as scientifically sound but rejecting Lovaas' protocol as experimental — demonstrates either a profound lack of knowledge and experience in this field of autism treatment or a clear agenda-based research imperative, or both. It is highly unlikely that the BCOHTA would have unquestioningly accepted the entire field of ABA based on their evaluation criteria, since so many studies in this area do not have a control group. The above exchange suggests that the published studies in the area of ABA were likely not even evaluated for the BCOHTA's study.

Family Counsel:

"...Did you look at any of the 271 published studies on ABA?"

Dr. Bassett:

"No, we did not."

BCOHTA Embraces Unsubstantiated Autism Programs and Research

In addition to accepting the broad field of applied behavior analysis uncritically, the BCOHTA researchers also accept the review article of Dawson and Osterling (1997) without question, choosing to ignore the dubious science behind some of the programs reviewed by Dawson and Osterling. The BCOHTA ignores the fact that not all studies Dawson and Osterling reviewed were themselves published in peer-reviewed journals. In addition to this sidestep, BCOHTA freely quote Howlin (1997) without any concern as to the reliability and veracity of Howlin's sources of information. ***They also unquestioningly cite the work of Jocelyn et al. (1998) without any probe into the quality of intervention studied in that paper. In short, research other than the work of Lovaas is not assessed in a rigorous, thorough manner.***

Family Counsel:

> "Now, you made reference to the work of Dawson and Osterling –"

Dr. Bassett:

"Yes."

Family Counsel:

"— at page 43 of your report?"

Dr. Bassett:

"Yes."

Family Counsel:

"And, in fact, those authors found that the early intervention program with the best results from one of the most rigorously designed and implemented programs is Lovaas; that was their conclusion?"

Dr. Bassett:

"That's not what we cite. We cite their work in defining the general characteristics of the eight major programs that have been established in the U.S. and these are the common features of them."

Family Counsel:

"Well, in fact, other than Lovaas, none of the treatment programs discussed by Dawson and Osterling had experimental and control groups, nor did any of them use comparable rigorous outcome measures such as those used by Lovaas; isn't that fair?"

Dr. Bassett:

"Yes. The study by Dr. Lovaas has two of the four major components that are needed to establish scientific validity. And

Family Counsel:

"And, in fact, those authors found that the early intervention program with the best results from one of the most rigorously designed and implemented programs is Lovaas; that was their conclusion?"

Dr. Bassett:

"That's not what we cite."

> you've identified two of them, which is independent assessment of outcome and a longitudinal study."

Family Counsel:

> "Both of which are lacking in all of the other studies that Dawson and Osterling comment upon?"

Dr. Bassett:

> "Yes."

Family Counsel:

"Well, in fact, other than Lovaas, none of the treatment programs discussed by Dawson and Osterling had experimental and control groups, nor did any of them use comparable rigorous outcome measures such as those used by Lovaas; isn't that fair?"

Dr. Bassett:

"Yes."

Family Counsel:

> "And, in fact, to your knowledge, none of those eight independent programs are offered by the government in British Columbia; is that true?"

Dr. Bassett:

> "I don't know."

In the next segment of the cross examination, Family Counsel reveals the BCOHTA uncritically uses "secondhand" information (rather than source materials) from an article written by Howlin (1997) likely because it supports the objective of their government — advocacy work.

Family Counsel:

> "Is 'relatively well' a term of some scientific meaning? You say:
>
> > 'The group has done relatively well despite receiving little in the way of specialist intervention and support.'
>
> What does 'relatively well' mean as you have used it there?"

Dr. Bassett:

> "As quoted by Howlin originally in Kanner? What we're referring to is the material that Howlin has brought together in his review of — of observational studies of children, long-term observational studies."

Family Counsel:

> "Let me just understand then what it is you do. With Lovaas you apply the strict stringent procedural safeguards but to criticize him, you just take at face value whatever anybody managed to get published?"

Dr. Bassett:

> "That's not correct at all."

Family Counsel:

> "What checking did you do as to the validity of Howlin's work?"

Dr. Bassett:

> "We retrieved the article, we read it and we cite it to try to provide background material. We didn't apply strict criteria to it because that's not what a systematic review does..."

Family Counsel:

"Let me just understand then what it is you do. With Lovaas you apply the strict stringent procedural safeguards but to criticize him, you just take at face value whatever anybody managed to get published?"

Dr. Bassett:

"That's not correct at all."

Regarding the Jocelyn et al study, the authors of the BCOHTA report clearly did not consider the study's insignificant outcome to be relevant or worthy of reporting. They also did not consider it important that what they had termed intensive treatment was neither "intensive" nor treatment. Family Counsel questions Dr. Bassett regarding BCOHTA's misleading use of the Jocelyn et al. study to further illuminate this point for the judge in the Auton hearings. Dr. Bassett's cross-examination continues:

Family Counsel:

> "Now, the intervention that was studied by Jocelyn and his or her colleagues was directed primarily at the parents and daycare staff as opposed to treatment of the child; isn't that so?"

Dr. Bassett:

> "Again, I'd have to look back at this study."

Family Counsel:

> "Well, according to Jocelyn I'm going to suggest to you that the child care workers got a total of five weekly three-hour classes which they attended with the parents. That was the extent of the intensive, community-based, integrated treatment program; does that sound familiar?"

Dr. Bassett:

> "It, well, yes."

Family Counsel:

> "Do you regard that as an intensive program?"

Dr. Bassett:

> "Doesn't matter how I regard it, that's not the issue here. It is not something... —"

Family Counsel:

> "You regard it as an intensive, community-based, integrated treatment program. Your idea of intensive is five weekly three-hour classes?"

Family Counsel:

"Well, according to Jocelyn I'm going to suggest to you that the child care workers got a total of five weekly three-hour classes which they attended with the parents. That was the extent of the intensive, community-based, integrated treatment program; does that sound familiar?"

Dr. Bassett:

"It, well, yes."

Family Counsel:

"You regard it as an intensive, community-based, integrated treatment program. Your idea of intensive is five weekly three-hour classes?"

Dr. Bassett:

"Presumably that's how they describe it."

Dr. Bassett:

"Presumably that's how they describe it."

Family Counsel:

"Sorry?"

Dr. Bassett:

"I presume that's how they describe it."

Family Counsel:

"Well, did you make any efforts, sir, to determine whether the description was a reasonable one when they used the adjective 'intensive'?"

Dr. Bassett:

"Yes, certainly when we read it."

Family Counsel:

"And was it five weekly three-hour classes?"

Dr. Bassett:

"The 'intensive' probably refers to the overall treatment program as opposed to this innovation which is this addition. And what they're trying to study is whether this additional element is sufficient to have an effect. And then they're randomizing two groups, did one get this additional three hours of whatever you've mentioned, referring to the intensive, community-based, integrated treatment program to which this innovation is being tested."

Family Counsel:

> "What was [in] the program that was so ground breaking, so intense, can you help Her Ladyship with that?"

Dr. Bassett:

> "No, the innovation, the thing that we noted from here is that the children were randomly assigned to one treatment group or the other; that's what's ground breaking."

Family Counsel:

"What was [in] the program that was so ground breaking, so intense, can you help Her Ladyship with that?"

Dr. Bassett:

"No, the innovation, the thing that we noted from here is that the children were randomly assigned to one treatment group or the other; that's what's ground breaking."

It is important to stress here that the Jocelyn et al. study, referred to by the BCOHTA as "ground breaking," reported no meaningful results, a fact that Dr. Bassett and colleagues elected to omit from their autism treatment report. Dr. Bassett does acknowledge, however, that this Canadian study they referred to as "ground breaking", is not so because of any meaningful outcome they achieved, but rather because of the study's design. This hardly qualifies as a challenge to Lovaas Treatment, but the BCOHTA Lovaas Report nevertheless misrepresented the significance of Jocelyn et al. in its effort to discredit the genuine autism treatment that Lovaas-type ABA represents.

Double Standard: Lovaas Studies meet BCOHTA Criteria for Attack

Despite the alleged shortcomings of Dr. Lovaas' research, the BCOHTA had to admit that the best research, and indeed the *only* research that met their criteria for analysis, was the work conducted by Lovaas and colleagues, or work which included the UCLA protocol.

Family Counsel:

> "All right. You go on in paragraph 4 and say:
>
> > 'As requested by the government, BCOHTA has produced a report assessing the effectiveness of Lovaas therapy.'

And that's what your report was about, wasn't it?"

Dr. Bassett:

"Yes."

Family Counsel:

"And no more?"

Dr. Bassett:

"It was also about other evidence for — of sufficient quality to determine the overall effect on children. There wasn't any."

Family Counsel:

"Of Lovaas therapy?"

Dr. Bassett:

"No, of alternatives as well."

Family Counsel:

"All right. You go on in paragraph 4 and say:

'As requested by the government, BCOHTA has produced a report assessing the effectiveness of Lovaas therapy.'

And that's what your report was about, wasn't it?"

Dr. Bassett:

"Yes."

BCOHTA's Report Excludes Relevant Articles That Support Lovaas Treatment

In this part of his testimony in B.C. Supreme Court, Dr. Bassett confirms what has been asserted throughout the *Science for Sale* analysis: the BCOHTA selectively, and in a clearly biased manner, includes or excludes academic papers from their report based on an advocacy agenda designed to discredit Lovaas Autism Treatment and defend Government in court at the expense of academic integrity, honesty and ethics.

Family Counsel:

"The U.S. Surgeon General's report isn't listed in the bibliography. Did you look at that?"

Dr. Bassett:

> "I don't remember looking at it."

Family Counsel:

> "Isn't that something that your researchers should have found for you?"

Dr. Bassett:

> "I don't know. I'd have to look at it."

Family Counsel:

"And if I were to suggest to you that the U.S. Surgeon General describes [Lovaas] as a well-designed study of psychological intervention, would that surprise you?"

Dr. Bassett:

"It's inconsistent with our opinion and the opinion of all the research discussion that we cite in our review."

The U.S. Surgeon General's Report on Mental Health (1999) is a highly significant landmark document in the area of mental health. The Surgeon General's report *specifically* commends Lovaas' work on the treatment of children with autism as being well done and significant. This glaring omission of the opinion of the chief medical officer in the U.S. highlights a brazen bias on the part of Office researchers. If the BCOHTA does indeed use the guidelines it claims to use for comprehensive literature searches (the AHCPR), it most certainly knew of the Surgeon General's report on mental health, but elected to omit the document from its submission to B.C. Supreme Court.

Family Counsel:

> "Now, you didn't, I gather from our discussion yesterday, find the U.S. Surgeon General's report commenting on the Lovaas study?"

Dr. Bassett:

> "No."

Family Counsel:

> "And if I were to suggest to you that the U.S. Surgeon General describes it as a well-designed study of psychological intervention, would that surprise you?"

Dr. Bassett:

> "It's inconsistent with our opinion and the opinion of all the research discussion that we cite in our review."

Family Counsel:

> "But, of course, you didn't have an opportunity to consider the views — published views of the Surgeon General of the United States on the issue?"

Dr. Bassett:

> "No, but we will if we can have a copy of their opinion and what they've said. We have no problem with including it. As we mentioned, the term "fugitive search," it's an ongoing process to find more opinions and more substantive claims."

Family Counsel:

"But, of course, you didn't have an opportunity to consider the views — published views of the Surgeon General of the United States on the issue?"

Dr. Bassett:

"No, but we will if we can have a copy of their opinion and what they've said. We have no problem with including it."

The Eaves and Ho (1996) autism article mentioned earlier in the chapter, selectively excluded from the BCOHTA report, damages the government's case since it was written by two doctors whose research followed a group of autistic children through the special needs system. These practitioners concluded that these children did not make substantive improvement in any programs funded by the Province of British Columbia.

Family Counsel:

> "There is an article by Drs. Eaves and Ho, who are British Columbian practitioners entitled, 'Brief report: Stability and Change in cognitive and behavioural characteristics of autism through childhood.' It is not listed in the bibliography; do you know why?"

Dr. Bassett:

> "It wasn't found through our systematic search because it wasn't directly relevant."

Family Counsel:

> "Well, it says that the treatment, I'm going to suggest to you, it says the treatment that is presently available in B.C. isn't working. Wouldn't that be relevant to your inquiry?"

Dr. Bassett:

> "That would be considered a background element. It is not what we're being asked to look at. We're being asked to look at the scientific evidence for a treatment."

Family Counsel:

> "The scientific evidence based on the clinical experience with practitioners in this province is irrelevant?"

Dr. Bassett:

> "It's not what we're doing in our systematic review. Systematic review looks at published scientific evidence of a certain quality."

Family Counsel:

> "You don't care about what the clinicians are doing, effectively?"

Dr. Bassett:

> "That's not relevant. What I care about doesn't matter. What we're looking at is scientific evidence and that's what a systematic review is all about."
>
> -
>
> -

Family Counsel:

"There is an article by Drs. Eaves and Ho, who are British Columbian practitioners entitled, "Brief report: Stability and Change in cognitive and behavioural characteristics of autism through childhood. It is not listed in the bibliography; do you know why?"

Dr. Bassett:

"It wasn't found through our systematic search because it wasn't directly relevant."

Family Counsel:

> "You didn't come across a work entitled 'A Work in Progress' by Ron Leaf and John McEachin as editors?"

Dr. Bassett:

> "I don't recall it. Is it in the bibliography?"

Family Counsel:

> "It doesn't appear to be. It is a book described as 'behavioural management strategies and curriculum for the intensive treatment of autism.' Would that have been relevant to your inquiry if you located it?"

Dr. Bassett:

> "If it had primary data on effectiveness, yes; if it is a textbook describing approaches, it is not relevant. We did look at a number of textbooks."

Family Counsel:

> "Did you locate an article entitled 'Parents as Therapists,' by O. Ivar Lovaas?"

Dr. Bassett:

> "I'd have to refer to the bibliography."

Family Counsel:

> "It is not there, Doctor. So if it is not there, can we assume you didn't find it?"

Dr. Bassett:

> "I don't recall the article."

Family Counsel:

"The scientific evidence based on the clinical experience with practitioners in this province is irrelevant?"

Dr. Bassett:

"It's not what we're doing in our systematic review. Systematic review looks at published scientific evidence of a certain quality."

Family Counsel:

"You don't care about what the clinicians are doing, effectively?"

Dr. Bassett:

"That's not relevant."

Family Counsel:

> "Let me read you a portion and see if it assists your recollection:
>
> > 'Not all parents of autistic children can be taught to become effective teachers of therapists for their children. This is true in cases where the parents are divorced and the mother has to work for financial reasons. Sometimes parents cannot be trained because of their own personal psychological problems or lack of interest in the child, or the child may have problems which are so severe, he is so self-destructive or so strong and assaultive that he has to be cared for elsewhere.'
>
> If that indeed is the review of Dr. Lovaas, would that have had any influence at all in terms of your report?"

Family Counsel:

"You didn't come across a work entitled "A Work in Progress" by Ron Leaf and John McEachin as editors?"

Dr. Bassett:

"I don't recall it. Is it in the bibliography?"

Dr. Bassett:

> "No."

The above exchange about Lovaas' article on "parents as therapists" is important because it is a common theme in governmental policy. By deprofessionalizing autism treatment with legions of parents and grandparents for frontline intervention duty — the substitution of family members for properly trained, professional therapists — the Government avoids the cost of bona fide treatment. The article by Dr. Lovaas critiquing the "parents as therapists" model directly undermines this theme. The BCOHTA excluded this Lovaas article from their "exhaustive" search of papers in autism treatment research.

Family Counsel:

> "Are you aware of the recent report from the University of Wisconsin by Drs. Sallows and Graupner on their replication efforts."

Dr. Bassett:

> "I guess not, we don't have a report of it. We haven't seen a report of it, haven't been able to find a report of it."

This BCOHTA omission is very relevant because Sallows and Graupner (2000) successfully replicated Lovaas' original results. This autism treatment replication is problematic for the BCOHTA insofar as their argument is that Lovaas' results have never been replicated and are therefore "experimental." Because the University of Wisconsin article hurts the Office's advocacy agenda, it was simply omitted by BCOHTA researchers, or somehow "overlooked" during their purportedly comprehensive, systematic review of the literature.

Family Counsel:

"Are you aware of the recent report from the University of Wisconsin by Drs. Sallows and Graupner on their replication efforts."

Dr. Bassett:

"I guess not, we don't have a report of it. We haven't seen a report of it, haven't been able to find a report of it."

Another highly relevant article omitted from the BCOHTA Lovaas Report (although cited in the bibliography) is the study conducted by Smith in 1997. In this study, Smith examined the results of Lovaas' treatment protocol on a very challenging group of children, those with autism *and* mental retardation. This is a highly relevant study because its findings disprove the contention often made that the Lovaas treatment protocol is only successful for children with autism who are mildly affected. This finding also casts doubt on the unfounded contention that Lovaas deliberately assembled a group of children who were mild, and therefore, responded well (the "creaming" argument).

Family Counsel:

> "Now, you didn't find, I gather, in your research, the article by Dr. Tristram Smith and others entitled 'Intensive Behavioural Treatment for Pre-schoolers With Severe Mental Retardation and Pervasive Developmental Disorder?'"

Dr. Bassett:

> "In 1997?"

Family Counsel:

> "Yes."

Dr. Bassett:

"Yes, we did."

Family Counsel:

"All right. Do you discuss it in the paper, Doctor?"

Dr. Bassett:

"I believe we do. It is an account of the children from the original group that were excluded because of low IQ or a prorated mental age below the minimum inclusion criteria, if I remember correctly."

Family Counsel:

"Well, doesn't Dr. Smith and his coauthor describe a study in which only children with severe autism and mental retardation were included in that study?"

Dr. Bassett:

"I would have to get the original study. Thank you. Sorry, your question?"

Family Counsel:

"Doesn't that paper describe a study group in which only children with severe autism and mental retardation were included?"

Dr. Bassett:

"Yes."

Family Counsel:

"Now, you didn't find, I gather, in your research, the article by Dr. Tristram Smith and others entitled 'Intensive Behavioural Treatment for Pre-schoolers With Severe Mental Retardation and Pervasive Developmental Disorder?'"

Dr. Bassett:

"In 1997?"

Family Counsel:

"Yes."

Family Counsel:

> "And it's really the reverse of what you have talked about earlier in your report, where high functioning children are sought out and might skew the results more favourably. This is the opposite, where it's really reverse creaming, you're getting the worst kids in this study; correct?"

Dr. Bassett:

> "I'd have to look at it in detail...
>
> -
>
> -
>
> So it did not address the population that we were — or the age group according to their prorated mental age, as I understand it."

Family Counsel:

"And it's really the reverse of what you have talked about earlier in your report, where high functioning children are sought out and might skew the results more favourably. This is the opposite, where it's really reverse creaming, you're getting the worst kids in this study; correct?"

Family Counsel:

> "All right. So let me start with this: You don't discuss the results reported in that study in your paper, do you?"

Dr. Bassett:

> "That's right."

Family Counsel:

> "And the results are an effort, I suggest to you, to address one of the concerns that you, in fact, raise in your paper; that is, that they've creamed off children who are likely to have better results?"

Dr. Bassett:

> "I don't see how this addresses that question."

Family Counsel:

> "Isn't that the very reason for the study, to address that concern, to see what would happen if you took — if you deliberately took particularly low-functioning children?"

Dr. Bassett:

> "I would have to study this report in detail."
>
> -
>
> -

Family Counsel:

> "Why don't you do that at the break, Doctor, and we'll come back to it."

Family Counsel:

"All right. So let me start with this: You don't discuss the results reported in that study [Smith 1997] in your paper, do you?"

Dr. Bassett:

"That's right."

At this juncture, there is a court recess, and Dr. Bassett studies the Smith et al. article to answer the questions posed to him at the cross-examination. Dr. Bassett's response after the break follows:

Family Counsel:

> "Dr. Bassett, you've had a chance to look at the article by Drs. Smith, Lovaas and others?"

Dr. Bassett:

> "Yes, I have."

Family Counsel:

> "And you can confirm that it's the Lovaas treatment?"

Dr. Bassett:

> "Yes. Yes, it is definitely Lovaas treatment."

Family Counsel:

> "Did the fact Dr. Lovaas helped, Dr. Bassett, [did] it give you a clue?"

Dr. Bassett:

> "They state very clearly that is what they provided."

Family Counsel:

"And the results are an effort, I suggest to you, to address one of the concerns that you, in fact, raise in your paper; that is, that they've creamed off children who are likely to have better results?"

At this point in the cross examination, Dr. Bassett admitted to excluding an important autism treatment study (Smith et al., 1998) — a study that supports the effectiveness of Lovaas Treatment — purportedly because it was irrelevant. The bias of omission found in the BCOHTA report is that it dutifully excludes publications that hurt the Government's case in court. Genuine academic inquiry should not be dominated by this type of advocacy imperative. The reputation of the academic community as a whole, and the University of British Columbia in particular, suffers immeasurable harm when ethical lapses such as the BCOHTA report are permitted to happen and, moreover, are ignored and go unchallenged by "self policing" academic bodies of ethics review. University silence regarding the unethical conduct of its faculty functions only as tacit approval and encouragement of improper practice.

Analysis of BCOHTA Critique of Lovaas Treatment Research

Accusation That Lovaas Assembled a High Functioning Group ("The Creaming" Argument)

As mentioned earlier, one of the many themes in the criticism levelled against the work of Dr. Lovaas and colleagues, is the concept that Lovaas' treatment protocol could have only achieved such remarkable results with "high functioning" autistic children. Family Counsel discusses this criticism with Dr. Bassett since the BCOHTA report, naturally enough, retrieved this common critique from chief academic rivals of Dr. Lovaas to feature in their Lovaas report.

Family Counsel:

"Now, how would you go about assembling a high-functioning group of autistic children, Doctor?"

Dr. Bassett:

"How would I, or how did this potentially happen in this study?"

Family Counsel:

"I'm going to suggest you couldn't do it; there is no predictability about autism, so you couldn't take a group of people and have any reasonable assurance they would do any better than any other group of autistic children; isn't that the truth?"

Family Counsel:

"I'm going to suggest you couldn't do it; there is no predictability about autism, so you couldn't take a group of people and have any reasonable assurance they would do any better than any other group of autistic children; isn't that the truth?"

Dr. Bassett:

"That's not my expertise."

Dr. Bassett:

"That's not my expertise."

Family Counsel:

"Have you read Dr. Baer's views, Professor Baer?"

Dr. Bassett:

"We've read the report, his part — we cited his argument, yes."

Family Counsel:

"He says you can't do it, doesn't he?"

Dr. Bassett:

"In that report, if I recall it right, yes."

Family Counsel:

"Have you seen anybody who has a contrary view to that, that you can actually deliberately set out to distort the outcome of a study by selecting children who will do well with respect to autism?"

Dr. Bassett:

"Have I, no."

Family Counsel:

"Have you seen anybody who has a contrary view to that, that you can actually deliberately set out to distort the outcome of a study by selecting children who will do well with respect to autism?"

Dr. Bassett:

"Have I, no."

Family Counsel:

"So the only opinion you have on that is that of Professor Baer?"

Dr. Bassett:

"It's — that's certainly his contrary — that's his opinion, yes."

Family Counsel:

"Well, it's the only opinion you have seen on this subject matter, isn't it, Doctor?"

Dr. Bassett:

"The issue here is around what was done in this trial report, not an opinion on that."

Family Counsel:

"The only opinion you have seen on whether or not you could select children who would do well, autistic children who would do well in a study is that of Dr. Baer, isn't it?"

Dr. Bassett:

"There are a number of trial analyzed — number of individuals analyzed in the trial that were concerned that the children selected for this study were nonrepresentative, and as we document, the children that were selected could have been a group of children that were more likely to do well."

Family Counsel:

"Well, Dr. Baer says you couldn't do that, and nobody else, to your knowledge, has said that you can, have they?"

Dr. Bassett:

"What they're saying is that looking at the subgroup in this trial, the 19 children in this trial, there needs to be reassurance that that isn't what happened."

> **Family Counsel:**
>
> **"Well, Dr. Baer says you couldn't do that [select children who do well], and nobody else, to your knowledge, has said that you can, have they?"**
>
> **Dr. Bassett:**
>
> **"What they're saying is that looking at the subgroup in this trial, the 19 children in this trial, there needs to be reassurance that that isn't what happened."**

Family Counsel:

"Doctor, let me try it again. The only opinion you have seen on whether it could happen is the opinion of Dr. Baer, and he says you couldn't do it; isn't that right?"

Dr. Bassett:

"No, I don't think that's right."

Family Counsel:

"Okay. Who says that you could?"

Dr. Bassett:

"Well, that's what the critiques, several of the critiques of this trial were based on that principle."

Family Counsel:

"They haven't said you can, they've said we're worried that it might have happened?"

Dr. Bassett:

> "And we need reassurance that it didn't happen, which is the essence of the need for a proper scientific study."

Family Counsel:

> "So as far as you're aware, no one challenges the express view of Dr. Baer that it couldn't be done?"

Dr. Bassett:

> "I haven't read any critique of his critique, no."

Family Counsel:

"So as far as you're aware, no one challenges the express view of Dr. Baer that it couldn't be done?"

Dr. Bassett:

"I haven't read any critique of his critique, no."

The "creaming" theme was heavily emphasized throughout the BCOHTA Report. However, specific criteria used by Dr. Lovaas for the inclusion of "test" children in his landmark autism treatment study were not presented fairly by BCOHTA researchers. One of the selection criteria used in the Lovaas study was proximity to the clinic so that children involved in the treatment group did not live too far away from the university. There was a preference that clinicians not need to drive more than one hour from U.C.L.A. to conduct the autism treatment research. So this key selection criterion was simply based on the constraints of Los Angeles traffic reality — not creaming.

Counsel representing families addresses this issue.

Family Counsel:

> "Well, just dealing with the geographic location, you're not seriously suggesting, are you, where any of the children lived would have an impact on their level of functioning?"

Dr. Bassett:

> "No. But when a child is selected for the treatment group, then they need to be followed to find out how they actually do. Whether they turn out to be children with problems, this follows a methodological criteria which is called intention to treat. And what you need to do is to identify the children

before the program starts, and then you determine subsequently how the entire treatment and control group do."

Family Counsel:

"Well, are you suggesting that the location of residence would in any way affect the level of functioning of an autistic child?"

Dr. Bassett:

"No, it should not."

Family Counsel:

"Well, just dealing with the geographic location, you're not seriously suggesting, are you, where any of the children lived would have an impact on their level of functioning?"

Dr. Bassett:

"No."

Family Counsel:

"Okay. Now, you're aware that Lovaas essentially took all comers if there were spots available in the study; it was first come first served, as it were?"

Dr. Bassett:

"Yes, that's what he describes in his methodology."

Family Counsel:

"And so that wouldn't allow him in any way to cream off children who he thought, if indeed he had such thoughts, might be higher functioning?"

Dr. Bassett:

"We have no idea. We have no way of knowing his — if it was, in fact, first come first serve, it's still potentially biased. And the only way to control for that bias is to subsequently randomize children."

Family Counsel:

"Okay. Now, you're aware that Lovaas essentially took all comers if there were spots available in the study; it was first come first served, as it were?"

Dr. Bassett:

"Yes,..."

Family Counsel:

"You're aware that Dr. Lovaas excluded children with low PMA scores, that is, those equivalent to a deviation IQ of below 30?"

Dr. Bassett:

"Yes."

Family Counsel:

"So they were excluded from either the control or the experimental group?"

Dr. Bassett:

"Yes."

Family Counsel:

"And the reason for that was because it was difficult to differentiate autistic children from other profoundly retarded children at that low an IQ level?"

Dr. Bassett:

"Yes."

Family Counsel:

"The group included echolalic children up to 46 months of age?"

Dr. Bassett:

"The inclusion group, yes."

Family Counsel:

> "Now, an effort was made to match the control and the experimental group by comparing measures such as prorated mental age?"

Dr. Bassett:

> "Yes, among others."

Family Counsel:

> "Some pathology?"

Dr. Bassett:

> "Yes."

Family Counsel:

> "Abnormal speech?"

Dr. Bassett:

> "Yes."

Family Counsel:

> "Self-stimulatory behaviour?"

Dr. Bassett:

> "I'll have to look at the list. There's about 12. I don't recall that one in particular. I will find the original study. But, yes, I mean, there are a number of criteria that they were compared on."

Family Counsel:

"Now, an effort was made to match the control and the experimental group by comparing measures such as pro-rated mental age?"

Dr. Bassett:

"Yes, among others." ...

"I'll have to look at the list. There's about 12."

Family Counsel:

> "All right. So there was some effort on the part of Lovaas to try and make the groups comparable based on a variety of criteria?"

Dr. Bassett:

> "Yes."

Family Counsel:

"All right. So there was some effort on the part of Lovaas to try and make the groups comparable based on a variety of criteria?"

Dr. Bassett:

"Yes."

The above cross examination exchange affords Dr. Bassett the opportunity to acknowledge that children in Dr. Lovaas' study were carefully "matched" on approximately twelve (12) relevant criteria, casting doubt on the argument or BCOHTA intimation that the experimental group in the landmark Lovaas study was biased.

Ethics in Canada: Feasibility of Random Assignment to a Control Group and Experimental Group

In the next portion of B.C. Supreme Court testimony, Dr. Bassett justifies why children with autism — in his opinion — can be randomly assigned to experimental and control groups in any future autism studies. Ignoring the large body of evidence supporting the effectiveness of the Lovaas treatment protocol, Dr. Bassett expresses support for placing children with autism in a control group — children that would intentionally not receive what researchers and clinicians have already declared as "best practice" in autism treatment, including the New York State Department of Health.

Family Counsel:

> "Now, you refer to Jocelyn and others in the fifth paragraph on this page; you see that?"

Dr. Bassett:

> "Yes."

Family Counsel:

> "And you refer in the fourth line from the end of that paragraph to their studies as being 'ground breaking' in this area of research?"

Dr. Bassett:

> "Yes."

Family Counsel:

> "Why do you say it was ground breaking?"

Dr. Bassett:

> "Because it was randomized."

Family Counsel:

> "The —"

Dr. Bassett:

> "Sorry — the selection to treatment or control group was random assignment."

Family Counsel:

> "But the authors offer absolutely no successful treatment outcome data, do they?"

Dr. Bassett:

> "It's ground breaking in its methodology. Their conclusion, their study was designed to look at the benefit of — of parent education versus community — with or without community education. So what it showed was in Canada, it is ethical and

Family Counsel:

"So what we can take from the Jocelyn work is not that it produces any meaningful or helpful results, but it's a great designed study?"

feasible to randomize treatment assignment and this was a community-based autism program, a comprehensive program."

Family Counsel:

"So what we can take from the Jocelyn work is not that it produces any meaningful or helpful results, but it's a great designed study?"

Dr. Bassett:

Dr. Bassett:

"Well, it shows that this type of research methodology is not only possible but it has been done and it's ethically feasible in Canada."

"Well, it shows that this type of research methodology is not only possible but it has been done and it's ethically feasible in Canada."

This exchange exposes Dr. Bassett's troublesome ethical stance: even if an autism treatment study shows no significant improvement in the condition of children, according to the BCOHTA it is ethical to randomly assign children to the experimental and control groups. What makes the BCOHTA position here all the more ethically questionable is that they strategically ignore the fact that Lovaas-type ABA treatment for autism has *already* been recommended by the U.S. Surgeon General and considered "best practice" by the New York State Department of Health. New York State states that not providing ABA, or provision of interventions that supplant ABA, *constitutes harm done to the child.* All this expert opinion was somehow ignored in the "exhaustive" review undertaken by the BCOHTA for their autism report.

Family Counsel:

"Are you familiar with the notion of informed consent for clinical trials?"

Dr. Bassett:

"Yes."

Family Counsel:

"And you can't put a child into a study without telling the parents what it is you're doing and why, can you?"

Dr. Bassett:

"Of course not."

Family Counsel:

"It would be completely unethical and unacceptable?"

Dr. Bassett:

"Right."

Family Counsel:

"And if you told a parent that they could have either participation in a program that had a 47 percent normalization rate as opposed to a 1 in 64 chance, you'd think seriously that you can conduct randomized trials if you give that kind of information to parents?"

Dr. Bassett:

"It would be unethical to give that kind of information to parents."

Family Counsel:

"If you did, you can be sure that no reasonable parent would want their child to be in the control group; correct?"

Dr. Bassett:

"If a study, a valid study had shown that degree of treatment effect, then everyone would be using it. The difficulty is that we have a number of treatment options available, none of which have been compared with one another, and it is ethical and appropriate to study those treatments options, and parents can be made aware of those options."

Family Counsel:

"Are you familiar with the notion of informed consent for clinical trials? ... And you can't put a child into a study without telling the parents what it is you're doing and why, can you?"

Dr. Bassett:

"Of course not."

Family Counsel:

> "You say we have a number, you're not aware of any in British Columbia?"

Dr. Bassett:

> "I'm not aware — we did not study the autism treatment options in British Columbia."

Family Counsel:

> "And if you told parents that their child could be enrolled in a group that had a prospect of 47 normalization rate or the group that has a 1 in 64 chance of just not staying and getting worse, you're not suggesting that any reasonable parent would opt for the latter group, are you?"

Dr. Bassett:

> "I wouldn't tell them that."

Family Counsel:

"And if you told a parent that they could have either participation in a program that had a 47 percent normalization rate as opposed to a 1 in 64 chance, you'd think seriously that you can conduct randomized trials if you give that kind of information to parents?"

It is worth emphasizing that Dr. Bassett said, "I wouldn't tell them that." This last statement seemed so outrageous to many in the court room that there was a perceptible hush. The fact that Dr. Bassett would not tell parents about the best designed study and most effective approach in the entire field of autism treatment research, raises serious questions of ethics.

Family Counsel:

> "Random assignment of children to treatment and control groups has been recently shown by Jocelyn and others to be both feasible and ethical in Canada?"

Dr. Bassett:

> "Yes."

Family Counsel:

> "In reviewing Dr. Jocelyn's work, did you conclude that the treatment described by Jocelyn produced no meaningful success in terms of outcomes?"

Dr. Bassett:

> "It produced moderate benefit. It didn't produce large gains in overall outcome."

Dr. Bassett:

"It would be unethical to give that kind of information to parents."

Family Counsel:

> "Now, were you able to determine whether Jocelyn, in recruiting subjects for the study described, offered to the parents any information about intensive behavioural early intervention?"

Dr. Bassett:

> "We did not examine that. And I don't know the answer."

Family Counsel:

> "Well, you've cited it to support the proposition that Jocelyn's work was both feasible and ethical in Canada. Are you saying it would meet Canadian ethical standards not to disclose that there are other treatments?"

Dr. Bassett:

> "I'm saying that this met Canadian ethical standards and preceded it at trial."

Family Counsel:

> "Well, Doctor, UBC policy on research specifically states:

> 'It is the purpose of the university to ensure that where a human subject is involved in a research or other study, the safety, welfare and rights of the subject are adequately protected.'

You're familiar with that statement?"

Dr. Bassett:

"Yes."

Family Counsel:

Now, were you able to determine whether Jocelyn ... offered to the parents any information about intensive behavioural early intervention?"

Dr. Bassett:

"We did not examine that. And I don't know the answer."

Family Counsel:

"And are you suggesting that not disclosing other available treatments and encouraging subjects into a study that is experimental would meet ethical standards such as that?"

Dr. Bassett:

"Oh, of course not."

At this juncture in the cross examination, it becomes clear that the BCOHTA Lovaas report's recommendations violate University of British Columbia ethical guidelines.

Family Counsel:

"And in fact, what Drs. Kazdin and Weisz said about Dr. Lovaas' work was:

> 'Constraints of real life may limit how experimentally pristine one may be in research with severe conditions possibly requiring intensive treatment. Neither other researchers nor Lovaas could arrange for random assignment of children to conditions. Both limitations were understandable under

> the circumstances and both were addressed by the investigators. These circumstances provide a reminder that the real issue in outcome research is not so much whether all the shibboleths of experimental methods were employed, but whether appropriate steps are taken to protect the validity of the study and to preserve the interpretability of its findings.'

Do you agree with those comments?"

At this juncture, it becomes clear that the BCOHTA Lovaas report's recommendations violate University of British Columbia ethical guidelines.

Dr. Bassett:

> "Those are his opinions on what Dr. Lovaas did and whether or not he could or could not have achieved randomization. I don't have an opinion specifically on that. Those are attributed to that article. I don't have any criticism of his opinion."

Once again Dr. Bassett contradicts himself. *On the one hand he has no opinion regarding whether or not the appropriate steps were taken to ensure that the study is valid, yet the BCOHTA report serves up stinging criticism regarding purported methodological problems with Lovaas' research relating to how experimental and control groups were assigned.*

Family Counsel:

> "All right, Now, when you deal with the issue of random assignment, are you aware of the reasons why pure random assignment was not undertaken by Dr. Lovaas?"

Dr. Bassett:

> "What do you mean by 'pure'?"

Family Counsel:

> "What you're suggesting should have been done."

Dr. Bassett:

"Randomization is randomization."

Family Counsel:

"Well, are you aware that there was an outcry from parent groups against the use of random assignment when Dr. Lovaas was trying to set up his study?"

Dr. Bassett:

"He describes that, yes."

Family Counsel:

"All right, Now, when you deal with the issue of random assignment, are you aware of the reasons why pure random assignment was not undertaken by Dr. Lovaas?"

Family Counsel:

"And because of that outcry, you're aware Dr. Lovaas went back to the funding agency, the U.S. National Institute of Mental Health, and obtained their specific approval for the randomization that he did employ? You're aware of that, aren't you?"

Dr. Bassett:

"I'm not aware of that."

Family Counsel:

"If that was the case, that the institute [NIH] whose criteria you say weren't followed, were prepared to approve the randomization employed by Dr. Lovaas, would you withdraw your criticism with respect to the randomization?"

Dr. Bassett:

"Not at all."

Family Counsel:

> "I see. So you're going to apply the National Institutes of Health criteria even though they themselves chose not to for this specific study?"

Dr. Bassett admits above that he is prepared to accept the NIH when it is convenient, but ignores it when it hurts — this, of course, represents classic advocacy research.

Family Counsel:

"Well, are you aware that there was an outcry from parent groups against the use of random assignment when Dr. Lovaas was trying to set up his study?"

Dr. Bassett:

"He describes that, yes."

Misleading Use of Citations

At this point in the cross examination, Dr. Bassett attempts to defend BCOHTA's heavy reliance on secondary sources of information, as opposed to primary sources, which is more academically appropriate. As becomes apparent in the exchange below, secondary sources of information were used by BCOHTA to support the erroneous contention that many people with autism do well without treatment.

Family Counsel:

> "You looked at Kanner's published work?"

Dr. Bassett:

> "I'd have to — I'd have to look back at the article. I don't remember all of these articles individually."

Family Counsel:

> "I don't believe it is in your bibliography, sir, but if you want to check."

Dr. Bassett:

> "Is it in the references?"

Family Counsel:

> "Well, it is not footnoted so I can't imagine it is, but you tell me."

Dr. Bassett:

> "The way it is referenced, it's almost — it looks like Howlin cited Kanner."

Family Counsel:

> "All right. Well, sir, when you undertake the work that you did, is it customary to rely on secondary sources and quote someone else's interpretation of a primary source?"

Dr. Bassett:

> "In this background section, again, we're using the material to give an overview..."
> -
> -

Family Counsel:

> "Okay. Well, the long and short of it is you didn't read Kanner's article, you don't know what he said other than what Howlin has made of it; is that fair?"

Dr. Bassett:

> "I think that's fair."

Family Counsel:

> "And in your research assessment work, if you were going to offer something that you believe to be reliable, you go to the primary source, wouldn't you."

Family Counsel:

"And because of that outcry, you're aware Dr. Lovaas went back to the funding agency, the U.S. National Institute of Mental Health, and obtained their specific approval for the randomization that he did employ? You're aware of that, aren't you?"

Dr. Bassett:

"I'm not aware of that."

Dr. Bassett:

> "Yes."

Family Counsel:

> "You didn't with Kanner?"

Dr. Bassett:

> "Exactly."

Family Counsel:

"Okay. Well, the long and short of it is you didn't read Kanner's article, you don't know what he said other than what Howlin has made of it; is that fair?"

Dr. Bassett:

"I think that's fair."

The point, made here by counsel for the families, is that when Dr. Bassett and colleagues find a comment in an article that supports their advocacy research, they simply take it from the secondary source: (1) without checking the accuracy of the statement, (2) without understanding the context in which the statement was made, and in Kanner's case (3) without even understanding or defining success for people with autism. Agenda based "shortcuts" are a hallmark of the BCOHTA's Lovaas Report.

BCOHTA and the Government Agenda

One of the themes apparent in much of the Government literature and also included in the BCOHTA report, is the concept that professionals are purposely misdiagnosing children with autism so that parents can access purportedly generous government services. Under cross-examination, Dr. Bassett admits there is only one source of information supporting this suggestion raised in the BCOHTA report. The source is a Government physician who happens to also be a so-called "external reviewer" of the BCOHTA autism report – Dr. Miller of Sunny Hill Health Centre for Children.

Family Counsel:

> "The comment that is attributable to Dr. Miller in the report is that he or she thinks that parents are being dishonest about their children's condition to get treatment; is that what Dr. Miller told you was his view?"

Dr. Bassett:

"No, not at all."

Family Counsel:

"I'd have to turn to the text."

Dr. Bassett:

"The point he was making is he was concerned about the labelling of children with autism as a potential bias towards making the incidence appear higher than it actually is. And the concern would be that by being labelled with autism or autism-like symptoms, you may have access to services which you may not otherwise have. So he was as much concerned about clinicians as taking that step towards labelling as parents being dishonest."

Family Counsel:

"Well, Doctor, what place does that anecdotal view of Dr. Miller have in your report?"

Dr. Bassett:

"A minor one and it's early on in the background estimate of the incidence of autism, which is clearly stated as background."

Family Counsel:

"Why, if you're just doing a systematic review of the literature, would you single out Dr. Miller's view?"

Dr. Bassett:

"We include what we hope will be enough background material for the audience to understand what is autism, what is the prevalence of autism..."

Family Counsel:

"And in your research assessment work, if you were going to offer something that you believe to be reliable, you go to the primary source, wouldn't you."

Dr. Bassett:

"Yes."

Family Counsel:

"You didn't with Kanner?"

Dr. Bassett:

"Exactly."

It is noteworthy that Dr. Bassett has no problem including "anecdotal" evidence that supports Government's court case, in a report which is purportedly only a "systematic review" of the literature on autism treatment. This is particularly disturbing since Dr. Marie Bristol-Power, of the U.S. National Institute of Children's Health and Human Development and coordinator of autism research at the NIH, states with respect to the rise in autism diagnoses: "I don't think it's just better diagnosis, or that autism or PDD is the disease du jour... there is something else going on, and we are hoping to solve this problem."[1] In fact, the increased number of cases of autism is entirely irrelevant to the issues at hand, yet was included in the BCOHTA Lovaas Report because it supports the agenda of its funding source — Government *i.e.,* to spend as little money as possible on treatment for children with autism.

Dr. Bassett:

"The point he was making is he was concerned about the labelling of children with autism as a potential bias towards making the incidence appear higher than it actually is. And the concern would be... you may have access to services which you may not otherwise have."

Clinicians vs. Researchers: In Defense of the NY Report

In this area of the cross-examination, Dr. Bassett attempts to defend the view that the entire "clinical guidelines" movement is flawed and that clinicians working with children with autism are not qualified to make recommendations regarding best practices treatment protocol. This is a theme that is prevalent in other BCOHTA publications.

Family Counsel:

> "Well, Doctor, as I understood you yesterday, your effort was to determine whether Lovaas treatment provided a cure for autism. Didn't you go to the work of eminent specialists in the field who got together to create the New York guidelines and see what they thought about it?"

Dr. Bassett:

> "It's important for the Court to understand that clinical practice guidelines per se do not meet our inclusion criteria."
> -
> -

Dr. Bassett:

"It's important for the Court to understand that clinical practice guidelines per se do not meet our inclusion criteria."

Family Counsel:

> "All right. So all these experts get together in New York to decide that the research supports in terms of what clinically should be done, and you don't care what their view on that is?"
>
> -
>
> -

Dr. Bassett:

> "If it's an opinion on what to do in clinical practice, it doesn't meet the minimum inclusion criteria or the appropriate inclusion criteria for systematic review."

Family Counsel:

> "Well, Gresham is secondary in the same sense, is it not?"

Dr. Bassett:

> "It's exactly the same sense. But he discussed the issues that were important to this systematic review as predefined in our protocol."

Family Counsel:

> "Well, Doctor, if the New York group came to the conclusion that research supporting the Lovaas treatment protocol is the most methodologically sound and has the most compelling outcome data of any autism research, you're saying that isn't worthy of inclusion in your paper?"

Dr. Bassett:

> "It would be worthy if they provided details of the basis of that conclusion."

Here it is important to stress that the New York Department of Health report on autism treatment provides fifteen pages of detailed information regarding the methodology used as "the basis of their conclusion."[2] In addition, appendices of the report carefully detail the literature searches employed for each topic.[3] The New York Department of Health report also provides evidence tables for each study that met its criteria.[4] In fact, supporting documentation offered by the New York report is far more detailed than any provided by the BCOHTA in its report on Lovaas Treatment.

Family Counsel:

"All right. So all these experts get together in New York to decide that the research supports in terms of what clinically should be done, and you don't care what their view on that is?"

Family Counsel:

> "Now, the New York study was conducted by a panel of 62 peer reviewers who were experts in autism?"

Dr. Bassett:

> "Presumably, yes."

Family Counsel:

> "And it was done in an open fashion; that is, it was done publicly?"

Dr. Bassett:

> "I don't know."

Family Counsel:

> "The New York report relied on a standard methodology for developing clinical practice guidelines used by the Agency of Health Care Policy and Research?"

Dr. Bassett:

> "I would have to refer to this. If you're quoting, then presumably yes."

Dr. Bassett:

"If it's an opinion on what to do in clinical practice, it doesn't meet the minimum inclusion criteria or the appropriate inclusion criteria for systematic review."

Family Counsel:

"Well, in fact, the AHCPR guideline methodology is a methodology that you've used in your own office, is it not?"

Dr. Bassett:

"Yes, it is."

Family Counsel:

"And it was on that basis that you examined practice guidelines for testing of cholesterol?"

Dr. Bassett:

"Yes."

Family Counsel:

"And so when you were asked to examine clinical guidelines, you used the same methodology in British Columbia as they did in New York to examine clinical guidelines for treatment of autism?"

Dr. Bassett:

"We should be clear that we did not develop clinical practice guidelines. We were not asked to. Our role was to use those guidelines that have just been referred to by the AHCPR to critique other guidelines."

-

-

Family Counsel:

"Don't you state in the report, Doctor:

> 'To review and evaluate the process used in developing clinical practice guidelines, and to determine the extent to which the guidelines were evidence based, BCOHTA used a set of 15 appraisal criteria derived from the work done by the Institute of Medicine and the Agency for Health Care Policy and Research.'"

Dr. Bassett:

> "M'mm-hmm."

Family Counsel:

> "That's what you did in that case?"

Dr. Bassett:

> "Yes."

Family Counsel:

"The New York report relied on a standard methodology for developing clinical practice guidelines used by the Agency of Health Care Policy and Research?"

Dr. Bassett:

"I would have to refer to this. If you're quoting, then presumably yes."

In this cross-examination of the director of the BCOHTA, the attorney representing families exposes the fact that Clinical Practice Guidelines developed by the New York State Department of Health used the same method of "systematic review" that the BCOHTA uses in its own research projects (developed by the AHCPR). Despite this fact, the BCOHTA views the New York report as flawed. According to BCOHTA, the entire Clinical Practice Guideline "movement" is flawed, except (apparently) when it comes to use of AHCPR clinical practice guidelines for BCOHTA's own report on cholesterol testing.

Misrepresenting the People They Quote

The BCOHTA report selectively quotes highly regarded academics in the autism research community in order to make it appear as though these researchers are critical of the Lovaas treatment protocol. However, views of these scholars are far more balanced than presented by the BCOHTA.

Under cross-examination these facts come to light. The first article that is not presented in a balanced manner is written by a researcher affiliated with the U.S. National Institutes of Health, Dr. Marie Bristol-Powers.

Family Counsel:

> "Now, in the same — are you familiar with the National Institutes of Health statement from the United States:
>
> > 'Although there is no cure, autism is treatable through educational interventions of various types. Early intervention may be particularly effective, presumably because of the plasticity of the neural systems at the time'?"

Dr. Bassett:

> "I'm not familiar with that statement but it sounds reasonable and it seems consistent with the NIH reference that you have pointed us to."

Family Counsel:

> "Well, in fact, they quote that as being Bristol's view from the work you rely upon at page 3."

Dr. Bassett:

> "Well, like I said, it seems consistent with it."

Family Counsel:

> "But you don't make any reference to the positive comments of Bristol. You selectively referred only to the weaknesses that Bristol described on page 3; did you not?"

Dr. Bassett:

> "On — of the NIH report?"

Family Counsel:

"Well, in fact, the AHCPR guideline methodology is a methodology that you've used in your own office, is it not?"

Dr. Bassett:

"Yes, it is."

Family Counsel:

> "No —"

Dr. Bassett:

> "Our reference to the NIH report is incomplete?"

Family Counsel:

> "Yes."

Dr. Bassett:

> "It's a huge report."

Family Counsel:

> "Incomplete and unfair because you take only one side of the comments, that is, the negative side, without including Bristol's own positive comments on the early intervention and treatment of autism?"

Dr. Bassett:

> "Well, that's your opinion..."
> -
> -

Family Counsel:

> "It's the statement that autism is treatable that I'm referring to, Doctor. You don't think it was fair to include that to add some context to the portion you did quote from Bristol?"

Dr. Bassett:

> "In this section to do with long-term outcome, we cite what seems to me a reasonable statement about the state of knowledge on long-term outcome."

Dr. Bassett:

"Our reference to the NIH report is incomplete?"

Family Counsel:

"Yes."

Dr. Bassett:

"It's a huge report."

Family Counsel:

"Doesn't Bristol also state:

'It is also clear that persons of all ages and all levels of ability can benefit from access to consistently available proven treatment. It is also known, however, that treatment response is not uniform within the population. Although many children may be brought to the point of near normal functioning, others are much less responsive to social behavioural intervention programs'?"

Dr. Bassett:

"That sounds like a reasonable statement. We make statements similar to that in our discussion section."

The next article that is presented by the BCOHTA Autism Report in an unbalanced manner is that written by Dr. Howlin in reference to rates and level of functioning amongst autistic adults.

> **Family Counsel:**
>
> **"Incomplete and unfair because you take only one side of the comments, that is, the negative side, without including Bristol's own positive comments on the early intervention and treatment of autism?"**
>
> **Dr. Bassett:**
>
> **"Well, that's your opinion..."**

Family Counsel:

"Now, you relied on some published work by Dr. Howlin?"

Dr. Bassett:

"Yes."

Family Counsel:

"And again at page 3, you have referenced the comment that:

'10 to 20 percent of people in the latter years are in their own homes and in work?'

Now, did you do any critical assessment of how Howlin came to that conclusion?"

Dr. Bassett:

"We said we read her article and we found that it included — as best we could tell without doing a critical appraisal of this literature..."

-

-

Family Counsel:

"Didn't Dr. Howlin suggest that the reason for the improvement, apparent improvement, was attributable, at least indirectly, to better treatment, education and a decrease in institutionalization?"

Dr. Bassett:

"Yes."

Family Counsel:

"So it wasn't the case of this just spontaneously happening. Better treatment, which she doesn't describe, and education were attributable to the improvements?"

Dr. Bassett:

"Yes."

Family Counsel:

"So it isn't really an answer to Dr. Rutter's comment that, untreated, only 1 in 64 will show any improvement, because these people Howlin is describing were, in fact, getting some form of treatment apparently?"

Family Counsel:

"Doesn't Bristol also state:

'It is also clear that persons of all ages and all levels of ability can benefit from access to consistently available proven treatment ... Although many children may be brought to the point of near normal functioning, others are much less responsive to social behavioural intervention programs'?"

Dr. Bassett:

"That sounds like a reasonable statement."

Family Counsel:

"So it isn't really an answer to Dr. Rutter's comment that, untreated, only 1 in 64 will show any improvement, because these people Howlin is describing were, in fact, getting some form of treatment apparently?"

Dr. Bassett:

"Exactly."

Dr. Bassett:

> "Exactly."

Family Counsel:

> "And if one reads the entirety of Howlin's work, she actually says that only 4.8 percent of the autistic people that researchers followed into adult life were sufficiently independent and teachable so as to be gainfully employed. Isn't that right?"

Dr. Bassett:

> "That's what she describes, yes."

Family Counsel:

> "So it's not anywhere near 10 to 20 percent of autistic adults who are in paid employment. The number is considerably less, under 5 percent?"

Dr. Bassett:

> "Well, I'll try and refer to her material. Are you quoting from her material in that — the article?"

Family Counsel:

> "Well, it's my summary of it, Doctor. I can't give you the line."

Dr. Bassett:

> "I don't have the summary in front of me so I would have to look at the original."

Regarding the article written by Rogers (1998), the BCOHTA report misrepresents her article by selectively quoting only the parts of the article that supports its government advocacy argument. Of note is the title of Rogers' article, which is "Empirically supported comprehensive treatments for young children with autism."

Family Counsel:

"Now, at page 38 of your report, you quote from Rogers."

Dr. Bassett:

"At the bottom, yes."

Family Counsel:

"'Studies did not demonstrate the level of improvement in multiple areas of functioning or the sustained long-term effects and treatment that Lovaas reported. The field awaits a full independent replication of the Lovaas study.'

But Rogers went on to say [about the Lovaas landmark study]:

'There are several methodological strengths of this study. Group sizes, although not large, were not unduly small. There was a treatment manual that outlined both the treatment techniques and the actual content of treatment. Treatment givers were all trained by the core staff and supervised closely. Children were diagnosed by professionals outside of the treatment team prior to referral, and the first set of follow-up data were gathered by outside professionals blind to the treatment status. Interrelated reliability was reported for pretreatment behavioural measures. Outcome variables at second follow-up included several different kinds of measures well chosen to

Family Counsel:

"And if one reads the entirety of Howlin's work, she actually says that only 4.8 percent of the autistic people that researchers followed into adult like were sufficiently independent and teachable so as to be gainfully employed. Isn't that right?"

Dr. Bassett:

"That's what she describes, yes."

> document current levels of functioning in areas that are generally significantly affected by autism: IQ, adaptive behaviours measures, school placement and behavioural measures. Follow-up was carried out for many years after the treatment was delivered so that long-term affect of treatment could be examined. The two control groups allowed for examination of two different treatment conditions, one of which represented typical community programs and the other represented both typical community treatment and some level of behavioural interventions. Thus, one control group could be considered to be allowing for the comparison of nonspecific treatment. A very important finding was that in the treated group, outcome was predicted by pretreatment mental ages.'

That's the context of which Rogers' comment that you've quoted was made, is it not?"

Family Counsel:

"So it's not anywhere near 10 to 20 percent of autistic adults who are in paid employment. The number is considerably less, under 5 percent?"

Dr. Bassett:

"Well, I'll try and refer to her material."

Dr. Bassett:

"If you're quoting from it, presumably yes."

Family Counsel:

"Why didn't you put that in to give some context? Reading this —"

Dr. Bassett:

"We quote extensively from Rogers and we actually make almost all the same points earlier in the discussion."

Family Counsel:

"Yeah, but you don't attribute them to Rogers, do you?"

Dr. Bassett:

> "Yes, we do."

The line of questioning regarding the misrepresentation of Rogers' comments is emblematic of how the BCOHTA use the legitimacy of well-known experts in the autism field to bolster their own agenda-based Lovaas report. It is expected, even desired, that experts in any field will offer constructive criticism regarding experimental designs. In fact, this is what moves any field forward; however, to take those comments out of context and present them as supporting a particular agenda is a completely different matter.

Family Counsel:

"'A very important finding was that in the treated group, outcome was predicted by pretreatment mental ages.'

That's the context ... is it not?"

Dr. Bassett:

"If you're quoting from it, presumably yes."

What Happened After BCOHTA Report Ruled Biased?

What happened to the BCOHTA report subsequent to a B.C. Supreme Court ruled a supposedly "impartial" work of University of British Columbia academics is "obviously biased?" Despite the ruling, *nothing happened.* The directors of both the BCOHTA and the CHSPR (Centre for Health Policy Research) did not "pull" the report; the Office still publishes it and the Ministry of Health still distributes it as though it were genuine academic research. The Director of the CHSPR, who has jurisdiction over the Director of the BCOHTA, did not get involved and attempt to restore academic legitimacy to the Office of Health Technology Assessment by pulling the document or reining in his people. Despite the B.C. Supreme Court finding of clear BCOHTA bias, the Centre for Health Services and Policy Research (CHSPR) at the University of British Columbia (UBC) has done nothing to stop this biased publication from making its way around the world.

In fact, the opposite is true. The CHSPR is apparently proud of BCOHTA's work. The 2000 Annual Report of the CHSPR describes as laudable the biased research BCOHTA delivered to B.C. Supreme Court. The report states:

> "A recent major research effort has focused on early, intensive behavioural therapy for children with autism, and in particular whether such forms of treatment result in improved outcome as compared with standard management. The assessment was undertaken in parallel with proceedings in the BC Supreme

> Court brought against the Province on behalf of several autistic children in British Columbia. In the course of the trial hearing, the Senior Medical Consultant of BCOHTA was called to give expert evidence to the Supreme Court, and provided two days of testimony. Full reports of these studies have now been published by BCOHTA, following conclusion of the legal proceedings."[1]

It is not surprising that neither BCOHTA or U.B.C.'s CHSPR mentioned that the result of the Senior Consultant's testimony was that the BCOHTA work was found to be obviously biased by a B.C. Supreme Court justice. Clearly those uncomfortable facts have no place in an Annual Report touting the achievements of U.B.C.'s Centre for Health Policy Services and Policy Research.

The line of questioning regarding the misrepresentation of Rogers' comments is emblematic of how the BCOHTA use the legitimacy of well-known experts in the autism field to bolster their own agenda-based Lovaas report.

In fact, by rejecting the B.C. Supreme Court's opinion of their report, the biased work has been tacitly given licence by U.B.C. to be widely disseminated — and it has been. The Report has been distributed across Canada and other Health Technology Assessment analysts are basing new reports on it. It is as though the Auton case never happened — that is the degree to which health technology has ignored this landmark B.C. Supreme Court ruling.

By working closely with Dr. Ken Bassett, first author of the BCOHTA, the Canadian Coordinating Council Office of Health Technology Assessment (CCOHTA) located in the nation's capital, Ottawa, got involved in the evaluation of Lovaas Treatment. The BCOHTA is affiliated with the national office and regularly conducts ongoing projects with them. The national office created a much more sophisticated, and more formidable report to address the claims of parents of children with autism in Canadian courts. This new autism report, relying significantly on the biased work of the BCOHTA, illustrates the danger of poor health technology assessment work. Significantly, Dr. Bassett's name initially appeared on the Canadian Coordinating Office of Health Technology Assessment's Lovaas Treatment document, but was later removed after the BCOHTA report was rejected by B.C. Supreme Court (page 207).

The final autism report published by the Canadian Coordinating Office of Health Technology Assessment toned down much of the anti-Lovaas rhetoric, possibly after they discovered that they had relied too heavily on the discredited BCOHTA report. In addition to reliance on the BCOHTA Report, the CCOHTA also relies on the Alberta Heritage Foundation Report (which itself relies heavily on the BCOHTA Lovaas Report). Perhaps to shield itself against further litigation (they have already been sued by a large pharmaceutical company for another allegedly biased report), the CCOHTA simply added this disclaimer to page (i) of the report, *Behavioural Interventions for Preschool Children with Autism:*

> *This report is a review of existing public literature, studies, materials and other information and documentation (collectively the "documentation") which are available to CCOHTA. The accuracy of the contents of the documentation on which this report is based is not warranted, assured or represented in any way by CCOHTA and CCOHTA does not assume responsibility for the quality, propriety, inaccuracies, or the reasonable of any statements, information or conclusions contained in the documentation.*[2]

The Report has been distributed across Canada and other Health Technology Assessment analysts are basing new reports on it.

If health technology information used as input for the CCOHTA is unreliable (largely because it is not in *peer-reviewed* journals and funded by government), then why use it? Why bother with disclaimers? The reason BCOHTA did not submit its Lovaas report to a peer-reviewed journal may well be that sidestepping the academic peer review process made it faster and enormously easier to deliver to government the agenda-based conclusions BCOHTA's MOH paymaster demanded to win a court case on health-care spending on autism. This is unfortunate because children with autism need disinterested academics to perform genuine, honest research based on scientific data, to determine *true* best practices. Children with autism are ill served by a national health technology technocratic elite that generates biased, substandard so-called autism treatment "research," drafted to defeat the legal challenges of families.

An important question must be considered: will the Canadian Coordinating Office of Health Technology Assessment eventually succeed in convincing a court outside British Columbia of health technology's supposed academic legitimacy and purported "objectivity" or, will judges across the country and around the world be wise to this biased game played by encumbered academics? Hopefully, other groups of families and their legal counsel will do with the CCOHTA Report what was done with the BCOHTA Lovaas Report in the Auton case — lay them bare and expose the truth behind government funded advocacy research. If parents are not successful against health technology guns for hire,

CCOHTA Web-site in April 2000: BCOHTA's direct involvement with the CCOHTA Autism Treatment report dates to April 2000.

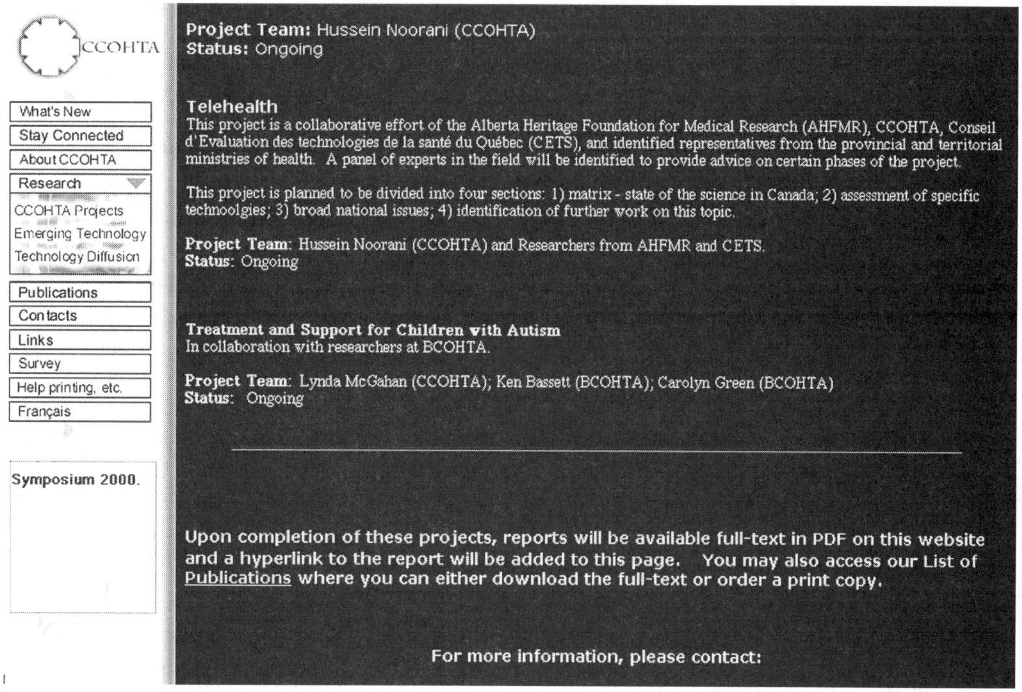

CCOHTA

What's New
Stay Connected
About CCOHTA
Research
CCOHTA Projects
Emerging Technology
Technology Diffusion
Publications
Contacts
Links
Survey
Help printing, etc.
Français

Symposium 2000.

Project Team: Hussein Noorani (CCOHTA)
Status: Ongoing

Telehealth
This project is a collaborative effort of the Alberta Heritage Foundation for Medical Research (AHFMR), CCOHTA, Conseil d'Evaluation des technologies de la santé du Québec (CETS), and identified representatives from the provincial and territorial ministries of health. A panel of experts in the field will be identified to provide advice on certain phases of the project.

This project is planned to be divided into four sections: 1) matrix - state of the science in Canada; 2) assessment of specific technoolgies; 3) broad national issues; 4) identification of further work on this topic.

Project Team: Hussein Noorani (CCOHTA) and Researchers from AHFMR and CETS.
Status: Ongoing

Treatment and Support for Children with Autism
In collaboration with researchers at BCOHTA.

Project Team: Lynda McGahan (CCOHTA); Ken Bassett (BCOHTA); Carolyn Green (BCOHTA)
Status: Ongoing

Upon completion of these projects, reports will be available full-text in PDF on this website and a hyperlink to the report will be added to this page. You may also access our List of Publications where you can either download the full-text or order a print copy.

For more information, please contact:

then a disturbingly powerful precedent will be set and the very real possibility exists that yet another generation of children with autism will be lost to autism — and not just in Canada.

Canadian Health Technology academics are, for the most part, internationalists, travelling to international conferences, disseminating reports in academic journals and through web-sites as well as enjoying sabbatical years in foreign countries to share ideas with trans-national colleagues. We have already seen the implications of the BCOHTA report in the United States, Austria and Finland. The BCOHTA report is now haunting parents of children with autism who are fighting for their children's right to medically necessary treatment against private health insurance companies in the United States. Aetna, a large health insurance company in the United States, uses the BCOHTA report and the Alberta Heritage Report to justify exclusion of autistic children's treatment in Coverage Policy Bulletin Number 0554.[3] Another large health insurance company — the Blue Cross Blue Shield of Tennessee — writes in its Medical Policy Manual that Applied Behavioral Analysis for the treatment of autism is considered investigational and does not meet their criteria.[4] The BCOHTA report was relied upon in their policy, effective in April 1st, 2002.

"CCOHTA does not assume responsibility for the quality, propriety, inaccuracies, or the reasonable of any statements, information or conclusions contained in the documentation."

Not surprisingly, the BCOHTA has found a journal, the *International Journal of Technology Assessment and Health Care*, Vol. 17, No. 2, April 2001[5] to publish their advocacy work. In addition, the International Network of Agencies for Health Technology Assessment has issued a brief in 2001 written by the Alberta Heritage Foundation for Medical Research (who relied heavily on the BCOHTA report) to advertise the availability of their paper.[6] In order to disseminate this biased document outside of Canada and the United States, the BCOHTA presented their work at the International Society of Technology Assessment in Healthcare (ISTAHC) 17th Annual Meeting in Philadelphia in June 2001.[7] This international conference helped add the document to the health technology movement in Finland[8] and Austria.[9] At this time, the Finnish web-site links the BCOHTA Report and the Austrian Health Technology web-site in their October 2001 newsletter; the BCOHTA, AHRMR and CCOHTA Reports are all listed. In addition, the AHFMR is linked to the Austrian web-site. In short, parents in European countries are now going to be up against their own health technologists who will present their research in European courts based on biased research flowing out of the University of British Columbias' Office of Health Technology Assessment.

It is unfortunate that this group of academics is going to achieve the rationing of health care for a very vulnerable group of children who desperately need treatment and, at the publication of this book, have no other effective treatment for their intractable disorder. The BCOHTA report on Lovaas Treatment in its published form, for years will haunt parents of children with autism fighting for their children's rights in courts around the world. Justice will elude these children as governments work to save money and academics pad their curriculum vitae. In view of the autism experience, it is my sincere hope that the health technology movement will question the unhealthy influence that government funding has in shaping their research; however, I am not optimistic that health technology academics are capable of self-policing. Consequently, this movement will continue to grow and exert disproportionate influence at the highest levels of government. If this is permitted to happen, it will be to the detriment — globally — of children with autism. It is my hope this book puts the necessary spotlight on the harmful role of health technology assessment in the ongoing autism wars, whereever the next battle is waged.

Sabrina Freeman, Ph.D.

Aetna, a large health insurance company in the United States, uses the BCOHTA report and the Alberta Heritage Report to justify not covering autistic children's treatment in their Coverage Policy Bulletin Number 0554.

Afterword

B.C. Court of Appeal Ruling

Highlights of the B.C. Court of Appeal Judgment on Autism Treatment

In October 2002, the B.C. Court of Appeal handed down a ruling in the landmark Auton case that is further proof of government's abject failure to provide genuine Early Intensive Behavioral Treatment to children with autism. The Court of Appeal decision not only validates the lower court ruling but also goes further than the B.C. Supreme Court did in July 2000 when it ordered government to fund bona fide, science-based autism treatment.

Three justices of the B.C. Court of Appeal were unanimous in supporting the Supreme Court ruling that government's failure to provide Intensive Behavioral Treatment for children with autism constitutes direct discrimination under the Canadian Charter of Rights and Freedoms. Moreover, and likely to the chagrin of academics at the BCOHTA, the Court of Appeal agreed with the lower court declaration that Early Intensive Behavioral Intervention is medically necessary and must be funded by government, rejecting all cost and other arguments posited by government's lawyers. In addition, the Court of Appeal went further in rejecting arbitrary age cut off for medically necessary autism treatment. Justice Saunders states:

> *[92] ...I would modify the order to direct that the four infant petitioners are each entitled to government funded treatment in the nature of that which they have been receiving..., if such treatment should still be useful to them. I would modify the order to direct that the Crown fund such treatment, from the time of the order declaring a breach of the Charter rights of the infant petitioners (Auton No. 2), provided that the petitioners establish the requisite usefulness by a written opinion from the child's family physician supported by a written opinion from an appropriately qualified paediatrician or psychologist, to continue until the medical view is that no further significant benefit in alleviating the autistic condition can reasonably be expected from a continuation of the treatment.*[1]

Government must continue to fund "treatment in the nature of that which they [the petitioners] have been receiving", which is Lovaas Autism Treatment.

This aspect of the Court of Appeal ruling is quite significant insofar as government's original purported remedy in the Auton case was designed to stop at the geriatric age of six. Moreover, the Court of Appeal's emphasis on a medical team's role in the determination of whether autism treatment is of further benefit to a child represents a sea change in government autism policy when adopted. However, the reality to date, despite two court rulings mandating bona fide autism treatment, is that generic social workers — untrained in medically necessary autism treatment — continue to preside over funding decisions that determine whether a child is entitled to publicly funded, physician-prescribed autism treatment. In other words, the inadequate social services autism paradigm exposed in the B.C. Supreme Court proceedings as being wholly inadequate for medically necessary autism health care, regrettably remains alive and well in British Columbia.

What is also important in the portion of the B.C. Court of Appeal ruling cited above is that the government must continue to fund "treatment in the nature of that which they [the petitioners] have been receiving." This means the court views Lovaas Autism Treatment provided for the children in the lawsuit as an Intensive Behavioral Treatment for autism it deems to be medically necessary and has ordered government to fund accordingly. Simply stated, the B.C. Court of Appeal has disallowed the government maneuver to strategically and willfully exclude Lovaas Treatment from the Auton remedy.

With respect to the conclusions of the BCOHTA that Lovaas-type autism remains "experimental," the B.C. Court of Appeal states:

> *[85] The Court has ordered this treatment, because, under its more generic name [Early Intensive Behavioral Treatment], it is the only known form of effective treatment for children with autism or ASD, the treatment having passed out of the experimental stage.*[2]

This unambiguously sets aside government's longtime refusal to fund Lovaas on the grounds that the autism treatment protocol is purportedly experimental and does not as yet enjoy adequate scientific validation to justify its cost in public funding.

The contempt mechanism give the B.C. Supreme Court additional power to force the government to comply with the ruling.

A key difference between the B.C. Supreme Court and the higher Court of Appeal rulings is that the latter introduces an important mechanism by which families can take government officials before the court on contempt charges if they continue to defy the Court order to implement medically necessary autism treatment for children. The B.C. Court of Appeal states:

> *[128] But if the process of enforcement requires the use of the contempt power of the courts and if it is thought necessary first to obtain an order in the nature of* ***mandamus****, then I would think that the application for that order would have to specify the public officer, by name or by office, against whom the order is to be directed.*
>
> *[129] I would affirm the continuing jurisdiction of the Supreme Court, in these proceedings, to entertain an application for an order in the nature of* ***mandamus*** *against a public officer, by name and office, if a direction to the government is not complied with.*[3]

What is highly significant here is that to fix government's serious and deeply entrenched constitutional failure — depriving medically necessary autism treatment — the court enforcement mechanism of "contempt" can now potentially be brought into play against senior government bureaucrats who apparently reject the notion that Superior Court rulings can possibly apply to them or can impinge on their decision making discretion and delegated authority. The B.C. Court of Appeal has given B.C. Supreme Court authority to compel intransigent government bureaucrats to abide by the Auton ruling. This makes considerable sense given the track record; all indications thus far show government has failed — and will continue to fail — to do what the courts have ordered.

On May 15th 2003, the Government of British Columbia was granted leave to appeal the B.C. Court of Appeal ruling to the Supreme Court of Canada. Neither the lower court nor the B.C. Court of appeal has granted a stay of the effects of the Auton ruling which means that even though the Attorney General has launched the Supreme Court of Canada appeal, government remains duty bound to fulfill the court orders on autism treatment as directed. As this book goes to press, the Government of British Columbia has yet to comply with the judgment of the B.C. Court of Appeal.

Endnotes

Chapter 1: BCOHTA's Attempt To Discredit Lovaas Autism Treatment

[1]Office of Comptroller General, *Grants and Contributions* [online]. Retrieved 2/11/02 from <www.fin.gov.bc.ca/ocg/pa/98-99/Sup-D/Grants/D7-22.htm>.

[2]Office of Comptroller General, *Grants and Contributions* (see n. 1 above).

[3]Bassett, K. et al., *Autism and Lovaas Treatment: a systematic review of effectiveness evidence.* Vancouver, B.C. BCOHTA, University of British Columbia, 2000, p. 1.

[4]Bassett, K. et al., BCOHTA, (see n. 3 above) p. 1.

[5]BCOHTA *B.C. Office of Health Technology Assessment Home Page* [online]. Centre for Health Services and Policy Research, University of British Columbia. Retrieved 5, 14, 02 from <www.chspr.ubc.ca/bcohta/>.

[6]BCOHTA *Office of Health Technology Assessment Mandate* [online]. Centre for Health Services and Policy Research, University of British Columbia. Retrieved 5, 14, 02 from <www.chspr.ubc.ca/bcohta/bcohta.htm#Mandate>.

[7]BCOHTA *Office of Health Technology Assessment Mandate* (see n. 5 above).

[8]BCOHTA *Office of Health Technology Assessment Home Page* (see n. 4 above).

[9]CHSPR *BC Office of Health Technology Assessment* [online]. Centre for Health Services and Policy Research, University of British Columbia. Retrieved 3, 22, 02 from <www.chspr.ubc.ca/bcohta/bcohta.htm>.

[10]CHSPR *BC Office of Health Technology Assessment* (see n. 8 above).

[11]CHSPR *BC Office of Health Technology Assessment* (see n. 8 above).

[12]BCOHTA *B.C. Office of Health Technology Assessment Home Page* (see n. 4 above).

[13]UBC Policy #97 *Conflict of Interest* [on line]. Approved Sept. 1992, revised July 1995. University of British Columbia. Retrieved 5, 15,02 from <www.policy.ubc.ca/policy97.htm>

[14]UBC Policy #97 *Conflict of Interest* [on line]. (see n. 12 above).

[15]UBC Policy #97 *Conflict of Interest* [on line]. (see n. 12 above).

[16]UBC Policy #97 *Conflict of Interest* [on line]. (see n. 12 above).

[17]Bassett, K. et al., BCOHTA (see n. 3 above) p. 27.

[18]Bassett, K. et al., BCOHTA (see n. 3 above) p. 28.

[19]American Psychological Association, *Ending Discrimination in Health Insurance*, [on line]. APA, Psychology Examines the Issues, 1997. Retrieved 5, 15, 02 from <www.apa.org/practice/paper/homepage.html>.

[20]Federal Mental Health Parity Act, *Health Care Financing Administration* [on line]. 1999. Retrieved 5, 15, 02 from <www.hcfa.gov/medicaid/hipaa/content/mhpastat.asp>.

[21]National Institute of Mental Health [on line]. 2002 Retrieved 5, 15, 02 from <www.nimh.nih.gov/publicat/equal.cfm>.

[22]American Psychiatric Association [on line]. 1999. Retrieved 5, 15, 02 from <http://www.psych.org/pub_pol_adv/sos_parity_999.cfm>.

[23]California Assembly Bill 88, Chapter, 534 -4, The people of the State of California, Approved by Governor September 27, 1999, Filed with Secretary of State September 28, 1999.

[24]California Assembly Bill 88, Chapter, 534 -4 (see n. 22 above).

Chapter 2: When Academics Go Bad: Selective BCOHTA Analysis

[1]Bassett, K. et al. BCOHTA, (see Chap. 1, n. 3), p. ix.

[2]Bassett, K. et al. BCOHTA, (see Chap. 1, n. 3), p. 7.

[3]Bassett, K. et al. BCOHTA, (see Chap. 1, n. 3), p. ix.

[4]Lovaas, O.I. *Clarifying Comments on the UCLA Young Autism Project*, [on line]. 2000. Retrieved 5, 15, 02 from <http://www.feat.org/lovaas/full.htm>.

[5]Lovaas, O.I. *Clarifying Comments on the UCLA Young Autism Project*, 2000 (see n. 4 above).

[6]Bassett, K. et al., BCOHTA, (see Chap. 1, n. 3), p. 37.

[7]Bassett, K. et al., BCOHTA, (see Chap. 1, n. 3), p. 39.

[8]Bassett, K. et al., BCOHTA, (see Chap. 1, n. 3), p. 10.

[9]Bassett, K. et al., BCOHTA, (see Chap. 1, n. 3), p. 39.

[10]Bassett, K. et al.,BCOHTA, (see Chap. 1, n. 3), p. 10.

[11]Bassett, K. et al., BCOHTA, (see Chap. 1, n. 3), p. 44.

[12]Bassett, K. et al., BCOHTA, (see Chap. 1, n. 3), p. 7.

[13]Bassett, K. et al., BCOHTA, (see Chap. 1, n. 3), p. 5.

[14]CCOHTA *Canadian Coordinating Office for Health Technology Assessment* [online]. Retrieved 4, 1, 00 from <www.ccohta.ca>.

[15]Guralnick, M. (ed). *Clinical practice guideline: Report of the recommendations. Autism/pervasive developmental disorders, assessment and intervention for young children* (age 0-3 years). Albany (NY), New York State Department of Health, 1999, p. IV-15 to 21, IV-24.

[16]Bassett, K. et al., BCOHTA, (see Chap. 1, n. 3), p. 39.

[17]Bassett, K. et al., BCOHTA, (see Chap. 1, n. 3), p. 44.

[18]Bassett, K. et al., BCOHTA, (see Chap. 1, n. 3), p. 5.

[19]Bassett, K. et al., BCOHTA, (see Chap. 1, n. 3), p. 6.

[20]Bassett, K. et al.,BCOHTA, (see Chap. 1, n. 3), p. 6.

[21]Bassett, K. et al., BCOHTA, (see Chap. 1, n. 3), p. 15.

[22]Bassett, K. et al., BCOHTA, (see Chap. 1, n. 3), p.15.

[23]Bassett, K. et al., BCOHTA, (see Chap. 1, n. 3), p.15.

[24]Bassett, K. et al., BCOHTA, (see Chap. 1, n. 3), p. iii.

[25]Public Health Service, *Mental Health: A report of the Surgeon General*, 1999, p. 164 [online]. Retrieved 5, 15, 02 from <http://www.surgeongeneral.gov/library/mentalhealth/home.html>

Chapter 3: Analysis of BCOHTA Critique of Lovaas Treatment Research

[1]Lovaas, O.I., T. Smith, and J.J. McEachin. "Clarifying comments on the young autism study: reply to Schopler, Short and Mesibov." *J. Consult. Clin. Psychology.* 1989, 57(1), p. 165.

[2]Bassett, K. et al., BCOHTA, (see Chap. 1, n. 3), p. 21.

[3]Smith, T., O.I. Lovaas. "The UCLA young autism project: a reply to Gresham and MacMillan." *Behav. Disord.* 1997, 22(4), p. 202.

[4]Baer, D.M. "Commentaries on McEachin, Smith, and Lovaas: quasi-random assignment can be as convincing as random assignment." *Am. J. Ment. Retard.* 1993, January 1997(4), p. 374.

[5]Baer, D.M. (see n. 4 above), p. 374.

[6]Baer, D.M. (see n. 4 above), p. 374.

[7]Bassett, K. et al., BCOHTA, (see Chap. 1, n. 3), p. 22.

[8]McEachin, J.J., T. Smith, O.I. Lovaas. "Long-term outcome for children with autism who received early intensive behavioral treatment." *Am. J. Ment. Retard.* 1993, 97(4), p. 369.

[9]Bassett, K. et al., BCOHTA, (see Chap. 1, n. 3), p. 23.

[10]Lovaas, O.I., T. Smith, J.J. McEachin, (see n. 1 above), p. 166.

[11]Lovaas, O.I. "Behavioral treatment and normal educational and intellectual functioning in young austic children." *J. Consult. and Clin. Psych.* 1987, 55(1), p. 4.

[12]Bassett, K. et al., BCOHTA, (see Chap. 1, n. 3), p. 4.

[13]Bassett, K. et al., BCOHTA, (see Chap. 1, n. 3), p. 24.

[14]Bassett, K. et al., BCOHTA, (see Chap. 1, n. 3), p. 18.

[15]Lovaas, O.I. (see n. 12 above), p. 4.

[16]Smith, T., S. Eikeseth, M. Klevstrand, O.I. Lovaas. "Intensive behavioral treatment for preschoolers with severe mental retardation and pervasive developmental disorder." *Am. J. Ment. Retard.* 1997, November, 102(3) pp. 238-49.

[17]Smith, T. (see n. 17 above), p. 238.

[18]Smith, T. (see n. 17 above), p. 244.

[19]Smith, T. (see n. 17 above), p. 212.

[20]Lovaas, O.I. (see n. 12 above), p. 6.

[21]Boyd, R.D. "Sex as a possible source of group inequivalence in Lovaas (1987)." *J. Autism. Dev. Dis.* 1998, June, 28(3), p. 214.

[22]Boyd, R.D. (see n. 22 above), p. 214.

[23]Bassett, K. et al., BCOHTA, (see Chap. 1, n. 3), p. 4.

[24]Guralnick, M. (ed). *Clinical practice guideline: Report of the recommendations. Autism/pervasive developmental disorders, assessment and intervention for young children* (age 0-3 years). Albany (NY), New York State Department of Health, 1999, p. IV-15.

[25]New York State Department of Health (see n. 25 above), p. IV-15.

[26]New York State Department of Health (see n. 25 above), p. I-10.

[27]Bassett, K. et al., BCOHTA, (see Chap. 1, n. 3), p. ?????.

[28]UBC Policy #87, *Research* [online]. Approved July 1993, Revised March 1995. <www.policy.ubc.ca/policy87.htm>

[29]Bassett, K. et al., BCOHTA, (see Chap. 1, n. 3), p. 44.

[30]Bassett, K. et al., BCOHTA, (see Chap. 1, n. 3), p. 25.

[31]Bassett, K. et al., BCOHTA, (see Chap. 1, n. 3), p. 25.

[32]Bassett, K. et al., BCOHTA, (see Chap. 1, n. 3), p. 25.

[33]Bassett, K. et al., BCOHTA, (see Chap. 1, n. 3), p. 25.

[34]Bassett, K. et al., BCOHTA, (see Chap. 1, n. 3), p. 25.

[35]Lovaas, O.I. (see n.12 above), p. 4.

[36]Smith, T., O.I. Lovaas. (see n. 3 above), p. 205.

[37]Rogers, S.J. "Empirically supported comprehensive treatments for young children with autism." *J.Clin. Child. Psychol.*,1998 June, 27(2), p.169.

[38]Lovaas, O.I. (see n.12 above), p. 5.

[39]Lovaas, O.I., T. Smith, J.J. McEachin. (see n.11 above), p. 165.

[40]Bassett, K. et al., BCOHTA, (see Chap. 1, n. 3), p. 26.

[41]Bassett, K. et al., BCOHTA, (see Chap. 1, n. 3), p. 26.

[42]Rogers, S.J. *J. Clin. Child.Psychol.* 1998 June, 27(2), (see n. 38 above), p.172.

[43]Gresham, F.M., D.L. MacMillan. "Autistic Recovery?: An analysis and critique of the empirical evidence on the Early Intervention Project." *Behav. Disord.,* 1997, 22, pp. 185-201.

[44]Smith, T., O.I. Lovaas. (see n. 3 above), p. 211.

[45]Bassett, K. et al., BCOHTA, (see Chap. 1, n. 3), p. 26.

[46]Bassett, K. et al., BCOHTA, (see Chap. 1, n. 3), p. 26

[47]Correspondence from Dr. E.J. Garland, *Open letter* [online]. 1996. Families for Early Autism Treatment of British Columbia. Retrieved 5, 15, 02 from <www.featbc.org/files/lobby_and_advocacy/FEATBCbriefMLA.pdf>

[48]Bassett, K. et al., BCOHTA, (see Chap. 1, n. 3), p. 26.

[49]Bassett, K. et al., BCOHTA, (see Chap. 1, n. 3), p. 26.

[50]Bassett, K. et al., BCOHTA, (see Chap. 1, n. 3), p. 26.

[51]Smith, T., O.I. Lovaas. (see n. 3 above), p. 204.

[52]Lovaas, O.I. (see n.12 above), p. 5.

[53]Smith, T., O.I. Lovaas. (see n. 3 above), p. 203.

[54]Bassett, K. et al., BCOHTA, (see Chap. 1, n. 3), p. 27.

[55]Lovaas, O.I., T. Smith, J.J. McEachin. (see n. 1 above), pp. 165-166.

[56]Bassett, K. et al., BCOHTA, (see Chap. 1, n. 3), p. 37.

[57]Smith, T., O.I. Lovaas. (see n. 3 above), p. 205.

[58]McEachin, J.J., T. Smith, O.I. Lovaas. (see n. 9 above) p. 369.

[59]Smith, T., O.I. Lovaas. (see n. 3 above), pp. 206-207.

[60]Smith, T., O.I. Lovaas. (see n. 3 above), pp. 205-207.

[61]Bassett, K. et al., BCOHTA, (see Chap. 1, n. 3), p. 28.

[62]Bassett, K. et al., BCOHTA, (see Chap. 1, n. 3), p. 33.

[63]Bassett, K. et al., BCOHTA, (see Chap. 1, n. 3), p. 29.

[64]Bassett, K. et al., BCOHTA, (see Chap. 1, n. 3), p. 32.

[65]Smith, T., S. Eikeseth, M. Klevstrand, O.I. Lovaas. "Intensive behavioral treatment for preschoolers with severe mental retardation and pervasive developmental disorder." *Am. J. Ment. Retard.* 1997, November, 102(3), p. 247.

[66]Anderson S.R, et al., "Intensive home-based early intervention with autistic children." *Educ. Treat. Children*,1987, 10(4), p. 363.

[67]Bassett, K. et al., BCOHTA, (see Chap. 1, n. 3), p. 41.

[68]Smith, T., O.I. Lovaas. (see n. 3 above), p. 204.

Chapter 4: BCOHTA Deceptive Use of Research

[1]Bassett, K. et al., BCOHTA, (see Chap. 1, n. 3), p. 3.

[2]Bristol, M.M. et al. "State of the science in autism: report to the National Institutes Health." *J. Autism Dev. Disorders,* 1996, April, 26(2), p. 147.

[3]Bristol et al., (see n. 2 above), p. 147.

[4]Bassett, K. et al., BCOHTA, (see Chap. 1, n. 3), p. 3.

[5]Howlin P. "Prognosis in autism: do specialist treatments affect long-term outcome?" *Eur. Child Adolesc. Psychiatr.,*1997, 6(2), p. 56.

[6]Howlin P., *Eur. Child Adolesc. Psychiatr.*, (see n. 5 above), p. 55.

[7]Howlin P., *Eur. Child Adolesc. Psychiatr.*, (see n. 5 above), p. 60.

[8]Bassett, K. et al., BCOHTA, (see Chap. 1, n. 3), p. 4.

[9]Jocelyn, L.J., O.G. Casiro, D. Beattie, J. Bow, J. Kneisz. "Treatment of children with autism: a randomized controlled trial to evaluate a caregiver-based intervention program in community day-care centers." *J. Dev. Behav. Pediatr.,* 1998 October, 19(5) p. 328.

[10]Jocelyn, et al.*J. Dev. Behav. Pediatr.,* (see n. 9 above) p. 328.

[11]Bassett, K. et al., BCOHTA, (see Chap. 1, n. 3), p.4.

[12]Jocelyn, et al.*J. Dev. Behav. Pediatr.,* (see n. 9 above) p. 328.

[13]Bassett, K. et al., BCOHTA, (see Chap. 1, n. 3), p. 36.

[14]Bassett, K. et al., BCOHTA, (see Chap. 1, n. 3), p. 36.

[15]Bassett, K. et al., BCOHTA, (see Chap. 1, n. 3), p. 36.

[16]Rogers, S.J. *J. Clin. Child Psychol.,* p. 176 (see Chap. 3, n. 43).

[17]Stone, W.L., O.Y. Ousley, P.J. Yoder, K.L. Hogan, S.L. Hepburn. "Nonverbal communication in two-and three-year-old children with autism." *J. Autism Dev. Disord.* 1997, December 27(6), p. 224.

[18]Bassett, K. et al., BCOHTA, (see Chap. 1, n. 3), p. 38.

[19]Rogers, S.J. *J. Clin. Child Psychol.,* (see Chap. 4, n. 38), p. 172.

[20]Mental Health: A report of the Surgeon General, (see Chap. 2. n. 25), pp. 163-164.

[21]Bassett, K. et al., BCOHTA, (see Chap. 1, n. 3), p. 42.

[22]Lonigan, C.J., J.C. Elbert, S.B. Johnson. "Empirically supported psychosocial interventions for children: an overview." *J. Clin. Child Psychol.,* 1998, 27(2), p. 144.

[23]Bassett, K. et al., BCOHTA, (see Chap. 1, n. 3), p. 41.

[24]Medical Services Plan of B.C. [online]. Ministry of Health. Retrieved 5, 15, 02 from <http://www.hlth.gov.bc.ca/msp/protoguides/index.html>

[25]Barer, M.L., K.M. McGrail, K. Cardiff, L. Wood and C.J. Green., *Tales From The Other Drug Wars.,* Vancouver, B.C., Centre for Health Services and Policy Research,1999, p. 40.

Chapter 5: BCOHTA and Provincial Policy

[1]Bassett, K. et al., BCOHTA, (see Chap. 1, n. 3), p. 4.

[2]Bassett, K. et al., BCOHTA, (see Chap. 1, n. 3), p. 5.

[3]Bassett, K. et al., BCOHTA, (see Chap. 1, n. 3), p. 5.

[4]Bassett, K. et al., BCOHTA, (see Chap. 1, n. 3), p. 6.

[5]Bassett, K. et al., BCOHTA, (see Chap. 1, n. 3), p. 20.

[6]Lovaas, O.I. "Parents as therapists." Rutter M, Schopler E, editors. *Autism: A reappraisal of concepts and treatment,* New York: Plenum Press 1978, p. 376.

[7]Lovaas, O.I. (see n. 6 above), p. 377.

[8]Bassett, K. et al., BCOHTA, (see Chap. 1, n. 3), p. 34.

[9]Bassett, K. et al., BCOHTA, (see Chap. 1, n. 3), p. 35.

[10]Bassett, K. et al., BCOHTA, (see Chap. 1, n. 3), p. 36.

[11]Bassett, K. et al., BCOHTA, (see Chap. 1, n. 3), p. 3.

[12]Bassett, K. et al., BCOHTA, (see Chap. 1, n. 3), p. 3.

[13] Talen, J. National Institutes of Health Sets $25 Million for Autism, *Newsday*, Tuesday, July 13, 1999.

[14]Bassett, K. et al., BCOHTA, (see Chap. 1, n. 3), p. 36.

[15]Bassett, K. et al., BCOHTA, (see Chap. 1, n. 3), p. 36.

[16]Bassett, K. et al., BCOHTA, (see Chap. 1, n. 3), p. 6.

[17]Bassett, K. et al., BCOHTA, (see Chap. 1, n. 3), p. 43.

[18]Bassett, K. et al., BCOHTA, (see Chap. 1, n. 3), p. 9.

[19]Bassett, K. et al., BCOHTA, (see Chap. 1, n. 3), p. 40.

[20]Bassett, K. et al., BCOHTA, (see Chap. 1, n. 3), p. 40.

[21]Bassett, K. et al., BCOHTA, (see Chap. 1, n. 3), p. 40.

[22]Bassett, K. et al., BCOHTA, (see Chap. 1, n. 3), p. 42.

[23]Bassett, K. et al., BCOHTA, (see Chap. 1, n. 3), p. 43.

[24]Bassett, K. et al., BCOHTA, (see Chap. 1, n. 3), p. 43.

[25]Bassett, K. et al., BCOHTA, (see Chap. 1, n. 3), p. 43.

Chapter 6: Clinical versus Health Technocrats: In Defense of the New York State Department of Health Report

[1]Bassett, K. et al., BCOHTA, (see Chap. 1, n. 3), p. 40.

[2]Bassett, K. et al., BCOHTA, (see Chap. 1, n. 3), p. 41.

[3]Bassett, K. et al., BCOHTA, (see Chap. 1, n. 3), p. 40.

[4]Guralnick, M. (ed). *Clinical practice guideline: Report of the recommendations. Autism/pervasive developmental disorders, assessment and intervention for young children (age 0-3 years).* Albany (NY): New York State Department of Health; 1999, p. 1-3.

[5]New York State Department of Health (see Chap. 3, n. 25), p. I-3.

[6]New York State Department of Health (see Chap. 3, n. 25), p. I-7.

[7]Savoie, I., K. Basset, A. Kazanjian. *Supporting Clinical Practice Guidelines Development: An appraisal of existing cholesterol testing guidelines.* 12D [online]. CHSPR, University of British Columbia. Retrieved 5, 31, 02 from <http://www.chspr.ubc.ca/cgi-bin/pub?program=BCOHTA>

[8]Savoie et al., *Supporting Clinical Practice Guidelines Development: An appraisal of existing cholesterol testing guidelines.* (see n. 7 above), p. 12-13.

[9]Bassett, K. et al., BCOHTA, (see Chap. 1, n. 3), p. 41.

[10]Savoie et al., *Supporting Clinical Practice Guidelines Development: An appraisal of existing cholesterol testing guidelines.* (see n. 7 above), p. 12-13, 21.

Chapter 7: Academic Rivalry in the Field of Autism Research

[1]Rogers, S.J. "A comparative study of the effects of a developmentally based instructional model on young children with autism and young children with other disorders of behavior and development." *Topics in Early Childhood Special Education*, 1991, 11(2): 29.

[2]Rogers, S.J. *Topics in Early Childhood Special Education*, (see n. 1 above), p. 37.

[3]Ozonoff, S., K. Cathcart. "Effectiveness of a home program intervention for young children with autism." *J. Autism Dev. Disord.* 1998. February, 28(1), pp. 25-26.

[4]Schopler, E. "Will your journal support parents advocating for intensive behavior therapy (the Lovaas method) as an entitlement under Part H of the Individuals with Disabilities Education Act?" *J. Autism Dev. Disord.,* 1998, 28(1), pp. 91-92.

[5]Schopler E., *J. Autism Dev. Disord.,* (see n. 4 above), p. 92.

[6]Gresham et al. "A Selective Review of Treatments for Children With Autism." *School Psychology Review*, 1999, 28(4): 559-575.

[7]Gresham, F.M., D.L. MacMillan. "Early Intervention Project: can its claims be subtantiated and its effects replicated?" *J. Autism Dev. Disord.,* 1998, February, 28(1), p. 12.

[8]Gresham et al., *. Autism Dev. Disord.,* (see n. 7 above), p. 12.

[9]Gresham et al., *. Autism Dev. Disord.,* (see n. 7 above), p. 12.

Chapter 8: The B.C. Supreme Court's Landmark Ruling

[1 - 18]*Auton et al. vs. the Attorney General et al.*, July 2000.

Chapter 9: BCOHTA on the Stand

[1]*Annual General Report 2000,* [online]. CHSPR, University of British Columbia. 2000 Retrieved 1, 31, 03 from <http://www.chspr.ubc.ca/annual2000.pdf>

[2]McGahan, L., *Behavioural Interventions for Children with Autism: A Synthesis of Evidence, Canadian Initiatives, Legal Analysis and Service Provision*, Canadian Coordinating Office for Health Technology Assessment, Ottawa, Ontario, 2001, p. i.

[3]*Lovaas Therapy - Applied Behavior Analysis for Autism-Intensive Intervention Programs,* AETNA Coverage Policy Bulletin No. 0554, [online]. 2001 Retrieved 1, 28, 03 from <http://www.aetna.com/cpb/data/CPBA0554.html>

[4]*Applied Behavioral Analysis (ABA) for the Treatment of Autism,* [online]. BlueCross BlueShield of Tennessee Medical Policy Manual, 2001 Retrieved 1/31/03 from <http://www.bcbst.com/MPManual/Applied_Behavioral_Analysis_(ABA)_for_the_Treatment_of_Autism.htm>

[5]Bassett et al., "Autism and Lovaas Treatment: a systematic review of effectiveness evidence." *International Journal of Technology Assessment and Health Care*, 2001, April, 17(2), p. 252.

[6]Ludwig, S. and C. Harstall. "Intensive Intervention Programs for Children with Autism." Alberta Heritage Foundation for Medical Research. 2001. Retrieved 2/2/03 from <http://www.ahfmr.ab.ca/publications.html>

[7]Bassett K, Green C, Kazanjian A. "Autism and Lovaas treatment: a systematic review of effectiveness evidence." Presentation ISTAHC 17th Annual Meeting, Philadelphia, PA. June3-6 2001. BCOHTA 2001:13C. Retrieved 9/14/01. <http://www.chspr.ubc.ca/cgi-bin/pub?program=BCOHTA>

[8]Finnish Office of Health Technology Assessment. Retrieved 1/31/03 from <http://www.stakes.fi/finohta/impakti/2000/05/index-Saapunei.html>

[9]Health Technology Assessment Newsletter, Osterreichische Akademie Der Wissenschafter,Vienna, Austria October 2001, No. 1. Retrieved 2/02/03 from <http://www.oeaw.ac.at/ita/hta/htaNL0101.pdf>

Afterword

[1 - 3]*Auton et al. vs. the Attorney General et al.*, October 2002.

References

Anderson, S.R., D.L. Avery, E.K. Di Pietro, G.L. Edwards, W.P. Christian, 1987. Intensive home-based early intervention with autistic children. *Educ. Treat. Children.* 10(4): 352-66.

Auton et al. vs. the Attorney General et al., July 2002.

Auton et al. vs. the Attorney General et al., October 2002.

Baer, D.M., M.M. Wolf, T.R. Risley, 1968. Some current dimensions of applied behavioral analysis. *J. Appl. Behav. Anal.* 1: 91-7.

Baer, D.M., 1993. Commentaries on McEachin, Smith, and Lovaas: quasi-random assignment can be as convincing as random assignment. *Am. J. Ment. Retard.* January 97(4): 373-5.

Bassett, K. et al., 2000. Autism and Lovaas Treatment: a systematic review of effectiveness evidence. BCOHTA, University of British Columbia.

Bassett. K et al., 20001. Autism and Lovaas Treatment: a systematic review of effectiveness evidence. *International Journal of Technology Assessment and Health Care*, April, 17(2): 252.

Birnbrauer, J.S., D.J. Leach, 1993. The Murdoch early intervention programme after 2 years. *Behav. Change* 10(2): 63-74.

Boyd R.D. 1998. Sex and bias: Reply to Smith and Lovaas. *J. Autism Dev. Dis.*, Vol. 23(4): 344.

Boyd, R.D., 1998. Sex as a possible source of group inequivalence in Lovaas (1987). *J. Autism Dev. Dis.*, June 28(3): 211-215.

Bristol, M.M., D.J. Cohen, E.J. Costello, M. Denckla, T.J. Eckberg, R. Kallen, H.C. Kraemer, C. Lord, R. Maurer, W.J. McIlvane, N. Minshew, 1996. State of the science in autism: report to the National Institutes Health. *J. Autism Dev. Disorders,* April 26(2): 121-54.

Campbell, M., J.E. Cueva, 1995. Psychopharmacology in child and adolescent psychiatry: a review of the past seven years: Part I. *J. Am. Acad. Child Adolesc. Psychiatry* September 34(9): 1124-32.

Campbell, M, E. Schopler, J.E. Cueva, A. Hallin, 1996. Treatment of autistic disorder. *J. Am. Acad. Child Adolesc. Psychiat.* February 35(2): 134-43.

Campbell, M., J.E. Cueva, A. Hallin, 1996. Autism and pervasive developmental disorders. In: Wiener, J.M., editor. *Diagnosis and psychopharmacology of childhood and adolescent disorders.* 2nd. ed. New York: John Wiley & Sons, p. 151-92.

Guralnick, M. (ed). Clinical practice guideline: Report of the recommendations. Autism/pervasive developmental disorders, assessment and intervention for young children (age 0-3 years), 1999, Albany (NY): New York State Department of Health.

Connor, M. 1998. A review of behavioural early intervention programmes for children with autism. *Educ. Psychol. Pract.*, 14(2): 109-17.

Cook, Jr., E.H., B.L. Leventhal, 1995. Autistic disorder and other pervasive developmental disorders. *Child Adolesc. Psychiatr. Clin. North Am.* 4(2): 381-99.

Cox, A., T. Charman, S. Baron-Cohen, A. Drew, K. Klein, G. Baird, J. Swettenham, S. Wheelwright, 1999. Autism spectrum disorders at 20 and 42 months of age: stability of clinical and ADI-R diagnosis. *J. Child Psychol. Psychiatry* 40(5): 719-32.

Dawson, G., J. Osterling, 1997. Early intervention in autism. In: Guralnick MJ, editor. *The effectiveness of early intervention.* Baltimore (MD): P.J. Brookes, p. 307-26.

Diagnostic and statistical manual of mental disorders: DSM-IV. 1994, Washington (DC): American Psychiatric Association.

Eaves, L., H. Ho., 1996. Brief Reports: Stability and Change in Cognitive and Behavioral Characteristics of Autism Through Childhood. *Journal of Autism and Developmental Disorders*, 26(5): 557-569.

Fenske, E.C., S. Zalenski, P.J. Krantz, L.E. McClannahan, 1985. Age at intervention and treatment outcome for autistic children in a comprehensive intervention program. *Analysis Intervention Dev. Dis.* 5: 49-58.

Forsyth, J.P., S. Kollins, A. Palav, K. Duff, S. Maher, 1999. Has behavior therapy drifted from its experimental roots? A survey of publication trends in mainstream behavioral journals. *J. Behavior Therapy and Experimental Psychiatry* 30, p. 205-220.

Fox, R.M., 1993. Sapid effects awaiting independent replication. *Am. J. Ment. Retard.* January, 97(4): 375-6.

Freeman, B.J. 1997. Guidelines for evaluating intervention programs for children with autism. *J. Autism Dev. Disord. December* 27(6): 641-51.

Friman, P.C., C.P. Lucas, M.J. Lubetsky, J.R. Holttum, 1994. Behavioral treatment for autism. *J. Am. Acad. Child Adolesc. Psychiatr.,* 33(9): 1349-51.

Furedy, J.J. 1999. Commentary; On the limited role of the "single-subject" design in psychology; Hypotheses generating but not testing. *J. Behavavior Therapy and Experimental Psychiatry* 30, p. 21 -22.

Garland, E. J. Open letter [online]. 1996. Families for Early Autism Treatment of British Columbia. Retrieved 5, 15, 02 from <www.featbc.org/lobby_and_advocacy/FEATBCbriefMLA.pdf>

Gillberg, C., 1996. The long-term outcome of childhood empathy disorders. *Eur. Child Adoles. Psychiatry*, 5: 52-6.

Gould, S.J., 1995. *Dinosaur In A Haystack.* New York: Harmony Books.

Green G., 1996. Early behavioral intervention for autism: What does research tell us? Maurice, C., G. Green, S.C. Luce, editors. *Behavioral intervention for young children with autism: a manual for parents and professionals.* Austin (TX): PRO-ED Inc., p. 29-44.

Gresham, F.M., D.L. MacMillan, 1997. Autistic recovery?: an analysis and critique of the empirical evidence on the early intervention project. *Behav. Disorders*, August 22(4): 185 -201.

Gresham, F.M., D.L. MacMillan, 1997. Denial and defensiveness in the place of fact and reason: rejoinder to Smith and Lovaas. *Behav. Disord.*, 22(4): 219-30.

Gresham, F.M., D.L. MacMillan, 1998. Early Intervention Project: can its claims be subtantiated and its effects replicated? *J. Autism Dev. Disord.* February 28(1): 5-13.

Gresham et al., 1999. A Selective Review of Treatments for Children With Autism. *School Psychology Review*, 28(4): 559-575.

Hanson, A., 1998. From research to policy: a look from an information perspective at the process of developing a mental health parity report. *Behavioral & Social Sciences Librarian*, 17(1): 1-20.

Harris, S.L., J.S. Handleman, R. Gordon, B. Kristoff, F. Fuentes, 1991. Changes in cognitive and language functioning of preschool children with autism. *J. Autism Dev. Disord.,* September 21(3): 281-90.

Howlin, P., M. Rutter, 1989. Mothers' speech to autistic children: a preliminary causal analysis. *J. Child Psychol. Psychiatry*, November 30(6): 819-43.

Howlin P., 1997. Prognosis in autism: do specialist treatments affect long-term outcome? *Eur. Child Adolesc. Psychiatr.* 6(2): 55-72.

Howlin P., 1997. When is a significant change not significant? *J. Autism Dev. Dis.* June 27(3): 347-8.

Howlin, P., 1998. Practitioner review: psychological and educational treatments for autism. *J. Child. Psychol. Psychiatry*, March 39(3): 307-22.

Hurth, J., E. Shaw, S.G. Izeman, K. Whaley, S.J. Rogers., 1999. Areas of agreement about effective practices among programs serving young children with autism spectrum disorders. *Infants Young Children* October 12(2): 17-26.

Jacobson, J.W., J.A. Mulick, G. Green, 1998. Cost-benefit estimates for early intensive behavioral intervention for young children with autism - General model and single state case. *Behav. Interventions*, 13(4): 201-26.

Jocelyn, L.J., O.G. Casiro, D. Beattie, J. Bow, J. Kneisz, 1998. Treatment of children with autism: a randomized controlled trial to evaluate a caregiver-based intervention program in community day-care centers. *J. Dev. Behav. Pediatr.,* October 19(5): 326-34.

Kazdin, A.K. 1978. Methodological and Interpretive Problems of Single-Case Experimental Designs. *J. Consult. and Clinical Psychology*, Vol 46(4): 629-642.

Kazdin, A.K. 1993. Replication and extension of behavioral treatment of autistic disorder. *Am. J. Ment, Retard.*, 97(4): 377-9.

Kazdin AK, J.R. Weisz, 1998. Identifying and developing empirically supported child and adolescent treatments. *J. Consulting Clin. Psychol.*, 66(1): 19-36.

Koegel, R.L., L.K. Koegel, 1990. Extended reductions in stereotypic behavior of students with autism through a self-management treatment package. *J. Appl. Behav. Anal.,* Spring 23(1): 119-27.

Koegel, R.L., A. Bimbela, L. Schreibman, 1996. Collateral effects of parent training on family interactions. *J. Autism Dev. Disord.,* June 26(3): 347-59.

Leaf, R., and J. McEachin, 1999. *A Work in Progress*. N.Y.: Different Roads to Learning LLC.

Lewis, M.H., 1996. Brief report: psychopharmacology of autism spectrum disorders. *J. Autism Dev. Dis.*, April 26(2): 231-5.

Lonigan, C.J., J.C. Elbert, S.B. Johnson, 1998. Empirically supported psychosocial interventions for children: an overview. *J. Clin. Child Psychol.* 27(2): 138-4.

Lord, C., 1995. Follow-up of two-year-olds referred for possible autism. *J. Child Psychol. Psychiatry*, 36(8): 1365-82.

Lovaas, O.I., 1978. Parents as therapists. In: Rutter M, Schopler E, editors. *Autism: A Reappraisal of Concepts and Treatment,* New York: Plenum Press, p. 369-378.

Lovaas, O.I., 1987. Behavioral treatment and normal educational and intellectual functioning in young austic children. *J. Consult. and Clin. Psych.* 55(1): 3-9.

Lovaas, O.I. *Clarifying Comments on the UCLA Young Autism Project*, [on line]. 2000. Retrieved 5, 15, 02 from <http://www.feat.org/lovaas/full.htm>.

Lovaas, O.I., A. Ackerman, D. Alexander, P. Firestone, M. Perkins, D.B. Young, .K.G. Carr, C. Newsom, 1981. *Teaching developmentally disabled children: the ME book.* Baltimore (MD): University Park Press.

Lovaas, O.I., T. Smith, 1988. Intensive behavioral treatment for young autistic children. In: Lahey B.B., A.K. Kazdin, editors. *Advances in clinical child psychology.* New York: Plenum Press, p. 285-324.

Lovaas, O.I., T. Smith, 1989. A comprehensive behavioral theory of autistic children: paradigm for research and treatment. *J. Behav. Ther. & Exp. Psychiat.* 20(1): 17-29.

Lovaas, O.I., T. Smith, J.J. McEachin, 1989. Clarifying comments on the young autism study: reply to Schopler, Short and Mesibov. *J. Consult. Clin. Psychology* 57(1): 165-7.

Lovaas, O.I., G. Buch, 1997. Intensive Behavioral intervention with young children with autism. In: Singh N.N., editor. *Prevention and treatment of severe behavior problems: models and methods in developmental disabilities.* Pacific Grove (CA): Brooks/Cole Publishing, p. 62-85.

Matson, J.L., D.A. Benavidez, L.S. Compton, T. Paclawskyj, C. Baglio, 1996. Behavioral treatment of autistic persons: a review of research from 1980 to the present. *Res. Dev. Dis.* November-December, 17(6):433-65.

Maurice C, G. Green, S.C. Luce, 1996. *Behavioral intervention for young children with autism: a manual for parents and professionals.* Austin (TX): PRO-ED Inc.

McEachin J.J., T. Smith, O.I. Lovaas, 1993. Long-term outcome for children with autism who received early intensive behavioral treatment. *Am. J. Ment. Retard.* 97(4):359-72.

McGahan, L., *Behavioural Interventions for Children with Autism: A Synthesis of Evidence, Canadian Initiatives, Legal Analysis and Service Provision*, Canadian Coordinating Office for Health Technology Assessment, Ottawa, Ontario, 2001, p. i.

Mesibov, G.B., 1993. Treatment outcome is encouraging. *Am. J. Ment. Retard.* Jan;97(4):379-80.

Nordin V., C. Gillberg, 1998. The long-term course of autistic disorders: Update on follow- up studies. *Acta Psychiatr. Scand.* 97(2):99-108.

Nourbakhsh, M.R., K.J. Ottenbacher, 1994. The Statistical Analysis of Single-Subject Data: A Comparative Examination. *Phys. Ther.* Aug (74):768-776

Ozonoff, S., K. Cathcart, 1998. Effectiveness of a home program intervention for young children with autism. *J. Autism Dev. Disord.* Feb 28(1):25-32.

Perry, R., I. Cohen, R. DeCarlo, 1995. Case study: deterioration, autism, and recovery in two siblings. *J. Am. Acad. Child Adolesc. Psychiatry* Feb 34(2):232-7.

Prizant, B.M., A.M. Wetherby, 1998. Understanding the continuum of discrete-trial traditional behavioral to social-pragmatic developmental approaches in communication enhancement for young children with autism/PDD. *Sem. Speech Language* 19(4):329-53, 424.

Public Health Service, *Mental Health: A report of the Surgeon General*, 1999, p. 164 [online]. Retrieved 5, 15, 02 from <http://www.surgeongeneral.gov/library/mentalhealth/home.html>

Reboussin, D.M., T.M. Morgan, 1996. Statistical considerations in the use and analysis of single- subject designs. *Medicine and Science in Sports and Exercise* 28(5): 639-644.

Ritvo, R.Z., S.B. Papilsky, 1999. Effectiveness of psychotherapy. *Current Opin. Pediatr.* 11(4):323-27.

Rodier, P.M., S.E. Bryson, J.P. Welch, 1997. Minor malformations and physical measurements in autism: data from Noval Scotia. *Teratology* 55(5): 319-25.

Rogers, S.J. 1991. A comparative study of the effects of a developmentally based instructional model on young children with autism and young children with other disorders of behavior and development. *Topics in Early Childhood Special Education*, 11(2): 29-47.

Rogers, S.J., 1996. Brief report: early intervention in autism. *J. Autism Dev. Disord.* Apr 26(2) :243 -6.

Rogers, S.J., 1998. Empirically supported comprehensive treatments for young children with autism. *J. Clin. Child Psychol.* Jun 27(2):168-79.

Rogers S.J., 1999. Intervention for young children with autism: from research to practice. *Infants Young Children* Oct 12(2): 1-16.

Rutter, M., 1996. Autism research: prospects and priorities. *J. Autism Dev. Dis.* Apr 26(2) :257-75.

Rutter, M.. 1999. The Emanuel Miller memorial lecture 1998: Autism: Two-way interplay between research and clinical work. *J. Child Psychol. Psychiatr. Allied Disc.* 40(2):169-88.

Schopler, E, 1998. Will your journal support parents advocating for intensive behavior therapy (the Lovaas method) as an entitlement under Part H of the Individuals with Disabilities Education Act? *J. Autism Dev. Disord.* 28(1):912.

Schopler, E., A. Short, G. Mesibov, 1989. Relation of behavioral treatment to “normal functioning”: comment on Lovaas. *J. Consult, Clin. Psych.* 57(1):162-4

Schreibman L., 1996. Brief report: the case for social and behavioral intervention. *J. Autism Dev. Dis.* Apr 26(2):247-50.

Scruggs, T.E., M.A. Mastropieri, 1998. Summarizing Single-Subject Research: issues and applications. *Behavior Modification*, July 22(3), p. 221-242.

Sheinkopf, S.J., B. Siegel, 1998. Home-based behavioral treatment of young children with autism. *J. Autism Dev. Disord.* Feb 28(1):15-23.

Smith, T., 1996. Are other treatments effective? In: Maurice C, Green G, Luce SC, editors. *Behavioral intervention for young children with autism: a manual for parents and professionals.* Austin (TX): PRO-ED Inc., p. 25-59

Smith, T., 1999. Outcome of ealy intervention for children with autism. *Clin. Psychol. Sci. Pract.* Spr 6(1):33-49.

Smith, T. T. Parker, M. Taubman, O.I. Lovaas, 1992. Transfer of staff training from workshops to group homes: A failure to generalize across settings. *Res. Dev. Dis.* 13(1):57-71.

Smith, T., J.J. McEachin, O.I. Lovaas, 1993. Comments on replication and evaluation of outcome. *Am. J. Ment. Retard.* 97(4):385-91.

Smith, T., S. Eikeseth, M. Klevstrand, O.I. Lovaas, 1997. Intensive behavioral treatment for preschoolers with severe mental retardation and pervasive developmental disorder. *Am. J. Ment. Retard.* Nov 102(3): 238-49.

Smith, T., O.I. Lovaas, 1997. The UCLA young autism project: a reply to Gresham and MacMillan. *Behav. Disord.* 22(4):202-18.

Smith,T., O.I. Lovaas, 1998. Seminar on applied behavior analysis treatment for autism: intensive and early behavioral intervention with autism: the UCLA Young Autism Project. *Infants Young Children* 10(3): 67-78.

Smith, T., O.I. Lovaas, 1998. Sex and bias: reply to Boyd. *J. Autism Dev. Disord.* Aug 28(4):343-44.

Stone, W.L., O.Y. Ousley, P.J. Yoder, K.L. Hogan, S.L. Hepburn, 1997. Nonverbal communication in two-and three-year-old children with autism. *J. Autism Dev. Disord.* Dec 27(6): 677- 96.

Stone, W.L., E.B. Lee, L. Ashford, J. Brissie, S.L. Hepburn, E.E. Coonrod, B.H. Weiss, 1999. Can autism be diagnosed accurately in children under 3 years? *J. Child Psychol. Psychiatry* 40(2):219-26.

Strain, P.S., F.W. Kohler, F. Gresham. 1998. Problems in logic and interpretation with quantitative synthese of single-case research; Mathur and Colleagues (1998) as a Case in Point. *Behavioral Disorders*, November, 24(1): 74-85.

Suzuki, David. 1996. The child who couldn't talk. *The Nature of Things*. Canadian Broadcasting Corporation.

Szatmari, P., D.L. Streiner, 1996. The effect of selection criteria on outcome studies of children with pervasive developmental disorders (PDD). *Eur. Child Adolesc. Psychiatr.* December 5(4): 179-84.

UBC Policy #87 *Research.* [on line]. Approved July 1993, revised March 1995. University of British Columbia. Retrieved 2, 14, 03 from <www.universitycounsel.ubc.ca/policy87.htm>.

Talen, J. National Institutes of Health Sets $25 Million for Autism, *Newsday*, Tuesday, July 13, 1999.

World Health Organization. ICD-10: 1992-1994. *International statistical classification of diseases and related health problems: tenth revision.* Geneva: World Health Organization.

Web-sites

AETNA ,*Lovaas Therapy - Applied Behavior Analysis for Autism-Intensive Intervention Programs,* AETNA Coverage Policy Bulletin No. 0554, [online]. 2001 Retrieved 1, 28, 03 from <http://www.aetna.com/cpb/data/CPBA0554.html>.

AHFMR, Ludwig, S. and C. Harstall. *Intensive Intervention Programs for Children with Autism.* Alberta Heritage Foundation for Medical Research. 2001. Retrieved 2/2/03 from <http://www.ahfmr.ab.ca/publications.html>.

American Psychiatric Association, *State of the states: Parity Laws* [on line]. 1999. Retrieved 5, 15, 02 from <http://www.psych.org/pub_pol_adv/sos_parity_999.cfm>.

American Psychological Association, *Ending Discrimination in Health Insurance*, [on line]. APA, Psychology Examines the Issues, 1997. Retrieved 5, 15, 02 from <www.apa.org/practice/paper/homepage.html>.

BCTV, *Leaving BC for Health Care* [online]. Families for Early Autism Treatment of British Columbia. Retrieved 5, 14, 02 from <http://www.featbc.org/files/media/video/BCTVNEWS_11_26_97.ram>.

BCOHTA, *About the Office* [online]. Centre for Health Services and Policy Research, University of British Columbia. Retrieved 5, 14, 02 from <www.chspr.ubc.ca>.

BCOHTA *Office of Health Technology Home Page* [online]. Centre for Health Services and Policy Research, University of British Columbia. Retrieved 5, 14, 02 from <www.chspr.ubc.ca/bcohta/>.

BCOHTA *Office of Health Technology Assessment Mandate* [online]. Centre for Health Services and Policy Research, University of British Columbia. Retrieved 5, 14, 02 from <www.chspr.ubc.ca/bcohta/bcohta.htm#Mandate>.

BlueCross Blue Shield *Applied Behavioral Analysis (ABA) for the Treatment of Autism,* [online]. BlueCross BlueShield of Tennessee Medical Policy Manual, 2001 Retrieved 1/31/03 from <http://www.bcbst.com/MPManual/Applied_Behavioral_Analysis_(ABA)_for_the_Treatment_of_Autism.htm>.

CCOHTA *Canadian Coordinating Office for Health Technology Assessment* [online]. Retrieved 4, 1, 00 from <www.ccohta.ca>.

CHSPR *BC Office of Health Technology Assessment* [online]. Centre for Health Services and Policy Research, University of British Columbia. Retrieved 3, 22, 02 from <www.chspr.ubc.ca/bcohta/bcohta.htm>.

CHSPR, *Annual General Report 2000,* [online]. Centre for Health Services and Policy Research, University of British Columbia. 2000 Retrieved 1, 31, 03 from <http://www.chspr.ubc.ca/annual2000.pdf>.

Correspondence from Dr. E.J. Garland, *Open letter* [online]. 1996. Families for Early Autism Treatment of British Columbia. Retrieved 5, 15, 02 from <www.featbc.org/lobby_and_advocacy/FEATBCbriefMLA.pdf>.

Federal Mental Health Parity Act, *Health Care Financing Administration* [on line]. 1999. Retrieved 5, 15, 02 from <www.hcfa.gov/medicaid/hipaa/content/mhpastat.asp>.

Finnish Office of Health Technology Assessment. Retrieved 1/31/03 from <http://www.stakes.fi/finohta/impakti/2000/05/index-Saapunei.html>.

HTA, *Health Technology Assessment Newsletter*, Osterreichische Akademie Der Wissenschafter,Vienna, Austria October 2001, No. 1. Retrieved 2/02/03 from <http://www.oeaw.ac.at/ita/hta/htaNL0101.pdf>

ISTAHC, Bassett K, Green C, Kazanjian A. *Autism and Lovaas treatment: a systematic review of effectiveness evidence."* Presentation ISTAHC 17th Annual Meeting, Philadelphia, PA. June3-6 2001. BCOHTA 2001:13C. Retrieved 9/14/01. <http://www.chspr.ubc.ca/cgi-bin/pub?program=BCOHTA>.

Medical Services Plan of B.C. [online]. Ministry of Health. Retrieved 5, 15, 02 from <http://www.hlth.gov.bc.ca/msp/protoguides/index.html>.

National Institute of Mental Health [on line]. 2002 Retrieved 5, 15, 02 from <www.nimh.nih.gov/publicat/equal.cfm>.

Office of Comptroller General, *Grants and Contributions* [online]. Retrieved 2/11/02 from <www.fin.gov.bc.ca/ocg/pa/98-99/Sup-D/Grants/D7-22.htm>.

Public Health Service, *Mental Health: A report of the Surgeon General*, 1999, p. 164 [online]. Retrieved 5, 15, 02 from <http://www.surgeongeneral.gov/library/mentalhealth/home.html>.

Savoie, I., K. Bassett, A. Kazanjian. *Supporting Clinical Practice Guidelines Development: An appraisal of existing cholesterol testing guidelines.* 12D [online]. CHSPR, University of British Columbia. Retrieved 5, 31, 02 from <http://www.chspr.ubc.ca/cgi-bin/pub?program=BCOHTA>.

UBC Policy #87 *Research.* [on line]. Approved July 1993, revised March 1995. University of British Columbia. Retrieved 2, 14, 03 from <www.universitycounsel.ubc.ca/policy87.htm>.

UBC Policy #97 *Conflict of Interest.* [on line]. Approved Sept. 1992, revised July 1995. University of British Columbia. Retrieved 5, 15, 02 from <www.policy.ubc.ca/policy97.htm>.

Index

A

B

C

D

E

F

G

H

I

N

O

P

R

S

T

U

V